learning

in

THIN

AIR

Katie,
Climb Strong!

by

Scott Kress

Scott Kress, www.scottkress.com

Library and Archives Canada Cataloguing in Publication

 Kress, Scott, 1967-
        Learning in thin air / by Scott Kress.

ISBN 978-0-9736554-3-8
        1. Kress, Scott, 1967-. 2. Mountaineers--Canada--Biography.
3. Everest, Mount (China and Nepal). 4. Success in business.

I. Title.
GV199.92.K74A3 2012   796.522092   C2012-905237-X

Editors: Christa Carroll, Jim Carroll, Heidi Rampersad, Dave Gibson, Olivia Hart
Design: Christa Carroll, Will Carroll

Photography: Scott Kress, Angus Murray
Cover Photo: Scott Kress

Printed in Canada

Oblio Press www.obliopress.com

Acclaim for Learning In Thin Air

Scott's journey is a testament to the age old statement "Every journey begins with the first step." For Scott it culminated with standing on top of the worlds highest mountain, Everest. *Learning in Thin Air* gives us real life lessons that can be applied to both our personal and business lives. It shows how critical it is to have the right people on our team and to have the entire team's vision and goals aligned through communication and dedication. *Learning in Thin Air* is an excellent learning vehicle on the road to successful achievement of our goals.

Stuart Lowther BSc., MSc.
President/CEO, Life Science Nutritionals Inc.

If you want to learn how to reach the highest goals in your life and in business, read this book. If you want to read a great story, read this book.

Olivia Hunt
Print Journalist

Scott Kress shares his exhilarating and often humorous story of mountain climbing all over the world for the last 20 years, and teaches you how to reach your "Everest" in life and in business. Reading this book will leave you inspired, motivated and empowered with Kress's learning models.

Steve Hart
Wealth Advisor, BMO Nesbitt Burns

I found Scott's story as a climber fascinating, engaging, and full of insight on what makes teams succeed in extreme high-altitude conditions with great obstacles to overcome. A great account of lessons learned and analogies that can be applied to team dynamics for success within business organizations. Great read!

Julieta Sevilla
Mortgage Agent, Mortgage Edge

As a CEO and Board member of a variety of organizations I am always looking for ways to focus our leadership and build our teams. This book was not only an interesting read, but it provided me with new ways to think about leadership and team development. I'll definitely encourage our Executives and other Directors to read it. I know it will help them redefine how they lead and motivate their teams.

Shaun Francis
President, Medcan

Leadership is a vital commodity, but in short supply these day in business, teams and family life. Scott Kress has managed to use his professional and climbing experience to distill key lessons for people of all experiences to learn from. *Learning in Thin Air* is not a story of how he did it, it's a journey that provides a framework for us to grow as leaders within the backdrop of some of the most challenging environments the world has to offer. An excellent read with a clear message for leadership growth, I highly recommend *Learning in Thin Air*.

Dr Paul Ziemer BSc., DC
CEO, Neuro Vas Clinic

In *Learning In Thin Air* Scott articulates how any achievement, whether individual or team-based, personal or professional, is one component of a greater arc of successes and failures. Using the mountains as a backdrop, Scott shows us how constant reflection, adaptation and progressive learning are required to optimize the chances of reaching any goal we may face in our lives.

Jennifer Hartman
Legal Consultant, Medico

I completed your book the same day you presented a copy to WRH. I could not put it down! Thank you for sharing your life (to date) and showing how we interact within our organization and how it parallels with achieving new heights!

Ron Foster
VP Public Affairs, Windsor Regional Hospital

I thoroughly enjoyed this book. Not only was it very interesting to read, but it also had a unique way of blending concrete successful leadership concepts with practical real life examples. It is inspiring to know that while we all have our own mountains to climb, anything can be conquered with a cohesive team and strong leadership.

Carie Reid
VP Retail Sales, Banking

Today I completed reading your story and I want to thank you for the book, the inspirational speech you gave and the story itself, which I really enjoyed. I have spent over forty years managing projects that have had dollar values as high as 600 million and the success of any project always came back to having a high performance team. My passion varies from yours as it takes place at sea level most of the time. Racing sailboats both in the local lakes and also some ocean racing has been my passion and what amazed me about your story is many of the similarities of the two sports. (Drowning or falling a 1000 feet would have the same result.) The one most important comparison is the need to have a high performance team. Teams that win competitive sailboat races always work like a Swiss clock and function together in every respect. Loved your book and I'm going to suggest to all the folks that I race with that they take time to buy and read it.

Blayne Willett
Project Manager, Hewlett Packard

Scott has an incredible story to tell and he does it brilliantly.....he is a leader, a thinker and a doer who lives by example and shares his experience and insight with others.

Timothy Fallis
President Black Rock Marketing Group

Scott is a masterful presenter with a compelling message about leadership and team building from his unique experiences climbing the tallest peaks in the world where team failure can cost you your life.

David Rubin
TEC Chair, TEC Canada

Scott shares his lessons from Everest and is able to clearly translate them into a personal or professional application.

Danielle Perron
Executive Vice President, Infield Marketing Group

Scott weaves the heartfelt experiences and challenges of the physical task of summiting Everest with the equally powerful messages of teaming and leadership using dramatic examples of success and failure.

Sean Donnelly
VP Manufacturing, ArcelorMittal Dofasco

As the adage goes...the road is littered with failed or distracted companies loaded with plenty of I-Q. It is often the E-Q that propels success or kills it! In a life-changing experience, you gain invaluable insights and learn to think differently. Scott Kress masterfully connects his experiences in the mountains to the challenges of everyday life.

Roger Woolsey
CEO, Million Air Aviation

Table of Contents

Mount Everest

Learning
In REALLY
Thin Air

WITH STUDIED precision, I gradually extend my right hand to the next handhold. Stretching to the limit of my reach, my fingers first touch then slowly grasp the next hand hold in a seemingly endless series of points that I will have to negotiate to reach my destination. Pausing for a moment to catch my breath, I turn to look over my shoulder at the panoramic vista beneath me. The spectacular blue of the Earth's infinite horizon appears painted with small cottony wisps of clouds far below me from my perch in the heavens. My safety tether can be seen extending back to its last point of attachment. A thin filament that is my lifeline should I lose my grip or miss a handhold.

Reflecting on this moment, I could have been climbing the Hillary step in the final stages of a Mount Everest climb. In fact I was performing a spacewalk, moving to the furthest point on the starboard truss of the International Space Station to get ready to rendezvous with the famous Canadarm and install a 3900 pound section of the backbone of the most complex structure ever assembled in space. As in the case of mountaineering, many assume that success spacewalking is an individual achievement. To defy the odds, to push the limits of performance making possible the seemingly impossible objectives of the mission, appears to be the epitome of personal achievement. That is a false assumption.

Success working outside in the extreme harsh vacuum of space is achieved using the lessons learned firsthand by astronauts and mission managers over the past fifty years. And these lessons are directly applicable to another potentially lethal environment - climbing the seven summits. Both are zero fault tolerant environments where errors can have catastrophic consequences, where a moment's indecisiveness, a minute loss of focus or a lapse of judgement can instantaneously turn success into failure. There is no question that individual performance is a significant contributing factor, yet these amazing accomplishments are achieved through the carefully choreographed efforts of a group of individuals supported by even larger teams, all coordinated in their efforts. Years of preparation, significant financial resources, countless hours of work and limitless enthusiasm all play a role enabling dedicated explorers to achieve their dreams.

The lessons learned in the rarefied thin air of high altitude peaks are similar to and validate those shared by space explorers who are relentless in their quest to have humans travel farther and stay longer in space. These lessons can transform the way you think about working together. The techniques of peak-performing teams, utilizing effective leadership and followership skills are as relevant in the board room, the office, the hospital or academic institution as they are on top of Mount Everest or on the International Space Station.

Learning in Thin Air takes us on a journey of discovery. It is the journey of an adventurer, an explorer whose dreams have taken him to destinations few humans have seen. It is a story of friends and family, loss and love, the joy of overcoming life's hurdles and doing so with the embrace of those who share the dream. The experiential learning model, the result of insights gleaned through the successes and failures of exploring some of the most remote locations on Earth, reminds us of the need for continuous reflection and non-critical introspection to grow as individuals in our pursuit of success.

As a physician astronaut, aquanaut, researcher and pilot, now turned hospital CEO leading a healthcare team of over four thousand dedicated volunteers and professionals, I have learned that anything really worth doing is never easy. Sometimes we all must reach deep to find that same determination that took Scott one footstep at a time to the summit of the world's highest peaks. This book will help each of us grow as individuals and learn to overcome our own hurdles. For the reader, each page is a step on a lifetime journey to achieve the unique blend of individual and team skills, leadership and followership qualities that are critical in transforming how we work together in groups into a new approach where we can thrive in peak-performing teams. Enjoy the journey!

Dave R. Williams MSc MD CM FCFP FRCP DSc (Hon) LLD (Hon)
Canadian Astronaut, Aquanaut and Exploration Scientist

To Susan, Amy and Colin
Thanks for being there for me.

To my Dad, Keith Kress
I wish you were here.

Introduction

THIS STORY is about life, it is about adventure, and it is about learning, but most of all it is about passion and vision. My passion for the mountains and my long internship in vision has helped me achieve great rewards in life. These rewards have not been without loss and tragedy, but that is what makes up our lives.

It is the story of an adventure that is born in a small child's backyard in Woodstock, Ontario. The adventure begins with a simple, innate love of climbing up and onto whatever was at hand in a child's world. As the child grows, so does the adventure.

The adventure moves beyond the picket fences, beyond familiar local crags and passes through dozens of remote mountainous realms in far flung, exotic countries. The story culminates half a world away and 40 years later on the summit of Mount Everest, the World's highest mountain.

The child who began that journey was neither overly ambitious nor extraordinarily gifted. Yet this is not a simple mountaineering story, nor is it a simple autobiography. This is a distillation of adventures and lessons learned by an average guy who keeps one foot firmly planted in the corporate world and the other planted in the mountains. Ultimately, it is a story about success and failure, and what separates the two. It is a story about passion, self-determination, and holding one's self personally accountable for results.

It is the story of how I began to get serious about climbing, and how I came to realize that I was gaining some powerful insight that I could share with others — success factors involving such things as goal setting, teamwork, and leadership to name but a few. My story is told using the climbing journals that I have kept through out my time on the mountains.

My lessons in thin air led me to a career that allows me to apply these lessons on a daily basis, helping to shape the perspectives of tens of thousands of team members, managers, executives and students. At the time of writing, among many other things, I am the President of two leadership and team development companies, and an international public speaker. I am an Executive MBA instructor at the Rotman School of Management at the University of Toronto, and teach a leadership class for the University of Edinburgh MBA program.

All this from a guy who was neither a star athlete nor a brilliant student. In fact, my first two attempts at higher education were abandoned pretty quickly, and it was not until I found climbing that my life seemed to come together.

In climbing, I have had notable successes, but not without first suffering some notable failures. (Of course, one could argue that in the climbing world, living to climb another day is always a success by some measure!)

In a nutshell, this is the story of my journey in life and of a triumph of passion and purpose — driven by the climb — that would take me on a voyage I never could have dreamed would occur. It is the story of how I learned some incredibly valuable lessons while up in thin air.

Enjoy,

Scott

The Early Years

Favourite climbing destinations in
North America and Mexico

The Origin of Passion

IT WAS a hot day, made hotter and more treacherous by a midsummer sun. I watched my Dad set the extension ladder against the side of our two story house and grew excited as he made the long ascent to the roof to repair the shingles. Clearly, Dad's mind and his actions were focused on getting the job done as quickly as possible. However, not more than a few moments after he settled into work, he was interrupted by a small voice saying, "Hi Dad." Turning around to locate the source of this unexpected greeting, he was no doubt horrified to find his smiling four year old son on the roof with him. This was my first big climb. I don't remember what happened after this, but none of the repercussions, actual or threatened, deterred my desire to climb.

I was always a natural climber. Even before I could walk I was climbing. My mother has often told me that as a baby they had to put extensions on my crib to prevent me from climbing out and when that did not work they had to put a top on it as well.

Throughout my adolescence, I continued to climb every vertical thing I could get my hands on. I can remember going to a local ravine with some friends and a length of discarded green garden hose. With just enough forethought, we tied one end of the hose to a strategically located tree and heaved the other end off the top of the adjacent cliff. We did not know how to tie good knots, but we ascribed to the theory that any knot is a good knot as long as you use enough of them. The hose just managed to meet the ground below, and the tangle of knots held. We happily scaled that "rope" all day long, oblivious to anything but the thrill of adventure. We were fortunate that garden hoses in those days were well made, as we all escaped any serious injuries.

Climbing for me has always been this way. It is just a natural extension of who I am and what I do. There was never, at least initially, much thought as to why, just the desire to do it. Without knowing it at the time, this natural desire to climb grabbed a hold of my life and guided me into the future. I see now that these initial climbing experiences were the emergence of my passion. Although, it took many years for this passion to mature and for me to fully understand it.

Wasaga Beach 1981

Up until my early twenties, I had always been a mediocre student and lacked any real life direction. I knew that I loved almost any outdoor pursuit; hiking, camping, canoeing, mountain biking, windsurfing, climbing – just about anything in the fresh air sounded good to me. In fact, unless forced, I rarely stayed inside for long.

I grew up in a small town called Wasaga Beach about 1.5 hours north of Toronto. In the summer months I would hop on my bike with my friends, my Mom would give me a dollar for lunch and I would be off. We would explore the sand dunes, ride the trails, jump over piles of dirt, swim in the bay, play at the park and eventually make it home for dinner, covered in mud, sweat and blood from the days adventures. But at the end of those summer months September always came and with it came the return of school.

School was never a highlight of my day. I knew school was important, but I was not the best of students. It was not that I had fallen in with the wrong crowd, or that I was not smart, it was just that I didn't care and therefore had

learning in THIN AIR

no real motivation. The closed in walls and the formality and structure did not work well with my learning style. I did not see the purpose so I didn't apply myself. Consequently my high school grades were lackluster at best. Meeting one day with my guidance counselor he kindly suggested that I forget about continuing on to university. Perhaps, if I were ambitious, I could try college, but most likely the best thing for me to do was to get a job in a factory. Not very inspiring advice.

After graduating from high school and experiencing a couple of failed attempts at college I found myself managing a ski shop. I was 21 and earning $21,000 a year. At first I thought I had won the lottery. I'm making a ton of cash, or so I thought, developing a great career, or so I thought, and getting to live the life of a ski bum, or so I thought.

For the first few months life was great and then reality sunk in. Although I loved working in the shop, it was not as good as initially advertised. There I was, indoors on the nicest days of the year, selling and tuning skis, merely providing the tools for those who were out doing what they loved. Yes, I had the best tuned skis in town, but they rarely saw the slopes.

I'm not exactly sure what my parents thought of the situation at the time. I do know that they were very patient with me and were allowing me to find my own way. I guess they figured I was young and had plenty of time to grow up. As a young man I did not really trouble myself with these deep thoughts and just lived life day to day.

My Mom and Dad had divorced when I was ten and I think that this placed some form of emotional and communication roadblocks in our relationship. We all seemed to keep our emotions and personal thoughts inside and did not often share the deeper side of ourselves. We had all been through a huge roller coaster of emotional highs and lows, mostly lows, and I guess this was our way of dealing with it. Consequently I did not really talk much with my Mom or Dad about the future and they did not raise their concerns with me.

I was however, smart enough to know that there must be a greater purpose in life for me. I felt trapped, struggling to figure out what exactly that purpose would be and where my life would lead me.

The Harnessing of Passion

THAT ALL changed in 1988 when my friend Al came home from university for the winter break and, unknown to him, threw me a lifeline. He told me in detail about the Outdoor Recreation Program at Lakehead University in Thunder Bay and all the various adventures he had been presented with through the course. I hung on every word as he described a degree program in outdoor recreation; a program designed specifically for climbers, paddlers, skiers, mountain bikers and hikers. It was a program for all those people who harbored an irrepressible spirit of adventure – like me. I wasted no time in applying.

Elora Gorge, Ontario

Fortunately, I was able to apply as a mature student as it is doubtful I would have been accepted to any university right out of high school. I started at Lakehead in September of 1989 and knew my life was about to change. Now I had a goal – a university degree – connected to my passion.

I was like a duck in water in Thunder Bay. Here, for the first time in my life, my passion for climbing was not only validated, it connected to an educational and professional pathway. I was immersed in a solid and focused learning environment with the northern wilderness at my doorstep. My studies and my climbing were mutually reinforced, giving me a whole new attitude toward academics. All my grades went up, even those that had no connection to climbing whatsoever. I became a leading student and landed a job as a teaching assistant for several classes.

My first winter in Thunder Bay opened my eyes to a whole new set of challenging climbing possibilities, and planted the seed of an ultimate goal, Mount Everest, in my brain.

If you have ever spent time in Thunder Bay, you know that the winter season can be longer than the summer season. Starting in late October and running through to mid-April we found a wonderland for ice climbing. January temperatures regularly reached -45° C. There were literally hundreds of frozen waterfalls for us to scale. The ice was hard, the days were cold and the climbs were tough, scary and unforgiving. I loved it!

Ice Climbing

ICE CLIMBING and rock climbing are both heavily tied to the act of temporarily cheating the laws of physics, specifically gravity. Both require often epic struggles of muscle and brain against the constant tug of the earth below. But that's pretty much where the similarity ends. Most, but not all, rock climbing places the climber in direct contact with the rock itself. It is hand and toe to rock, using friction and the available nubbins, cracks and crevices to keep you on the crag. Meanwhile, the anchors (called chocks, nuts, pins, friends, etc) and belay ropes protect you from any unexpected lapse in ability.

Ice climbing, on the other hand, requires the climber to use artificial means to stick to a near frictionless vertical surface. Steel crampons (metal bases laden with spikes) are fitted to the climber's boots so he can kick them into the ice and gain purchase. Specialized axes with deadly sharp serrated picks become extensions of the arms and are swung against the frozen surface to give a secure hold. Alternating crampon and axe work helps the climber move up. Ice screws and snow anchors replace "chocks" and "friends" in the safety system. For me, ice climbing represented a whole new set of technical skills to master, and I set about it earnestly. Regardless of how cold it was, I spent most of my free time on the ice, challenging myself with my climbing buddies.

And challenging it was. One January day, I was working my way up a frozen waterfall with my friend Walter when I experienced my first true lead climbing fall. January temperatures in Thunder Bay are very cold, and this translates into rock hard ice that repels all but the most powerful swings of the ice axe and kicks of your crampons. Being relatively inexperienced, I was not conserving my energy well. By the time I approached the top of the pitch my arms had turned to rubber. (A pitch is a measurement of distance in climbing and basically relates to the length of a rope which is 50 - 60 m.) I swung and pounded with my ice axe but I could not generate enough power to get it to bite into the ice. Walter was down below observing my fruitless actions and no doubt getting ready to stop my inevitable fall. He didn't have long to wait. My wild flailing

> **Lead climbing** is when both climbers start on the ground. One climber ascends while the other feeds out the safety rope ready to arrest any fall. The lead climber connects the rope to the rock or ice with pieces of protection such as chocks, friends, and ice screws. The scary part of lead climbing is that as the lead climber climbs above their last anchor point they are looking at a potentially dangerous fall. If I were to climb 5 m above my last anchor and fall, I would fall 5 m to the anchor and 5 m past the anchor with the possibility of hitting all kinds of things on the way down.

caused my one secure axe and then my feet to detach from the frozen waterfall. I'm sure it happened in an instant, but it seemed to play out in slow motion. I launched out from the ice on a smooth outward arc and then down. I started the fall about 4.5 m above my last piece of protection so I knew I had a fall of at least 9 m coming. I instinctively threw my hands outward to get those razor sharp ice axes as far away from my vital organs as possible. Before I knew it, I was slamming back into the ice with an incredible force. I was stunned, but essentially unhurt by my first real "whipper." Walter held the rope taunt until I regained my senses, and then lowered me to the ground. We both stared at one another in silence for a few moments. I was not ready to venture back up and Walter had no desire to give it a go as he had been spooked by my fall. As we slunk home, we knew that the ice had beaten us that day, but we vowed to train hard and get to the top the next time.

We returned to the ice frequently, each time with better skills and more strength. But we also learned that there was more to ice climbing than just learning the technical skills. Being a winter sport, there were always any number of weather related challenges that we had to deal with. It was not enough to be hanging precariously from a frozen waterfall dozens of meters from the ground, we also had to deal with the Canadian winter.

For those unfamiliar with what a Canadian winter can be like, it can provide a severe, even painful, cold that will penetrate to the bone, making fingers hard to operate and toes near impossible to stand on. It can add in a biting wind that cuts through your best outer layers to lower your core body temperature and sap your strength. Finally, it can feed some horizontally driving ice pellets or snow into the mix and, suddenly, you have a recipe for some real winter fun. It was likely after climbing in such conditions that I began to ask myself, "How can I get more of this?" And, naturally, the world of mountaineering became an alluring prospect.

Once you get to the top of the mountain how do you get down? There are two basic ways to come down from the mountain peak. Often there is a less steep route that can be walked down and when this is not available you must rappel down. Rappelling is the act of anchoring your rope and then sliding down it. Once you reach the end of the rope you pull it down and do it over and over again until you reach the ground.

Joshua Tree National Park

MY TIME at university was fantastic. I did well as a student and had a great group of friends. I found climbing partners and mentors in my classmates, my professors, and within the local climbing community. Climbing in Thunder Bay was still in its infancy and this provided us with a vast opportunity for exploration, discovery and development. Centennial Park, Pass Lake, The Giant, and Thunder Mountain became our regular stomping grounds. Centennial Park is only 10 minutes from the school so it was an easy escape. The cliffs there were not tall at 9 m, but there were over 100 established climbing routes from easy to hard. It would be difficult to find a better and more convenient training ground.

As climbing took a stronger hold on my life I began to plan climbing trips with my friends. No longer content with the small crags of Thunder Bay we decided to explore the climbing of Western Canada and the United States. Every school break found us piling into my Hyundai Excel; the car bursting at the seams with camping and climbing gear. We would head out to the Bugaboos, Squamish, Mount Rushmore, The Needles, Devils Tower, Hueco Tanks, and many other popular climbing destinations, but by far our favourite was Joshua Tree National Park in Southern California, a 48 hour drive from Thunder Bay.

Wanting to maximize our climbing time, these drives were done without stopping for sleep. We would take turns at the wheel in 4-6 hour shifts. When not driving we tried to sleep as best we could. We drove through rain storms, wind storms, snow storms and mile upon mile of beautiful country. Denny's was the food of choice once we discovered the great value of the $2.99 Grand Slam (a huge pile of eggs, sausage, hash browns and toast).

It was at Joshua Tree that we learned one of our first big lessons in climbing. We were attempting to climb a multi-pitch route about 183 m high. We were lead climbing which means that both climbers start at the bottom of the route. The lead climber makes their way up the rock face, placing protection along the way, until they come to a good place to stop (usually close to a full rope length). The second climber then ascends the route removing the protection the lead climber put in. Both climbers are connected to one another and the non-climbing partner acts as the belayer (holding tight to the rope to arrest a fall if required).

The route we were climbing was about six pitches tall and required several hours of climbing. Having a late start and moving slowly, the light soon began to fade as night approached. We were four climbers on two rope teams. My partner and I decided it was too late for us to be able to finish the climb before dark so we began to rappel off the route. The process of rappelling off a multi pitch climb involves connecting your rope to an anchor, sliding down the rope, pulling the rope down and doing it all over again. As we were retrieving our rope from the previous rappel the rope suddenly jammed in a crack. No amount of tugging and pulling would set it free. Fortunately we had a second rope and were able, after many hours of struggling, to get to the ground safely.

The next day we went back to finish our climb and retrieve our rope. As we made our way up we contemplated using the jammed rope as a safety line, but then thought better of it. When we did finally extricate our rope we found that it was cut three-quarters of the way through from the abrasion on the sharp rock. This discovery turned us white with fear. The previous night we had been hanging on this rope, hundreds of feet above the ground, not knowing that the rope was perilously close to cutting in half. Thinking of what could have happened was horrifying. This was a huge lesson for us as young climbers and it helped us to understand the danger of what we were doing. It did not, however, deter us from climbing. We just knew we needed to learn more to ensure safety as we climbed.

Personally, I had no idea that I had a LOT more to learn, and that I would be living a life that would literally have me learning, constantly, relentlessly, in thin air.

Learning in Thin Air - Pondering Success and Failure

Little did I know, but those early years of adventuring would lead me through a thought process about teamwork and leadership that would form the cornerstone of my business activities today.

As I learned about the rudimentary elements of climbing, and experienced some early wins and a few losses in the push for various summits, I was also learning about what it takes to achieve success. I found that while exerting myself physically, I was also constantly thinking about what it was that made some efforts succeed, while others failed. Over time, I came to realize that I was picking up some extremely real, powerfully relevant insight that could apply to any individual and business organization — what I would later crystallize in my mind as "learning in thin air."

In just a few short years, I would find myself continuing to take on many additional climbs. I began to structure in my mind what it was that would ensure that I would have the greatest chance of success — but I was also prepared to analyze what might lead to failure. I began to think constantly about success vs. failure and came to understand that to achieve the former and avoid the latter, I needed to be very deliberate in how I went about things.

Without realizing it, I was forming in my mind key concepts for climbing that related to business and life — powerful stuff, indeed.

But as you will see, I still had much to learn.

My first climbing trip to Mexico
The summit of Ixtaccihuatl 5230 m with
Popcatepetl 5426 m in the background

Higher Elevation

MY TIME at Lakehead University was pivotal. It helped me to access the passion I had for climbing, manage it and channel it. Though I couldn't yet see the details of where I was headed after university, at least I had interim goals and a guiding influence in life.

Goals are important to drive performance, both on the rock face and at work. The goals that best engage us are those that keep us in the "zone," they allow us to use our existing knowledge and skills, yet challenge us and require growth. Being in this zone is called "flow" by the psychologist Csíkszentmihályi. He was once quoted as saying that flow is "being completely involved in an activity for its own sake. The ego falls away. Time flies. Every action, movement, and thought follows inevitably from the previous one, like playing jazz. Your whole being is involved, and you're using your skills to the utmost." This is what climbing is like for me. I am thoroughly engaged in the present yet constantly looking for the next level of challenge.

I had long been aware of people who climbed huge mountain peaks so with my initiation into the world of vertical ice, mountaineering seemed a natural progression for me as a climber. This is when I started to think about Mount Everest. I mean, what is the pinnacle of mountaineering if not Mount Everest? At 8848 m it is the highest mountain on earth; the perfect goal for an aspiring climber. I was smart enough, however, to know that I had a long way to go before I was ready to tackle Everest. Rock climbing was my foundation and ice climbing started to give me the winter skills I would need, but I still had a lot to learn. To achieve my long term goal I first needed to set some interim goals. I set my sights on mastering high altitude mountaineering and aid climbing. This found me going to many parts of the world few people will ever see.

Higher Education - Mexico

MY FRIEND Chris and I had done many climbs together, but we decided that we needed to up our challenge level and so we headed south to Mexico. With our excitement level set to 'high,' we drove 4200 km from Thunder Bay to the Texas Mexico border in his beat up old Toyota pickup truck. This is a long road trip by any standard but we just could not get there fast enough.

We parked the Toyota at the border and took a bus to Amecameca, a town just outside Mexico City. From there, our plan was to take a taxi to the head of the trail that would lead us to the summit of Popocatepetl, a 5426 m peak known to most non-Mexican climbers simply as "Popo." As Popo is the second highest peak in Mexico, we thought that it would be a great place to learn about high altitude climbing. Unfortunately, the volcano was no longer dormant. There was a gate across the road and a soldier blocking all entry. This would not be the last time in my climbing career that a change in plan was enforced by high powered weaponry.

Our taxi driver informed us through hand gestures and broken English that the mountain was erupting and that we were not permitted to climb. He would gladly take us back to town or on to another mountain. Of course, there would be an additional fee. Even as naive Canadians, we were somewhat mystified that our driver had managed to live in the shadow of the mountain and not notice that it was erupting. But we succumbed to the ploy and paid him to take us to Ixtaccihuatl, simply known as "Ixta," a 5239 m volcano.

We arrived at the trailhead for Ixta just before dusk and planned to make it to a climbing hut before dark. This was an aggressive plan, but we were young and fit and felt this was well within our grasp. What we had not factored into the equation was the effect of altitude.

We hoisted our huge packs onto our backs and began to walk uphill at an ambitious pace. This is the classic mistake of novices at altitude. Within moments we began to breathe very heavily, trying desperately to drink in the oxygen that our bodies were simply not equipped to absorb at such low atmospheric pressure. Our pace slowed to a crawl, our chests heaved constantly and our heads began to ache. It quickly became apparent that we were not going to make it to the hut. Even worse, it was beginning to rain. We knew we were going to have to spend the night in the open as we did not bring a tent. With no flat ground in sight, we opted to wedge ourselves between a tree and a boulder. We got into our sleeping bags, stuffed our feet into our packs, zipped our jackets together and laid them over our heads to create a crude shelter. When daylight finally returned, we had survived a sleepless night and learned an important lesson about high altitude: it can incapacitate even the fittest climber. We would need to go slowly and allow our bodies to acclimatize if we were going to make it to the top of Ixta.

Pacing ourselves more reasonably, we arrived at the hut early on day two and, as a nod to the previous night's lesson, spent the rest of the day resting and acclimatizing. That night we set off for the summit. Unfortunately, Chris had to stop several times at the side of the trail to vomit as he was rapidly developing a severe altitude induced headache. Eventually the pain in his head was just too great. Acknowledging the danger of this developing into something much more serious, Chris made the difficult decision to descend immediately – the only remedy for altitude sickness.

Bivouac on Ixta

From where Chris turned around, the route to the top of Ixta was pretty straight forward. Believing him to be coherent and safe, I elected to carry on to the top alone. I was getting pretty tired as I crested the final slopes of Ixta and at 11:00 am stood on the highest peak I had ever attempted. It was a gorgeous sunny day with staggering views extending for a hundred miles in all directions. This moment was a life altering experience. I was hooked on high altitude mountaineering, and even the extreme effort of sucking oxygen from the thin alpine air did not diminish the smile on my face.

The descent from Ixta was quick. I caught up with Chris on the lower slopes of the mountain and found him pretty much recovered, if somewhat chastened. We had begun this climb as two confident young guys, riding a string of lesser climbing successes and ready to take on the world, but we had smacked straight into a surprising and unyielding reality — the effect of altitude on the human body. Our training and our experience with hardship at lower altitude could not possibly have prepared us for this. The high altitude was the direct cause of our unplanned and sleepless night in the rain, and of Chris's forced retreat from his summit bid. But, on the upside, we had managed. Overall on our expedition we had been flexible where we had to be: we had switched mountains when our original target, Popocatepetl, erupted; we had adjusted our pacing when the mountain dictated; we had improvised functional shelter when needed; and we had recognized the need for Chris to descend when the original plan had called for the opposite. We had been sensible in the end and handled the risks in a way that allowed us to climb another day.

As rewarding as the climb up Ixta was for me, once accomplished and briefly celebrated, its memory quickly gave way to thoughts of bigger and better things. Chris and I internalized our substantial learning about altitude, and recalibrated our goals to match our new knowledge and rapidly acclimatizing bodies. By the time a few days had passed, Chris and I were focused on the next project, a nearby peak called Pico de Orizaba. For this climb, Chris and I were joined by our friend Paul.

Pico de Orizaba is a beautiful conical volcano, very closely resembling the well known and perfect shape of Mount Fuji. Like many mountains, its beauty belies danger. At 5612 m, Orizaba is the third highest mountain in North America and much steeper and more dangerous than Ixta. Just days before we arrived, several climbers and a guide had died when they fell from very near the summit of the mountain. We fully expected this climb to test our technical mountaineering skills.

We set out from our camp at 2:00 am bound for the summit, headlamps illuminating a small section of path for us to follow. Our crampons bit into the hard blue ice as we moved forward. It was exciting and beautiful, but the conditions were not exactly what we had been expecting. We were prepared to climb soft snow, not hard ice. That meant we didn't have the appropriate protection to secure our rope to the mountain. We had planned on using the standard mountaineering technique of climbing connected together with a rope.

When roped together, one climber's fall in soft snow could easily be arrested when the other two drop to the ground and thrust their ice axes into the snow to create an anchor. However, this technique is not effective on hard ice. In these conditions, if one person were to fall the other two could not likely arrest the fall. This is exactly what had happened to the guide and clients who had died just a few days earlier. They were almost at the top when one member of the team lost his footing and fell. Without proper ice protection and with no ability to dig their ice axes into the rock hard ice, they all fell to their deaths. Our only choice was to untie from the rope and go solo.

Through the initial darkness, the growing light of dawn and on through the morning we picked our way carefully up the icy slope, ice axes at the ready. Our skills and, notably, our level of acclimatization were up to the challenge that Orizaba posed. We had a spectacular climb, no one slipped and after 10 hours we found ourselves standing on the top of Orizaba.

It was so warm on the summit that we all settled down for a short nap before we descended.

Learning in Thin Air - The Experiential Learning Model

As our climbs continued to take us into ever thinner air, we were quickly ramping up our experience and knowledge. In my own case, I was building a foundation that would provide greater potential for success in the future. I had become a relentlessly experiential learner.

All of us are experiential learners from the moment we are born. When we decide to learn to walk we don't read a book, watch a YouTube tutorial or get a coach — we just try it. We stand up and fall over. We try it again slightly differently and learn from our earlier attempts. Soon we are scooting around like we had been walking forever.

The experiential learning model is a very deliberate process that begins with an experience, we then reflect upon that experience to analyze how it went, what we did well, and what we did not do so well. We then bring in additional tools, models, theories and experiences to make sense of it all and finally we take it forward as learning and apply it to future events.

Experiential Learning Model

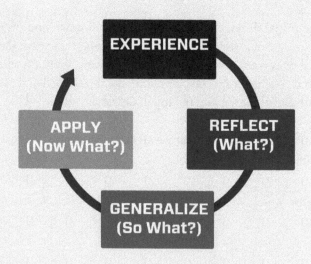

For each progressively more complex climb, I was thinking through in my mind how to evaluate each experience and how to apply it for future benefit. It turned out to be a great framework for development that could be applied for any type of activity.

What did I learn? What did it mean? And what could I do with this knowledge?

Possessed by the opportunities of altitude, I became relentless in building up experience upon experience. My experiential learning was only just beginning.

New Mexico

Outward Bound

NOT ALL my time was spent climbing and learning. I also lived a fairly regular life at times.

While at university I worked as a waiter at a great restaurant with nice owners and a great team of staff, but it was not really me. I began to learn about the advantages of being an extrovert, which I am not. Several of the more extroverted waiters would easily take home double the tips I would. They could easily chat up, joke and flirt with their customers and in return they were rewarded with larger than average tips. I knew I would need to adapt to this environment, but I was struggling with it.

One night the leadership team from the Canadian Outward Bound Wilderness School was in town and they came in for dinner. I was assigned as their waiter and spent the night serving them and chatting. I knew many of them from the field and was asked by the executive director how I liked waiting tables. I told him that it was ok, but that it was not really me. He asked me if I would rather be teaching rock climbing for Outward Bound. My positive response was so enthusiastic he offered me a job on the spot. That night was my last shift waiting tables.

I could not have envisioned it at the time, but Outward Bound became the launching pad for the rest of my life. I spent the next several summers working as a wilderness instructor for them and continued to do so on and off for the next ten years. Outward Bound has been known for helping wayward youth to find their way but it can also help their instructors. Outward Bound gave me confidence in myself, helped me discover my personal values, and allowed me

Kayaking on Lake Powell, Nevada

to grow as a person. They gave me so much it is really difficult to explain except to say it was a truly pivotal time in my life.

In the summer of 1996 I was working with Outward Bound in New Mexico establishing a new program area. The work was hard, but exciting and rewarding. While in New Mexico I learned that my stepfather had been diagnosed with terminal cancer. As soon as my contract was up I made my way back home to help.

The power of the mind is truly amazing. When I arrived home my stepfather Barry was obviously sick, but he seemed to be holding on. Very quickly, however, he reached a tipping point and his condition went downhill rapidly. Even though he did not express this to me, it seemed like he had been waiting until I got home to help my Mom. Once I was home his body seemed to relax and allowed the cancer to take over. He passed away only two weeks after I got back.

After Barry passed away I decided to stay at home with my Mom to help tie up loose ends and to sell the family business. During this time I decided to start my own guiding business. I called it Planet Adventure after my desire to explore the world. My primary activity was teaching rock climbing in the summer and ice climbing in the winter, but I also ran a few trips to the South West United States and into Mexico. It was a good life, fun and easy. I would wake every morning, load my pack with climbing gear, hike out to the local rock cliff and set up my ropes in anticipation of the clients who would soon join me. I loved to teach them how to climb, to share my passion with them, and to watch them learn and experience their personal triumphs on the rock.

I also began offering climbing trips for a Toronto based fitness club. One day the Recreation Director suggested that it would be a good idea for me to take the Managers of the various clubs out climbing. They would then be able to promote this activity within their clubs and help expand my business.

When the Managers arrived I was in my glory. Each Manager was a young, beautiful, fit woman. As a young single male I thought I had hit the jackpot. They were a great group and we had an amazing day. Each of the managers were fantastic, but there was one that stood out to me. Susan seemed to really embrace the experience and we spoke comfortably. I was really happy when Susan called to set up another couple of climbing days. As we spent time together I began to feel that perhaps there was more to this relationship than climbing.

I wanted to ask her out on a date, but was unsure what her response would be. She and I lived in two very different worlds. She was in the city with a big job and a big salary. She went to expensive events and hung out with successful people. I lived in the country (with my Mom), and brought home a very meager salary.

I figured what the heck and asked her out. To my surprise she accepted. I drove the two hours down to the city and we met at a restaurant close to her work. Looking back on it now I wonder what she was thinking. Here I was with my long hair in a ponytail and holes in my jeans meeting this beautiful and successful woman for dinner. We had a great evening, but I thought I may have blown it when I had to borrow money from her to get my car out of the parking lot.

Two weeks after our first date I left with some friends for a one month trip to Mexico. While I was gone I was constantly thinking about Susan and wondering if she would move on while I was gone or still be interested upon my return. Fortunately for me, I had done something right. I am still not sure what it was, but Susan could somehow see that we were meant to be together.

Susan and I on the summit of
Illiniza Norte, Ecuador 5126 m

learning in THIN AIR

Learning in Thin Air - Believing in Yourself

Outward Bound was a pivotal time for me and helped me to grow so much. This is exactly what Outward Bound was designed to do. The foundation of Outward Bound came in WWII when it was observed that when a ship was sunk at sea the older more experienced sailors seemed to have a much greater survival rate than the younger less experienced sailors. It was determined that much of this survival success was due to greater confidence in self and emotional strength to withstand adverse situations. Thus a program was designed to provide sailors with experience that would strengthen them as individuals and to give them the fortitude to withstand adversity.

Post war this program formed into Outward Bound and was opened up to civilians. It soon spread throughout the world and morphed into many different programs depending upon the geography of the local area. Youth and adults alike tested themselves and grew as individuals on the water, in the mountains and on the rock face. Not only were people growing individually, but they were also learning about the power of a team and leadership.

I think self-regard and self-actualization are the biggest and most important things I took from Outward Bound; the ability to like oneself and to constantly aspire to learn and grow.

Meeting Susan also taught me the power of partnership. Up until this point I had had strong partnerships with my climbing buddies, but with Susan it was different. Having someone in your corner who totally believes in and encourages you is so important. Without her support, I have no doubt that I would not have been able to accomplish many of the things I have done in my life.

Ultimately, my life lesson here was to believe in myself, to constantly strive as a life long learner, and to find unconditional support from a partner.

*High up on Moonlight Buttress
in Zion National Park*

The School
of Hard Rock

HAVING DONE some high altitude climbing, I determined that the next step in my development, and the ultimate challenge for many climbers, was to climb a "big wall." A big wall is any face that cannot be scaled in a single day. These walls are often in the 600 - 1200 m range and almost invariably entail aid climbing.

Aid climbing is a very slow and methodical process. It requires mastery of a whole new set of climbing equipment and techniques. In aid climbing, the climber selects a piece of equipment such as a metal "chock" or "friend" and inserts it into a crack. He then connects a small nylon ladder to the gear, ascends a few steps and repeats the process with a second ladder. The equipment you place into the wall is your "aid" in climbing, but also your protection in the event of a fall. Aid climbing is very painstaking and gear intensive. Climbers set out for a multi-day climb with hundreds of pounds of gear. Now, this form of climbing may not sound overly challenging, but it is. Although the climber is not physically gripping each hand hold, there is a lot of physical strain involved. The mental side of aid climbing is very strenuous. Each route is a huge problem to solve as you puzzle out what gear to select, what crack to follow, and how to organize hundreds of feet of rope, hundreds of pieces of equipment and all your camping gear without being overwhelmed.

Additionally, it also exposed me to bigger and bigger challenges that helped me gain a level of confidence that comes with spending many hours with nothing but a half mile of empty air beneath my feet.

Zion National Park

WHILE IN Thunder Bay there were many great opportunities to learn and practice my aid climbing skills, but it could not provide a "big wall." For that, I went to Zion National Park in Utah with my climbing partners, Julian and Andrew.

The aid routes on the red sandstone walls of Zion were spectacular. Standing at the bottom looking up I had to arch my back to see towards the top. Snaking up these tall towering rock walls were fine cracks, most of which were too small to insert a foot or hand. Other than these fine cracks the wall was void of any features. Without using artificial means, it would be almost impossible to scale them.

When big wall climbing, you need to take everything with you that you will need for the duration of the climb, whether you expect it to be several hours or several days. There is no coming back to the ground for supplies. We climbed all day and then set camp for the night, repeating the process for as many days as it took to reach the top. The mainstay of our camp was our port-a-ledge, essentially a camping cot that was secured to the vertical wall. We were tied in at all times but, still, my first few nights on the port-a-ledge were unnerving.

Andrew and I were about 300 m up the rock face when it came time to stop for the night. With our harnesses on, connected to the wall with a length of rope, we set up our port-a-ledges and had a dinner consisting of cheese, crackers and salami (it is possible to cook while on the climb, but we had elected to leave this luxury behind). As it started to get dark, I laid out my sleeping bag and crawled in for the night. The air was fresh and crisp, but not cold. I could hear the Zion river flowing below me as I watched the birds dance on the wind currents. Before attempting to doze off in the waning light, I enjoyed a view of miniature people and cars as if I were looking out an airplane window.

Despite my fatigue, I managed only a fitful sleep. All night long my port-a-ledge swayed in a persistent wind. When a particularly strong gust would buffet me around and bounce me against the wall, I would turn on my headlamp to make sure my anchors were still holding fast to the rock. It took several nights before I learned to trust my equipment and my skills in such a dramatic setting, however it remains one of the most exciting experiences of my life.

As the climb progressed and we got higher and higher, the mental strain started to creep up on me. I had just spent six hours belaying Andrew on a particularly difficult pitch. As he struggled his way upward, I hung in my harness connected to two pieces

Belaying means to hold fast or to stop. To belay is the act of holding the climbing rope so that the other climber is secure in the event of a fall.

of protection that were adequate at best. If Andrew fell, I doubted that the protection would hold. That would have been disastrous for both of us. Finally, I heard him yell down to me that he was secure at the next belay anchor and I could make my way up.

As I ascended the route with over 300 m of air below me I began to freak out. My mind was struggling with the fear I was feeling, and I was losing the battle to keep it under control. This is often the biggest challenge in climbing. It is not the physical strain, but the emotional strain that creates the biggest challenge. Days or weeks spent in uncomfortable conditions, hours of hunger, constant danger and fear often can overwhelm a climber, as I was starting to experience.

As I reached the ledge where Andrew was standing I was an emotional wreck. My heart was pounding, my respiration was rapid and shallow, and my mind was spinning. I needed some time to rest and regroup. I sat for a quick snack of chocolate, a great cure for all that troubles you, before continuing to climb.

Eventually I was ready to continue up for another two days of physical and emotional punishment. As we pulled over the final ledge and stood on top of the climb I was exhausted, but elated. I had learned so much from this climb. Not only about the technical skills, but more importantly I had gained some insight into how emotions impact performance and how to combat a mind that is spiraling out of control. It was far from mastery, but it was a start that would help me in difficult situations for the rest of my life.

Big wall climbing gave me the technical knowledge and rope management skills I would need on large mountaineering expeditions. But it also gave me confidence to handle more discomfort, bigger problems and the higher risks that come with bigger aspirations.

Fear does not disappear on a big wall or on a mountain. It is always there to help you make smart decisions. It is not about eliminating the fear, it is about learning how to perform at a high level with the fear. I have a saying that summarizes how I see fear in the mountains – "fear breeds hesitation, and hesitation will make your worst nightmares come true." I am not sure where the phrase came from or if I was the one who came up with it, but I find this statement so true in everything we do. Hesitation in the mountains, and in life, often leads to inferior results or grave consequences. Full commitment is required as the slightest pause in confidence could bring the world crashing down on you. The challenge is to control the fear and to use the energy that is produced to allow you to accomplish great things.

Learning in Thin Air - The Four Stages of Development

In any task or learning experience I believe we have to travel through four phases. Each phase builds upon the last and plateaus at the point of real, sustainable expertise.

For me, succeeding with complex climbs really made me wonder about these efforts compared to my early experiences. Quite obviously, I had no clue what I was doing when I started, which I call my "unconscious incompetent" stage. By the time I was mastering "hard rock climbing" I was clearly progressing into having a skill level that involved "conscious competence." I was steadily moving up what is known as the "Four Stages of Development" created by Noel Burch in the 1970's

Unconscious Incompetence
This initial phase essentially means we are not good, but we have so little experience that we don't even know how bad we are. Although not a place you want to stay for long, it is the natural entry point. The key for progress is to be curious, to ask questions, to learn and apply. For me this phase was reflective of my time in Thunder Bay and my early ice climbs.

Conscious Incompetence
At this level you are bad and you know it. The beauty of this phase is that you also know what you know and what you don't know, what you need to learn, how you need to learn it and who you need to learn it from. In other words you become a sponge and start sucking in learning. That's probably the best way to describe my climbing efforts in the US and Mexico.

learning in THIN AIR

Conscious Competence

You are very deliberate in this phase, doing specific things to get a specific result. You know what to do, when to do it, how to do it, and who to do it with. It builds confidence and starts to move you into a phase where you are good and you know it.

Moving on to my "hard rock" climbing experiences took me into a different level of climbing. The element of risk was just so much higher, but I felt I had moved into a phase of knowing what, when, how and with whom to do these climbs.

Unconscious Competence

This fourth phase is where you are so good you don't even need to think about it anymore. You can operate on automatic pilot.

As I continue to wrap my life of climbing with my passion for learning, this model keeps turning over in my mind. I sometimes wonder if being at the top of the pyramid, unconscious competence, is the best place to be. Or if conscious competence would be a better place to spend your time and net you greater results on a more consistent basis?

Four Stages of Development

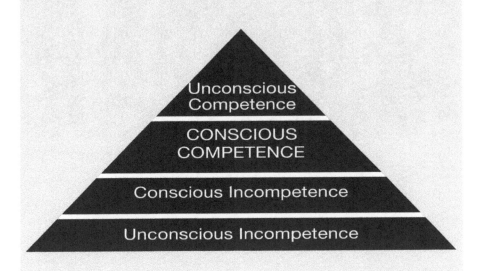

*The Logan Team 1991
with our helicopter pilot*

Mount Logan

THERE IS no doubt that success is sweet. Success builds confidence which allows us to push our boundaries further. But success on one mountain never guarantees an easy ride on the next.

With Everest in mind, I felt I needed to learn more about extreme environments. I decided to climb Canada's highest peak, Mount Logan (5959 m) situated at the head of the Hubbard and Logan glaciers in Kluane National Park in the Yukon Territory. Its location near the Arctic Circle means very extreme conditions can be expected all year round. In this particular year not all of our team made it onto the mountain due to a severe, extended storm.

Expect the Unexpected

I AND six friends (Scott, Sarah, Chris, Rudy, Colin and future Everest partner Angus) set out to climb Mount Logan in late April 1999. At this time of year the winter still held a tight grasp on the mountain with subzero temperatures and frequent storms. Our initial plan was to fly by fixed wing plane to Base Camp on the mountain, however, as we arrived in the city of Whitehorse we learned that the plane was down for repairs and would not be able to fly us in for at least two weeks. Scrambling to find an alternative we met with a local helicopter pilot who said he could take us in.

After several days of waiting out bad weather the helicopter finally took off and deposited Colin and Chris on the mountain. As the helicopter made its way back a huge storm moved in and Colin and Chris were trapped on the mountain for the next four days. Fortunately, we had been smart enough to send them in with tents, food and fuel so they could survive this unexpected solo time.

After several more days and multiple attempts Angus, Scott and I were able to join Colin and Chris. We set up Base Camp and waited for Rudy and Sarah to join us, but as the weather got worse it soon became apparent that they were not going to make it. In fact, no flights could get onto the mountain for the next three weeks. As there was nothing else we could really do, we decided to start our climb without them.

Heavy load on Mount Logan

Our team of five spent the next three weeks on the mountain in relentless snow storms and -45°C temperatures. Using wide, steel edged backcountry touring skis to provide us with enough flotation to stay near the surface of the deep snow, we dragged our gear packed sleds behind us. It was torturous work. For protection against falls, we travelled roped together in pairs. Day after day we struggled uphill against deep snow, bone chilling cold, and high winds. It was so constant that it almost became routine.

On one particular day, with the weather quickly deteriorating, we found ourselves in low visibility conditions from the blowing snow. I vividly remember watching Colin skiing along, leaning into the driving snow when suddenly he was gone. Chris, attached by a climbing rope to Colin, was sliding backwards across the snow. Colin's weight plus the weight of his sled, an additional 45 kg, had pulled Chris off his feet, dragging him violently towards a dark, gaping hole. Just as Chris was about to reach the open mouth of the hole, he abruptly stopped. Colin had hit the bottom of a crevasse.

learning in THIN AIR

We had not realized that we had moved onto a huge crevasse field, perhaps because we were rushing too much to escape the quickly building storm. These deep cracks in the mountain's glacier were all the more dangerous because they were made invisible by a thin layer of freshly fallen snow. Somehow, Chris had made it across one of these hidden crevasses on a thin snow bridge that had miraculously held his weight. Colin had not. A trap door had opened beneath him as he plunged 12 m into the crevasse.

I was traveling right behind Chris and Colin on a rope with Scott and Angus. We quickly dropped our packs, unhooked our sleds and with hearts racing we carefully made our way over to Chris. He was understandably rattled but otherwise fine. I laid flat on the snow, crawled tentatively forward and peered into the hole to see how Colin was. To my great relief, he looked up at me and waved his hand to indicate that he was unhurt and suffered no injuries at all. Luckily, as he fell his pack made him flip over like a turtle, and when he hit the bottom of the crevasse, his pack absorbed most of the impact. Now all we had to do was get him out of the hole.

This is exactly where technical training and proper equipment can make a difference. We put together a series of snow anchors and pulleys, and combining our strength, soon had Colin winched out of the hole. By this time it was late in the day, Colin and Chris were cold from their ordeal, and the storm had intensified around us. We had very little visibility and agreed further travel would be unwise. Carefully probing the ground to make sure there were no other hidden holes nearby, we set up our tents. For three days we were trapped in those tents

Camp 3 on Mount Logan

as the storm raged around us. When eventually the winds relented and the skies cleared, we crawled out of our tents into a winter wonderland. We packed up our gear and set off once again for the top.

Due to the poor weather and our slow progress we were running out of time, food and fuel. It was time for a team huddle. We agreed that our original goal, the true summit, was no longer a viable option. We made the decision to climb to the top of Queen's Peak, a sub-summit of Mount Logan, rather than take the much heightened risk of sticking to the original plan. And so, we climbed to the top of this spectacular and steep ridge and together celebrated success. When we finally got off the mountain, we were told by the park rangers that our climb had taken place during one of the longest periods of bad weather in the mountain's recorded history. That alone validated our decision to go for Queen's Peak.

Mount Logan holds the record for the lowest registered temperature in the Northern hemisphere, -71° C.

In retrospect, I have no doubt that the success of this expedition, in fact our very survival on the mountain, was a result of good team work. By fortunate accident or design, we did so many things right as a team. We had the technical skills and equipment to do the job, and we applied them. We positioned ourselves for success by having a common goal (the summit). We came into the expedition with strong interpersonal relationships founded on the trust that comes with years of climbing and belaying together. We were able to frankly assess situations and make critical consensual decisions quickly, sometimes as a matter of reflex. The challenges of weather and the crisis of the crevasse fall drew us closer together and reinforced our bonds. More importantly, we all brought complete commitment to the table. That commitment extended to the expedition goal, but also to the safety and well being of every team member.

With several mountaineering successes under my belt, I was getting a feel for the mountains. A growing bank of experience and knowledge was allowing me to better anticipate and judge challenges. Wanting to test myself on higher and higher ground, I climbed several peaks in Ecuador and then moved on to Argentina where Mount Aconcagua towers above the rugged Andes range.

Learning in Thin Air - Deliberate Learning

Most climbers don't go far or live long without developing some good team and leadership skills. But the starting point for most climbing success stories is with an individual. There is a lot of ground work to lay in terms of personal skills, attitudes and experience. For me, this began in a haphazard way. However, as my vision of success as a climber came into sharper focus, my personal development became very deliberate.

Deliberate. I often reflected on that word while immersed in the planning for a climb, or while facing extreme personal, physical and mental changes in some of the most extreme conditions on the planet.

What did I come to learn through those early years? That I had to first connect solidly to my passion, then build the technical skills, experience base, self confidence and judgment I would require as the danger ramped up. This was not a strictly linear journey. I experienced setbacks. But I did two things consistently once the vision was born: I reflected often and I applied the learning. I was deliberate in my efforts. I just didn't have a complete model - yet!

On the summit of Aconcagua 6959 m Argentina

Ready for the Big Time!

LET'S FACE it: life is a mountain. It presents us with challenge and opportunity, sorrow and joy, failure and success. In climbing, I have had notable successes, but not without first suffering some notable failures. Of course, one could argue that in the climbing world, living to climb another day is always a success by some measure!

It's with that thought in mind that one of my first forays into the world of big mountaineering began on Aconcagua in Argentina in January of 2000. At 6959 m Aconcagua is the highest mountain in all the Americas and was the first of the Seven Summits I have climbed. Aconcagua is called the "Stone Sentinel" due to its immense size and the atrocious weather that guards its summit. This three week climb opened my eyes to extended mountain expeditions and to the world of higher and higher altitude. It was also the first time that I was climbing with a group of strangers. This proved to be an interesting experience and demonstrated the critical importance of forming a team at an accelerated rate.

The Seven Summits are the highest mountains on each of the seven continents. Summiting all of them is regarded as a mountaineering challenge, first postulated as such and achieved on April 30, 1985 by Richard Bass.

Our team consisted of a leader, who I already knew, and 12 men and women from across the United States, Canada and Mexico. Some were fit and experienced, and some were not. Nonetheless everyone was friendly and welcoming.

It was classic alpine expedition methodology. From Base Camp we slowly made our way up the mountain to acclimatize to the altitude and stock our mid and high camps. This process entailed multiple trips up and down the mountain over 2 weeks, sometimes sleeping at higher camps, sometimes returning to recover at lower camps. After 2 weeks of preparation we were set to launch a bid for the summit from our High Camp.

Setting off in the dark of the night, I had my headlamp lit and my down parka on to fight off the bitter cold. One behind another we moved slowly higher and higher. As we neared the top, we were moving at a snail's pace. We had entered a notorious part of the climb just before the summit called the "Caneleta." Depending on the weather, this narrow gully can be covered in snow and ice or loose rock. For us it was loose rock. With every step I took, I slid back half the distance. This was physically difficult, but even more mentally devastating. Here I was, almost at the top, completely exhausted, struggling to breathe, and I was sliding back down the hill with each and every step. This is the time when it is easiest to give up and, I confess, the thought occurred to me. But it is also the time that the mind must overrule the body's insistence that the game is over. I kept my eye on the goal and did not allow temporary difficulties and discomfort to defeat me. I pulled it together and pressed on. So did my teammates.

Scott on the trek to Aconcagua

learning in THIN AIR

It was cold and windy at the top, but we all made it as a team. I was ecstatic. We stayed on the summit for about 30 minutes to rest and take photos. We then began the long trip back to High Camp.

It was on the way down from the summit of Aconcagua that I saw more of the debilitating effects of high altitude on the human body and mind. One of our team members began to talk to me at a rest stop. He asked me if I thought we should ride the horses back down the mountain instead of walking. When I asked him what horses he was referring to, he pointed into the distance and said, "Those horses." There were no horses. He was hallucinating from the effects of high altitude induced cerebral edema; the lack of air pressure at this high altitude had allowed fluid to pool next to his brain. The symptoms of cerebral edema include hallucination and can rapidly result in death if the person is not taken to lower altitudes immediately. In this case, we were able to get our climbing partner down to safety and he recovered fully. Another lesson learned.

With the successful climb of Aconcagua, I had my first of the Seven Summits in the bag. It was time to build on that success and think about the others on the list.

Learning in Thin Air - From the Mountain to the Boardroom

Perhaps my early mountaineering efforts began as a method to channel the enthusiasm for adventure that is found in many teenagers, desires which stay with them into their early adult years. But, as I climbed I also began to learn that everything I was thinking about on a mountain was relating to life in general. I was having a lot of fun, but I was also starting to think how I could channel my learning and enthusiasm into something that would help other people to manage their own successes and failures.

I believe that three main things have enabled my success in both climbing and in business and when these things have not been present, failure was the most common outcome. I have experienced a few failures along the way during the early years — and was beginning to learn from them.

What were the elements of my successful summits? Vision, action, and reflection.

I believe that the positive things in our lives — joy, success, and opportunity — are not determined purely by accident. They are determined in large part by how we view life and by the role we are prepared to play in creating our own stories, happy endings and all.

As a result of my experiences over the years I have developed an approach to mountains, business and life in general. This model can be applied as an individual, a team, a leader, or to an organization.

This very simple model describes the three essential steps for success:

The Deliberate Success Model

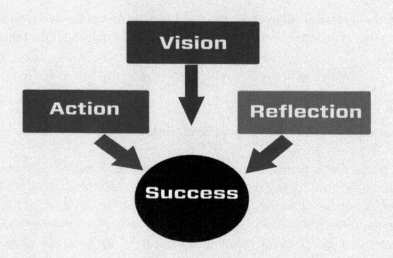

1. Create your vision of success. *A vision is a description of a desired future state. This includes both the results you intend to get, and the culture you intend to create while you strive for your results. It describes who you want to be as a person, a team, a leader or an organization. This identifies your values, your norms and your expectations. As Stephen Covey writes in the 7 Habits of Highly Effective People, "Begin with the end in mind."*

Without a vision you have no focused direction; you are simply wandering through life. While this is not necessarily a bad thing, I believe that you are more likely to achieve great successes and get more out of life if you have a vision. This vision must be filled with passion and be motivational when you read it. This will be your road map for development and your score board for performance.

*2. **Take action.** Make a deliberate, focused, detailed action plan and implement it. In other words your action plan must be S.M.A.R.T. (Specific, Measurable, Attainable, Relevant, and Time Bound). These actions must be directly connected to your vision. Deliberate and specific actions are essential to success. You can just do what you do and hope for the best, or you can do the right thing to get the desired result.*

*3. **Reflect.** Without reflection it is easy to lose your way; to stray off course towards some shiny object that catches your attention. Periodically ask yourself if you are achieving what you set out to do. Is your vision still the right one for you? Are you being who you said you would be? Are your actions getting you the results you had hoped for? If not, why not, and what do you need to change? Set a schedule to reflect upon your vision and your actions on a regular basis. If you do not schedule it, it is unlikely it will happen.*

The three steps described above repeat themselves as we grow and reinvent ourselves. If you have a very specific goal in mind it may even be a good idea to get a coach involved to help you brainstorm, to be a sounding board and to hold you accountable.

In my early years of climbing and business I did not know the importance of focusing deliberately on vision, action and reflection. I just assumed that if I had the skills and experience necessary, the desire, and the right intention I would get the results I was looking for.

Little did I know I had quite a lot to learn!

Cho Oyu

Cho Oyu 8201 m

Framing the Risks

MY LONG term goal was to climb Mount Everest.

I had learned enough through my 20+ years of climbing that one does not, or at least should not, just decide one day to climb Everest and go. It was likely that I would only ever have one chance to attempt this climb, so I wanted to give myself the best opportunity for success. I had strategically orchestrated the last 15 years of my climbing to slowly work towards Everest, climbing bigger and bigger mountains and learning all aspects of the sport. In the spring of 2001, I was off for what I considered my big test. My success or failure on this expedition would, in my mind, determine if I was worthy and prepared enough to go on to Everest. It was time to test myself on an 8000 m peak, Cho Oyu. I would see how I performed on this lower and "easier" mountain; if I did not perform well here, I had no business on Everest.

There were always risks and challenges associated with any of the climbs that I went on: falling; equipment failure; weather. However, one of the most challenging risks was altitude.

Human beings (in fact all animals) are adapted to function well within a relatively narrow range of environmental conditions. On mountains, the fluctuation of temperature, air pressure and oxygen concentration can all be life threatening. We can protect ourselves from the extremes by, for instance, wearing special clothing and breathing bottled oxygen but, short of staying in a pressurized cabin (as we do with commercial air travel), we are limited in our ability to adapt to high altitude. The complications that arise from exposing one's self to extreme altitude are among the most constant threats to life in high places. The effect of altitude is a fascinating and a frightening science.

Our bodies' cells depend on oxygen to survive, and the oxygen in the air around us can only get to our cells if it can first enter our bloodstream. The first step along the way is relatively simple: get the oxygen into the lungs where it can come into contact with rich beds of blood filled capillaries. In other words, breathing. The next step, getting it into the blood, is problematic at high altitude. Atmospheric pressure is one of the forces that push the oxygen across the capillary walls and keep it dissolved in the blood. As we climb in altitude from sea level and the atmospheric pressure drops, less oxygen can be coaxed into the bloodstream. Contrary to popular belief, the percentage of oxygen in the air at high altitude is roughly the same as it is at sea level. It's just that the lower pressure creates a limited ability to transfer the oxygen into our blood and therefore our blood does not carry its normal payload.

This lack of oxygen has ripple effects. A normal, healthy body in its natural environment is constantly dying and then rebuilding itself. Of the body's several trillion cells, millions are dying every day. We all engage in a weekly battle to keep our homes from being overtaken by the huge amounts of sloughed off skin cells and hair that this generates. Happily, in the presence of adequate oxygen, these dying cells are quickly replaced with new, healthy ones at about the same rate they are lost. That is, until we venture above 8000 m into the "death zone," where our bodies lose the ability to regenerate new cells. Cells are dying at an increased rate, but they are not being replaced. This is the beginning of death.

There's more. With the decrease in available oxygen, our bodies automatically prioritize which parts are critical and will therefore get the majority of the available supply. (A similar thing happens with the onset of hypothermia where the body reacts to a sudden drop in core body temperature by shutting down blood flow to the extremities, thus protecting the body core and its vital organs with any available warmth.) When we are at extreme altitude, the little oxygen available to us is routed via the bloodstream to the vital organs and the brain. Oxygen supplies to the muscles of our arms and legs are slowly shut off, forcing us to move at a much slower pace. As the reduction in available oxygen is prolonged, less critical organs are denied oxygen. Ultimately this sets off a dangerous downward spiral of functioning that includes extreme fatigue, a slowing of pace, the loss of motor control and cognition, loss of consciousness, complete organ failure and, finally, heart stoppage.

A person who spends prolonged periods on a high altitude expedition feels these low levels of oxygen, even before they are critical, in a number of disconcerting ways. For instance, a climber's body struggles to digest food, effectively robbing it of precious calories and nutrients. Because of this, the brain suppresses appetite and the desire to eat. As unimaginable as this may sound, you just do not feel like eating at high altitude. You must force yourself. Lean, fit climbers regularly lose 20 to 30 or more pounds on an extended climb due to the increased caloric need and the decreased caloric intake. Now, losing a few pounds may sound appealing to some people but, on a climb you really need all of the energy you can get. The loss of body fat and muscle robs you of much needed energy reserves and power. The climber will also experience the symptoms of the brain's reaction to the ongoing oxygen deprivation. It is almost impossible to fall into a deep sleep at high altitude. Good rest is elusive. Climbers are almost constantly sleep deprived and often tell stories of vivid and dramatic dreams at high altitude. Despite this, they must perform at very high physical and mental levels.

If the oxygen issue is not enough to deal with, there is one more major effect of altitude: the lower amounts of pressure allow fluids to leak from veins, capillaries and other body tissues. The medical term for this is "edema." Pulmonary edema occurs when fluids accumulate in the lungs and make it even more difficult to breathe. Cerebral edema is when the fluids accumulate on the brain. Not surprisingly, both are life threatening.

Ultimately, above 8000 m you will die. It is not a question of if, but rather of when. It could be two days or maybe four, but sooner or later your body will shut down and you will die. Even in perfect conditions, you will die. This means that whenever you climb above this line, you are, at best, pitting yourself against a fast running biological clock. In fact, the highest parts of the highest mountains on earth are littered with hundreds of bodies of climbers who have died in pursuit of their dreams.

This climb was my first excursion into this extreme altitude and the fabled "death zone." I needed to understand and prepare for the associated risks if I did not want to become another statistic on the mountain.

Camp 1 Cho Oyu 6400 m

Welcome to the Big Leagues!

Our Personal Capacity

CHO OYU, "the Turquoise Goddess" in Tibetan, straddles the border of Nepal and Tibet and stands a staggering 8201 m above sea level. That is 26,906 feet; more than five vertical miles. It is the 6th highest mountain in the world and one of only 14 peaks that reach above 8000 m. All of these giants lie within the borders of Nepal, Tibet and Pakistan.

My passion for climbing led me to Cho Oyu. It loomed as the biggest adventure of my life, a great personal opportunity. By this time, Susan and I were married and we had a one year old daughter, Amy. Susan has always been extremely understanding of my passion for climbing and has supported me fully in my pursuits.

My Personal Preparation

ONCE I committed to climb Cho Oyu, I trained intensely to make sure I was physically ready for the rigours I would encounter. I started to run every day, did hill repeats, sprint interval workouts and ran my first half marathon. I followed a regime of regular push ups, sit ups, chin ups and weight workouts. As strange as it sounds, I actually tried to put weight on to make up for the approximately 25 pounds I expected to lose on the mountain. Muscle is best, but a little fat is good as well. So, following the advice of a trusted friend, I added pizza and beer to the workouts.

I had most of the gear I would need for the climb, but purchased some new and specialized equipment that I had not needed for climbs in North America. New Koflach Arctis Extreme boots and 40 Below over boots would keep my feet warm in sustained cold, although each was the size of a small car. I also picked up a one piece Mountain Hardware down suit. Thanks to the strategically located trap door, I could live for weeks in this "sleeping bag with arms and legs." It would keep me warm on the summit push and even prove quite comfortable for sleeping.

By the early spring of 2001, I was fitter than I'd ever been, well equipped and connected to a group of four other highly skilled climbers. If I had any misgivings, they were dwarfed by the anticipation of meeting Cho Oyu face to face.

By March 22, I found myself on a plane bound for Kathmandu.

Mountains above 8000 m	
Everest	8848 m
K2	8611 m
Kangchenjunga	8586 m
Lhotse	8516 m
Makalu	8485 m
Cho Oyu	8201 m
Dhaulagiri I	8167 m
Manaslu	8163 m
Nanga Parbat	8126 m
Annapurna I	8091 m
Gasherbrum I	8080 m
Broad Peak	8051 m
Gasherbrum II	8034 m
Shishagangma	8027 m

Journal Entry for March 22 (Day 1) - Hong Kong

The flight out today was long. It eventually deposited me in Hong Kong in a time confused state. I was lucky to have a friend in Hong Kong. He and his wife were wonderful hosts for the night. We talked for a while, but soon my sleep deprivation got the better of me and I went off to bed. As I dozed in my bed, I felt as though I was dreaming; was I really doing this? This is one of the biggest adventures of my life, and yet it is so emotionally difficult. Leaving home was very tough. Saying goodnight to my one year old daughter Amy before I left was heart wrenching. As Susan drove me to the airport, few words were spoken. We were both consumed with our own thoughts, wondering what the next eight weeks would bring. I know these emotions will dull as time goes on, but for now it is immensely difficult. Leaving home will quite possibly be the most difficult part of this trip.

I will try not to let my heavy heart bring me down however, as this is an amazing opportunity for me. It is not one that many people will ever get, or perhaps ever want for that matter, but I do want it, and I owe it to Susan and to Amy to get as much from this experience as I can. I am determined to come back from this trip a better person in some way. I hope to use this experience to enrich our lives somehow. I will do it. I will get to the top and back home again.

54

The Initial Steps

THE FLIGHT to, and arrival in, Kathmandu really marked several significant aspects of this expedition. I finally felt that I was moving physically closer to the summit of Cho Oyu. I was also about to meet the expedition leader and the rest of our climbing team for the first time. These are the people with whom I would spend the next two months, yet they were almost unknown to me. Would our leader be capable? Would we all get along with each other? What was the plan of attack? How would we deal with the major cultural change we were about to encounter? How would we all measure up against the mountain itself?

As I sat on the plane, full of nervous anticipation, bound for the other side of the world, I found myself spending as much time thinking about the world I was leaving behind as the unknown chapter about to unfold. This hinted at one more recurring battle I would face on the mountain: the psychological challenge of enduring the mountain while intensely missing my family back home.

Journal Entry for March 23 (Day 2) - Kathmandu

My five and a half hour flight from Hong Kong to Kathmandu today went relatively smoothly. There was no movie on the plane and the food was terrible, but they did serve free beer. I was met at the airport by our expedition leader, John, a tall, fit, good looking and gregarious guy. He has obviously been here many times before and knew how to work the system. He had wandered through customs into the "passenger only" area. When a guard approached him, his strategy was to first ignore him. When that didn't work, he talked really fast and used lots of gestures to confuse him. Eventually the guard would give up and wander away to focus on someone less difficult to corral. It seemed to work, as neither of us were arrested.

John has been on several Himalayan expeditions, including climbing Cho Oyu before. He appears to be the perfect leader, commanding respect and acting in charge. I feel fortunate to be on his team, and willing to follow his lead.

We gathered my two large duffel bags from the luggage belt and piled them onto a cart. As I emerged from the airport, I was treated to my first experience of Kathmandu. What a crazy place! I don't know whether to describe it as

City of Kathmandu

organized chaos or just chaos that somehow seemed to work. The noise and the congestion was staggering. Hundreds of people pushed and shoved and yelled to get my attention. Everywhere there were taxi drivers and porters looking to make a few dollars from my arrival. Fortunately, John was an old hand at this and swiftly guided me through the throngs of people to our waiting car and driver.

The streets of Kathmandu were even more chaotic than the scene at the airport. A two lane road had 4-5 lanes of actual traffic and, although there were lines painted on it, they did not seem to hold any sway. Communication between cars was through a system of horn honks, whistles and hand slaps to the sides of the vehicles. The streets were crowded with cars, trucks, buses, bikes, motorcycles, rickshaws, pedestrians, and even cows and dogs. As we entered the heart of the city, the streets got very narrow and the poverty became very apparent. Small shops littered the streets, hawkers were everywhere, everything was covered with a thin layer of grime and the noise was horrific! I quickly experienced sensory overload.

Don't ask me how, but we soon pulled up to our hotel. I gratefully disembarked from our vehicle and stumbled into the lobby. After checking into my room, I *cleaned myself up a bit and then went for dinner where I met the rest of the team. We are quite an international group coming from various countries in the world. John, Steve, Sarah, Rick and I will spend the next few days exploring Kathmandu and getting to know one another. If you ask me, we look to be a pretty great team. Everyone seems nice and seems to have the experience and skills necessary for this climb. We are young, fit, experienced and full of desire; it can't get much better.*

Learning in Thin Air - Personal Capacity

Young, fit and full of desire. Would that be enough?

Let's start with my own personal efforts. Most climbers don't go far or live long without developing some good team and leadership skills. But the starting point for most climbing success stories is with an individual. There is a lot of groundwork to lay in terms of personal skills, attitudes and experience.

In order to build your personal capacity you must first determine your definition of success; your vision. Who do you want to be as a person, as a team member, as a team, and as a leader? Without this vision you are just going through the motions with no clear direction, sometimes it all works out and sometimes it does not. I would rather create it than leave it up to fate.

Personally, I was well aligned for success. I set out on this voyage with a belief that I certainly had what it would take from a personal success viewpoint.

Now it was time to learn about the team.

Scott in Kathmandu

Forming Our Team

Our Team Capacity

Preparing for the Climb

HAVING MET my team, I began to think about how well we would work together. Team performance would be the critical success factor on top of my own personal capabilities.

Through both mountaineering and business, I began to recognize the importance of having a team of strong, skilled, and capable people on any project. The combined power of many people makes the physical labour easier and the camaraderie makes the time go faster. That is why it is so rare to see solo attempts in adventure sports. Whether it is climbing Mount Everest or sailing around the world, going alone is far more difficult and infinitely more dangerous. So, one of my first organizational tasks in pursuit of my goal was to decide how to align myself with a solid team.

In the world of climbing there are several possible approaches to an expedition. There is the self-led expedition, the organized expedition, the professionally led expedition and the fully guided expedition.

The self-led expedition is a completely independent undertaking whereby the expedition members themselves handle all the pre-trip logistics and preparation, and do all the work on the mountain. An organized expedition enlists the assistance of a commercial operator to put together specific aspects of the expedition. This can include permits, transportation, the hiring of cook staff and climbing Sherpa, among other things. In this case, the climbing team is still ultimately in charge and is largely independent once on the mountain. A professionally led expedition takes the organized expedition one step further and adds a professional leader. The climbers are still somewhat independent, but the expedition leader is there to help them when necessary, to provide advice and call the shots in a crisis. This makes the trip safer, and provides the climbers with a greater chance of success due to the input of a capable mentor. The fourth expedition option is the fully guided expedition, where pretty much everything is done for the climbers. These expeditions are often sought out by less experienced climbers, climbers who do not have the time to do it themselves, climbers who do not have a suitable climbing partner or climbers who want a highly controlled climbing experience.

My preferred options were to go either with a self-led or a professionally led expedition. I knew that a strong supporting team would have a direct effect on my safety and success on Cho Oyu, so I set about assembling one. By this time in my life I had been climbing for years, many of them as a guide. I had already achieved success on a long list of mountains and had made connections with a deep roster of skilled climbers. It would be no problem gathering a few dedicated climbing friends to share this experience. Or, so I thought.

The problem with climbing these huge mountains is that there are a lot of details for a person to line up. This expedition would cost close to $15,000 and would require us to be away from family – and work – in a remote location, performing physically and technically demanding challenges for almost two months. I was fortunate to have the financial resources for the climb and, being self employed, the ability to take time off work. My climbing friends did not. Once the filters of desire, ability, time and money were applied, every single name had been crossed off my list of potential partners.

With no friends to climb with, I started to investigate my options. The internet provided a useful tool for connecting with a community of like minded people from around the world. After some research, I hooked up with an outfitting company that was organizing an expedition to Cho Oyu. This would be a cross between an organized and a professionally led expedition; the company would provide the logistical infrastructure and an expedition leader. I researched the company, spoke to the trip leader and looked at the climbing resumes of the other climbers. Although I had never met any of these people, they all appeared qualified, fit and determined. I could – and did – expect to be in good company. With a strong roster and a common goal of attaining the summit of Cho Oyu, things looked promising. I signed onto the trip.

The formation of our team certainly started out in an interesting way!

Journal Entry for March 27 (Day 6) – Into Tibet; toilet humour; karaoke and disco dancing

After several days in Kathmandu to gather last minute supplies, we are finally on a bus heading towards the mountain. We are planning to climb Cho Oyu from the Tibetan side so we need to drive overland across the border to get to the base of the mountain.

On the bus with us were two new members of our team, our Sherpas Kami and Lhakpa, who will be our expedition cooks. They are warm and friendly and have huge smiles. There is no doubt they are a good addition to our team. They will stay at Base Camp to make sure everything is comfortable for us and that we are well fed.

Our first stop today was the town of Kodari on the Nepal Tibet border. We had a short lunch of Dhal Bhat as our Nepal exit visas were being processed and then walked across the Friendship Bridge that separates the two countries. Our gear was also carried across the bridge as our vehicles were not allowed to enter Tibet.

Dhal Bhat is the go to meal for most people in Nepal and several of the surrounding countries. It is a meal of lentils, a few vegetables and curry. These easy to find ingredients are nutritious, easy to prepare and tasty. Many people in Nepal will have this dish for every meal of the day.

Once on the other side of the bridge we boarded a waiting truck and began the one hour drive up the side of a huge hill. The town we were headed for, Zanghmu, was at the top of the valley. The road was very narrow with endless, mud laden switchbacks, and massive drop-offs. At times I doubted we would make it, so I closed my eyes and hoped for the best. It is astonishing to think that this road is a major trade route between Nepal, Tibet, China and India. It must be nearly impassable during the monsoon season.

At the top of the hill we disembarked with motion sick stomachs and entered Chinese immigration control. Unfortunately, by the time we finished filling out all the paperwork it was 3:30 pm and the office was closed for the day.

The Friendship Highway *also known as the China Nepal highway is an 800 km trade route that connects Lhasa, the capital of Tibet, with the border of Tibet and Nepal at the Sino-Nepal Friendship Bridge. This highway is carved out of the mountains and crosses three passes over 5000 m before dropping 1750 m to the border.*

There is no doubt that the communist government runs on a tight and strict schedule. We need to return tomorrow for the final approvals. An army officer kept our passports as we were ushered to a hotel for the night.

This is my first time in a communist country. Tibet is ruled by China and has been, off and on, for much of its existence. The town of Zanghmu itself is built on the side of a very steep hill. Most of the buildings, which are built to match the topography, are typical communist utilitarian structures. We walked up 30 flights of stairs to get to our hotel which is a huge, cold, damp and musty concrete block. The room, which Rick and I will be sharing tonight, is on the third floor of the hotel. It is very spartan. Light fixtures that once worked have long since broken and been replaced with bare light bulbs that hang from the ceiling. These lights only seem to work some of the time. The TV works with a fuzzy picture, but there are no programs that I recognize and none are in English.

learning in THIN AIR

The communal bathroom is quite an adventure. No more toilets, only squat facilities here. Everything is organized but dirty. When I turned on the water tap in the sink, a leech came out with the water. I watched it swim across the sink and disappear down the drain. As I peered out the window into the beautiful valley, I noticed a pipe coming out of the wall with water cascading into the river below. No septic system here. All waste goes directly into the river. I will try not to think about this as I eat and drink.

We went for dinner in a traditional Chinese restaurant. The food was surprisingly good, although I did not know what all of it was. After dinner, John gave us a tour of the town. He is quite well suited for this. He loves to be in the spotlight and to entertain. He seems to know everyone or, at least, pretends to.

The city of Zanghmu, Tibet

As Zanghmu is a major trade hub, there is endless traffic in town and many people on the move. Truck drivers, Chinese businessmen and army personnel are everywhere. One of the major entertainment vices for these men seems to be the company of prostitutes. Brothels are everywhere, identified by the red light bulb hanging at the front of the building. The women are dressed in Western clothing and are quite beautiful. Prostitution seems to be a pretty open part of the culture.

Disco's, pool halls, and karaoke bars are also abundant. This last establishment is where we ended our tour of the city. The room was dimly lit and had a strange mix of Western and Asian music blaring from the speakers. The patrons were made up of us, a number of soldiers, some businessmen and several prostitutes.

We sat at a table and ordered beer from the waitress. She placed small sake glasses in front of us, filling them from a beer can. She stood there with her head bowed, waiting for us to take a drink, refilling our glasses each time. It was uncomfortable having her stand there serving us, but I was not sure of the custom and did not want to offend her. After about ten minutes, when our beer consumption slowed down, she left a few cans on the table and departed.

After a while, the karaoke started up and the soldiers were quick to jump up and sing. When you sing a song, a silk kata (scarf) is placed around your neck like a badge of honour. Some men had many katas proudly displayed. All the songs were in Chinese and seemed to be of the love ballad genre. We were soon approached by soldiers looking for dance partners. Since all the women in the establishment were "professionals" and would only dance for money we were the only other choice. I did not really think I could refuse a man with a gun. Through broken English and mime, I was told that as long as I kept my hands above the waist it was ok. As one singer after another sang his heart out I "enjoyed" a few dances with the soldiers and then called it a night.

Tomorrow we will head to Nylam. I am told a landslide has taken out the road. We will need to walk across this portion. I'm not sure exactly how this will work, but I'm up for the adventure.

Journal Entry for March 28 (Day 7) – Travel to Nylam; the Friendship Highway; landslide
After a quick, delicious breakfast of tea and scrambled eggs we headed to immigration control get our passports back and to complete the final paperwork to get our visas, and our Liaison Officer (commonly referred to as the LO). We are required to have a military liaison officer with us at all times because we are entering a communist country. For the duration of the expedition, his job will be to make sure everything goes smoothly for us and to make sure we do not do anything we are not supposed to do. He will help with transportation, hotels, purchasing food, and even negotiation with porters. Surprisingly, no bribes were necessary. We were off to a good start!

Our drive to Nylam took three hours on the Friendship Highway. This road clings to the side of an immensely steep valley. A glance out the window allows a spectacular view down thousands of feet to a raging white water river below.

About two hours into the drive, we came across the landslide. It was only about 30 m wide but had rendered the road impassable. The only way to the other side was a narrow foot path. As our truck stopped, porters seemed to appear out of nowhere to carry our supplies to the other side and into another waiting truck. We were told the road would be closed for about a week while repairs were made. Most of the labour would be done

**Landslide on
The Friendship Highway**

by hand. What heavy equipment I saw was antiquated and in poor repair.

The transfer across the landslide was pretty much seamless. We settled into our next truck with our new driver and were once again on our way.

Not long after our transfer we arrived in Nylam, a larger town than most, which seemed to be cleaner and more sturdily built. We checked into the Snow Leopard Hotel getting a room with 5 single beds. I went for a walk around town and met many children as they came out of school. They all wanted to play with my camera and wear my sunglasses. This provided me with the opportunity to take some really great photos.

Lunch was good, consisting of rice, vegetables, egg drop soup, and many more excellent dishes that I don't know how to describe. I don't think I want to know what they contained.

Children of Nylam loved to wear my sunglasses!

The distance from here to Cho Oyu is not that great, but we will take almost a week to get there in order to allow our bodies to acclimatize to the increasing altitude. I am getting along well with my climbing partners, but we have little in common. Conversations are light and we all spend a lot of time alone. Our leader, has begun to show some confusing personality traits. While claiming that he is extremely humble, in my opinion, he actually appears to have a huge ego that needs to be constantly fed. I find this an interesting mix, but it is what it is. This is turning out to be very different from all the other expeditions I have been on. Not only is it much bigger, longer and more dangerous, but I am not climbing with my customary climbing partners with whom I have shared experiences and built trust.

Journal Entry for March 29-30 (Day 8-9) – Tingri; the "plan" remains a mystery

Our last stop before reaching Base Camp is the town of Tingri. It is here that I was rewarded with my first view of Cho Oyu. It is massive beyond belief. Looking out across the Tibetan plateau, I am shocked by the sheer size of it. Towering above everything else around it, there is a huge plume of snow which is being rocketed off its summit by the jet stream. This mountain is so tall it actually invades the jet stream. Its summit is at the same altitude that commercial jets fly. I am beginning to wonder what I have gotten myself into.

Is this climb too big for me? Have I bitten off more than I can chew? After some tense personal moments I remembered that in order to be successful I just have to tackle this like any big project. I have to break it down into smaller sub-goals. My first goal will be to make it to Base Camp.

With this thought in mind I spoke with John to learn about our plan of attack as this had not yet been shared with the team. He said to trust him; he knew what he was doing and all would be well. I thought to myself, "What else can I do?" so I stopped asking questions and just waited for instructions.

The time we have spent in Tingri has been pretty uneventful. We have gone for several acclimatization hikes and I have tried to eat as much as I can to pack on a few pounds before we hit the mountain. The food is good, but greasy and much of it is unidentifiable. Our hotel consists of mud walled rooms with a dirt floor; not very comfortable and extremely dusty. I will be glad to get to Base Camp.

Journey to Base Camp

MOTORIZED TRANSPORTATION can only get you so far in the Himalayas. Sooner or later the roads peter out and the ancient and decrepit trucks pass their loads to lumbering, but sure footed, yaks. Eventually, even the yaks are turned back and humans – climbers and porters – must shoulder the loads. The guest houses, however humble they once appeared, become distant, wistful memories. The only shelter you will enjoy from here on is the one that you or a porter has carried in. This is where the going gets tough.

As you can imagine, extreme mountaineering expeditions require that significant amounts of food and specialized gear be transported uphill, over long distances, in harsh conditions at strength sapping altitudes. So, like most large projects, they are broken into smaller bits or stages. Each stage involves slowly shuttling mounds of gear and food from one camp to the next, higher camp. Usually the team will make several trips over several days. Fortunately this requirement fits neatly with the need for climbers to acclimatize systematically to the increasing altitude. The first trip to higher camp will usually be a day trip; you trek to the higher camp, spend half an hour, then descend to the previous camp to sleep and recover for a few days. The next trip up will involve an overnight at the higher camp, followed by a return to the lower camp to recover some more. This shuttling up and down the mountain means that you will actually climb most of the mountain several times over the weeks leading up to the final push to the summit.

On most mountains, the first camp, and the main launch point, is called Base Camp. Subsequent camps are numbered Camp 1, Camp 2, and so on. However on Cho Oyu we had two additional base camps. There was Chinese Base Camp where our Chinese Liaison Officer waited for us, Interim Base Camp which was situated half way between Chinese Base Camp and Advanced Base Camp, and Advanced Base Camp where we established our true expedition base. We spent a total of more than four weeks shuttling between camps in a prolonged struggle to balance progress and acclimatization on our way toward the summit.

Journal Entry for March 31 (Day 10) – Base Camp; Kippa and Lhakpa
Today we boarded a truck at 8:00 am for a two hour drive to what is called Chinese Base Camp. This is where our Liaison Officer will stay with the Liaison Officers from all the other expeditions. From here it will be a two day trek to Advanced Base Camp and our home for the next six to seven weeks.

View from Base Camp tent

At this camp there are very few flat spots to be found as the ground is littered with boulders of all sizes. A light dusting of snow covers everything. I searched around for an old tent platform and erected my home away from home. Along with our personal sleeping tents we have a dining tent, a cook tent, and a toilet tent. Kami and Lhakpa are now in their element, preparing and serving us great food. They are not climbing Sherpa and will not venture onto the mountain with us. We have decided to be a self-sufficient expedition and do all the work ourselves once on the mountain.

Journal Entry for April 1 (Day 11) – Base Camp days; cold nights; sighting the summit

We've spent two days acclimatizing at Base Camp. Our days have been made up of resting, eating, resting some more and eating some more. I asked John what the plan was for the next few days and was told not to worry about it, he was in charge and knew what he was doing. I am starting to become concerned by the lack of communication, but there does not seem to be too much I can do about it.

Base Camp is extremely windy and quite cold most of the time. Last night the temperature in my tent dropped to -15° C. I was very cold in my sleeping bag as it seems to have lost some of its insulation value over the years. I only hope the weather will get warmer as we move more into the spring.

From my tent Cho Oyu looms 4000 m over my head; it is immense. I cannot see our climbing route as it is on the other side of the ridge, but I can see that the weather on the mountain is just as bad as it is here at Base Camp: cold and extremely windy.

Journal Entry for April 2 (Day 12) – Departing Base Camp for the walk from hell

Today we woke at 6:30 am to the sound of clanging bells as the Tibetan yak herders and their yaks get ready to ferry our gear to Advanced Base Camp. Our Liaison Officer will help in the loading and then we will not see him until the end of the expedition. Once we leave him, we can pull out the computer, the video cameras, the satellite phone and all the other illegal stuff we are hiding away (expensive permits are required to bring this equipment into Tibet). I look forward to sending an email home and receiving one in return. I will even try to make a call home later in the week, but I think I will wait until we get to Camp 1 when I will have something to tell.

The walk today was supposed to be about six hours. The first two hours were relatively gentle. We entered a valley where we stopped to have lunch. The walking became quite steep as we continued on our trek. We were planning to stop at the head of the valley for the night, but when we got there we discovered that there was no water and no ice to melt. We needed to go about 30 minutes further. Well, 30 minutes turned into three hours, but we eventually made it to Camp. What was intended to be a modest walk with a small elevation gain turned out to be a death march with a huge elevation gain. I was the last one into Camp, but I feel pretty good considering what we have done today.

Once in Camp, I set up my tent, changed into some warmer clothing, and crashed for a while to recover. After my rest I went to the dining tent for something to drink. Six cups of tea, a bunch of biscuits and several bowls of soup later I was feeling pretty good. I have no headache, but do get a bit dizzy when I try to lift something heavy or if I stand up too fast.

Journal Entry for April 3 (Day 13) - Interim Camp to Advanced Base Camp; sunglasses and socks

Due to our very long day yesterday breakfast was not until 8:30 am. I slept well and I am feeling strong. The hike today was about three hours over mostly easy ground with one big steep climb. The ground is ankle deep snow with small loose rocks — the perfect combination for a twisted ankle. The yak drivers are constantly after us for sunglasses and socks. Most of them do not have sun glasses; to protect their eyes from the sun they drape a thin layer of cloth over their eyes and try to peer through and around it, or they place a bunch of hair across their eyes and use the hair as a filter. Both systems are extremely inadequate. Most of the Tibetans wear thin Chinese running shoes that resemble Converse All Stars. Their feet must be freezing. If I had known they were in need of sunglasses and socks, I would have brought a bunch of wool socks and cheap sunglasses from home.

Once in Advanced Base Camp we set up the dining and cooking tents, as well as our personal sleeping tents. It will be nice to have some personal space for a bit and to have access to all my bags again. Tomorrow will be a rest day with time to fix up our tents, build the toilet and shower tents, and generally get Camp organized.

Learning in Thin Air - Team Capacity

As a climber, it is always an interesting experience to meet and work with your new team for the first time. Your life will literally depend on the collaboration and cohesion of the team. You might have everything that it takes in terms of personal capacity, but team capacity is equally as critical.

We certainly had a good start. We seemed to work well together, and shared some fascinating experiences, however, I was starting to have some worries about our team leader.

The dynamics of the team are particularly critical on more complex climbs. One way we can manage risks when we take on a big task or responsibility is to test ourselves in progressively more challenging situations. When we are working alone this is relatively straightforward. Most of us have a pretty good idea of our current abilities and level of commitment. We can judge the task at hand and take a pretty good guess at our chance for success. We can often make up for any of our own shortcomings that might emerge by applying additional sweat and effort. But on very big projects, there are usually many others involved: a team. I don't mean to give the impression that my climbing successes up until this point were individual efforts. They were not. In fact, high performance teamwork was an integral component of each and every climb from the simplest top rope pitch in Thunder Bay to the summits of Denali and Mount Logan.

Just as with building personal capacity, building team capacity starts with vision. Who do you want to be as a team? What is your definition of success? What is your definition of high performance? Without a clear and agreed upon definition, your team has no guidance as to what to do, what not to do, and where to go. If you cannot define your vision you cannot measure it, and measurement is critical in knowing if you are on track towards your vision or not.

Ultimately your vision is your guiding light. Only time would tell if our team had that critical shared vision.

*Yaks help to transport equipment
to Advanced Base Camp*

The Early Stages
of Leadership

Our Leadership Capacity

MAKING IT to Advanced Base Camp is an important step in any climb. It is a signal that things are about to get serious; full commitment is necessary. In retrospect, I've also learned that, by this point, it is critical to have an alignment of personal, team and leadership dynamics.

From one perspective, we were well set. Advanced Base Camp was well supplied and relatively comfortable. While we rested and acclimatized, our Sherpa cooks did their best to keep us energized on high calorie fare that would sharpen appetites suppressed by nearly constant altitude induced sickness.

Yet it was also here where I felt our leader was displaying some disturbing behaviours that I thought might cause us some problems down the road. He had revealed earlier that he saw himself as a humble leader. In my opinion this was beginning to contrast significantly with what I was witnessing on a daily basis. John's ratio of speaking to listening appeared seriously skewed. Ironically, with all his speaking, he rarely revealed the information that I felt I needed most: a sense of our overall plan of attack. This continued to remain a mystery.

John also attempted to gain control over the fixed ropes above Camp 2. This set up a seriously divisive force on the mountain in the weeks to come.

Fixed ropes are climbing ropes that are permanently attached to the mountain and are used to protect climbers as they ascend and descend the mountain. New ropes are placed at the start of each climbing season by the first team to climb, and usually shared by all expeditions.

Journal Entry for April 4 (Day 14) - Rest day Advanced Base Camp; food; Swiss team; the fixed rope

I have not mentioned the food in a few days but it has been great. Lhakpa and Kami always have plenty of hot water ready for tea and hot chocolate and there is usually a snack lying around. Last night for dinner we had popcorn as an appetizer, followed by a tomato ginger garlic soup, and then the main course was boiled potatoes, spiral pasta, fried onions carrots and cauliflower and a light tomato sauce. We also had fried yak steak that was very tasty and tender. Once we get up on the mountain the quality and quantity of our food will drop drastically so I am taking advantage of this while I can.

Today was an acclimatization day which basically means we did very little. The body needs several days to adjust to the lower levels of pressure and the lack of oxygen. We did have a visit from a Swiss climber that is here on another expedition. They have been here for nine days and are on a very tight schedule as they plan to move on to another 8000 m peak once this climb is complete. They were moving between Camp 1 and Camp 2 today putting in a fixed rope. John wants to speak to their leader to purchase the fixed rope

A Puja is a traditional Sherpa ceremony conducted to ask the spirits of the mountain to forgive us for trespassing and to ask for kindness in weather and mountain conditions.

when they are done, that way he will own the rope and be able to charge a toll to all the other teams to use it. This seems a bit odd to me, but John seems confident in his plan.

Journal Entry for April 5 (Day 15) – Advanced Base Camp; bath time; the rope purchase

Today was another rest day. We set up the shower tent so I had a bath. Basically you stand inside a small 2 foot x 2 foot tent, strip down and have a very quick sponge bath before your parts freeze and fall off. I also did some laundry, which quickly froze to the line. I was going to wash my hair, but I chickened out as it was too cold. Perhaps in a few days it will get warmer.

The Swiss leader came over today and had a meeting with John about the rope. I am not sure what the deal was, but when the Swiss leader left somehow the rope belonged to John. I'm sure the Swiss leader left wondering what had just happened and what he had agreed to as it appeared that most of the talking was done by John.

Tagging Half Camp

FROM HERE on in we would launch a series of forays from Advanced Base Camp. This is where the extreme challenge began. We acknowledged this point in the expedition with a traditional Sherpa Puja ceremony intended to bring us blessings and protection on the mountain. We would need it.

Progress would be slow. Sometimes we would just try to tag a goal further up the mountain before retreating that same day. Sometimes we would aim to camp overnight, then descend again the following day to rest and recover. It was very tedious.

Journal Entry for April 6 (Day 16) – Puja ceremony; Advanced Base Camp to Half Camp to Advanced Base Camp

At 8:00 am this morning we had our Puja ceremony to invite blessings for our trip. A Chorten (a small stone altar) was erected and prayer flags were strung from it in three directions. A small fire burned juniper, cedar and incense. We threw rice and flour into the air as we walked around the Chorten in a clockwise direction. Our Puja was shorter than normal as it was run by our Sherpa cooks since we do not have access to the religious Lamas who would normally run it.

We then set out for our first carry to Half Camp. Camp 1 is a great distance and most teams elect to place a food and equipment cache just before the steep face leading up to it. The morning was cold, windy and overcast with snow in the air. We left at 10:00 am in hiking boots. The trail, small, loose gravel like stones called scree, was covered in light snow. Although I was only carrying about 13 kg, I was struggling. I was last in line and having difficulty breathing. Coughing frequently, I found it challenging to keep going. We arrived at our cache location (5800 m) after about three hours of walking and took a break. Looking up the steep loose slope to Camp 1 was intimidating. I think I could have made it all the way, but it would have been a push. Many people do not make it this far in their first carry so I guess I did alright.

The trip back down to Advanced Base Camp took about half the time but was still tough. Even with very little in my pack the slightest uphill climb would grind me to a stop. The trail itself was difficult to follow. At one point we found ourselves on the wrong trail. We had to descend into a very steep gorge and climb up the other side in order to regain the correct trail. Although it was not too big, it was very difficult.

I am now in my tent and not feeling too badly. I am tired and have a small cough, but no headache. This is unbelievably hard work, and we have only just begun. I know in the end the experience will be worth it, but sometimes I wonder.

Journal Entry for April 7 (Day 17) - Advanced Base Camp rest day; no phone

It is hard to believe we have another rest day. It seems all we have had is rest days. We have really only had three out of fifteen days with any significant physical exertion. I hope all this time spent acclimatizing will pay off in the end. The Swiss team has been up on the mountain and they have told us that the conditions are excellent. Our slow schedule should provide us with good acclimatization and give us a good chance at the summit. It will not, however, give us much of a chance to finish early. I need to remind myself that this is a marathon, not a sprint.

Today was our warmest day yet. This was the first day I did not need to wear my heavy fleece jacket all day. I sent off a group email today using the Swiss camp system. Our communication system is not up and running yet as

Advanced Base Camp

promised by John, although it appears to me that he really does not seem to care.

I have been out of contact with Susan and Amy now for longer than anticipated and I desperately want to call home to speak to them. Amy is only a year old, but just to hear her voice would be a huge comfort to me. This is why the satellite phone system was so important to me and was a requirement for the trip. In my younger days I could easily go without contact with the outside world for long periods of time. I was happy to be where I was with little care about connecting with home. Being married now and having a daughter has changed all this. No longer is my world just me, but there are others who are important to me and I desperately want to connect with them.

There is no doubt that setting up the satellite phone system is complex, but it is important to me. John has experience with the phone and I do not so I am dependent upon him to set it up for me. It appears to me that he has little desire to work on the phone. It is not for lack of time as that is all we seemed to have; hour after hour, hanging around at Camp.

This is difficult for me, not being able to call home. I am at a loss really about what I should do. The Swiss have offered to allow me to use their phone, but it is $10 per minute. If our phone is not up and running in a few days I will suck it up and spend the cash to call home. I'm sure it will be money well spent.

I have not spoken to John about my emotional need for the phone as I do not want to come across as being soft and I do not want to get into a debate with him. In my opinion he has shown on several occasions that he is king of the debate team and king of the mountain. I am finding him quite unpredictable in his moods, even intimidating at times, but mostly I am feeling disappointment as I don't feel I have the support of my team leader.

Illness at Camp 1

MOST PEOPLE who frequent mountains such as these are very fit and healthy by any standard. Yet, as you'll see in these entries, sickness is very common. Climbers must constantly walk a fine line between being conservative in health and climbing and pushing the envelope. They must decide which action will most improve their eventual summit chances: push higher in spite of illness to improve overall acclimatization, or back off to conserve resources and avoid climb ending medical conditions such as HAPE (high altitude pulmonary edema) and HACE (high altitude cerebral edema).

Journal Entry for April 8 (Day 18) – Illness Camp 1; psychological downer; meet the Swiss; more phone woes

Today was our first shot at Camp 1. When I woke up this morning I did not feel 100%, but figured I could just walk it off. I was out of breath just walking up the short hill to breakfast. I had several cups of tea to make sure I was not dehydrated and ate what I could force down. I am not sure if it was nerves, exhaustion, or the altitude, but all I know is that I felt like crap. As I walked back to my tent to get ready for the day, I felt like I would throw up, but I figured I would get over it.

I set off at 9:15 am with a very light pack but had to stop frequently. I started to get cramps in my stomach and could not catch my breath. I sat down to let the rest of the group catch up to me figuring that I may get my second wind if I followed them. They quickly left me behind as I stopped at the side of the trail to vomit. I decided that the best thing for me to do was to return to Camp. Even though it was mostly downhill it took me a really long time to cover the distance back to my tent.

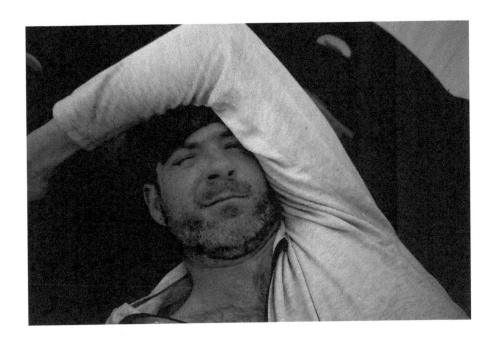

Not feeling very well at Camp 1

It is now 10:30 am and I am sitting in my tent feeling defeated. It is so hot in the tent that it feels like a mini sauna. My tent keeps the wind out but it also intensifies the sun's rays. Every now and then a slight puff of wind makes it bearable, but just barely. I stopped at the Swiss camp on the way back to see if there was an email for me, but no luck. It is the weekend and Susan may not check her email until Monday. The Swiss are heading up the hill tomorrow and taking their phone system apart. If I do not get a message today, I may not have access to the system again for a week or more. I hope I get a message today. I could sure use the psychological boost.

Steve is now back in Camp as well. He made it to Half Camp and turned around. He too has something going on. He has a terrible cough and sounds awful. I feel OK as long as I don't move.

It is now later in the day and the Swiss have invited us up for dinner. It will be a nice change to talk to other people. Their phone system is down now and I did not get a message; disappointing, but there is not much I can do about it. I am disappointed our system is not up and running yet. Today has been a very lonely and homesick day.

Journal Entry for April 9 (Day 19) - Rest day; illness and doubts; Swiss Camp; call home

Another rest day of course, but today I am OK with it. I am still weak and recovering from whatever hit me yesterday. I still feel that we are having way too many rest days, but John says that this is the way to do it, so I will follow his lead. I feel a little better today, but I am still not where I want to be. In two days we plan to spend the night at Camp 1, if I can't make it I will be in trouble. It would change the whole expedition for me and I may need to go to a lower elevation to recover. This could ultimately put me out of the summit bid.

We went to the Swiss camp for dinner last night. They have a great set up, a huge dome tent with a couple of kitchen tents attached. Most of the Swiss team are up on the mountain preparing for their summit bid, but a few people were around. We had an excellent dinner of soup, pizza and apple pie. The Swiss cook team is very good. They even have an assistant cook that stands around like a French waiter and takes care of your every need. They have a huge solar energy system that charges a panel of batteries to run the florescent lights and the other electronic equipment. They also have a propane heater that keeps the dining tent very comfortable. This is a huge step up from what we have. I tried to call home but only got voice mail. It is very disappointing to call home only to listen to your own voice on the machine.

I called home again this morning using the Swiss team's phone and got through. I spoke with Susan for a while and was on the edge of tears the whole time. I guess this experience has been more emotional for me than I thought. It was great to hear about Amy and how she is doing. Susan said she has sent me a long email, but I don't think I will get it until the Swiss get back from their summit attempt.

Journal Entry for April 10 (Day 20) - Advanced Base Camp rest day; Steve descends to Base Camp

Steve has gone down to Base Camp or to Tingri to try to recover. I have elected to stay here and hope that I will recover without the long walk to Base Camp. I am worried, however, as yesterday when I went for a walk I quickly ran out of breath and energy. This morning I even had a hard time keeping my breath while lying in my sleeping bag. I don't know what I should do. I don't even know if I could make it to Base Camp in my condition. I don't want to be out before I even start. The mountain is in such great condition I wish I could be up there right now.

Tagging Camp 1

FORTUNATELY FOR me, I did begin to feel better in time to make the important trip to Camp 1. Steve was also feeling better and had made the decision not to descend to Tingri after all, but to stay at Advanced Base Camp and to push up to Camp 1 with me. While some from our team were planning to spend a night there, Steve and I had to be content with making the extremely difficult climb, leaving some gear in our tents at Camp 1 and returning to Advanced Base Camp to recover. Still, we were acclimatizing despite the hardship.

Journal Entry for April 11 (Day 21) – Advanced Base Camp to Camp 1; Camp 1; Camp 1 to Advanced Base Camp
There is a light snow falling right now as there has been every afternoon for the last few days. My penmanship is a bit sloppy right now as my fingers are pretty much frozen and I am exhausted. I made a push to Camp 1 this morning. It took me 120 minutes to make it to Half Camp which was much faster than before. I walked alone and that seemed to help as I did not feel compelled to walk at someone else's pace. I coughed frequently throwing up small amounts of liquid on a regular basis, but overall I was feeling better. Taking a 35 minute break at Half Camp, I was hoping that someone would join me, but no such luck. I struck out alone for the rest of the trip to Camp 1. The only way I can describe it is that the climb to Camp 1 is the worst piece of hell and the most physically demanding thing I have done in recent memory. From Half Camp to Camp 1 there is a 400 m elevation gain, made over a giant scree slope (loose gravel over dirt) that averages about 40 degrees. Each step onto the loose ground is met with a slide. It therefore takes three steps just to make one. Not all the slope is like this, some of it is marginally better, but 70% of it is pure evil. The slope seems to go on forever, just when you think you see the top, you find it is a "false summit" and the ridge continues to rise in front of you. It is crushing. From Half Camp to Camp 1 it took me an additional two hours, and each step was taken with three to four breaths.

Eventually I made it to Camp 1, stashed my gear in my tent and spent about 15 minutes looking up at the route to Camp 2. From here on up we will be on snow which will be much better — I hope. On my way down I spoke with John, Sarah and Rick. They are planning to spend the night at Camp 1. Steve and I will miss out on this important acclimatization night as we are still recovering from our illnesses.

The trip back down to Half Camp was way faster. The slope was so steep that much of it you could slide down. What took two hours to go up took me only 20 minutes to go down. About ¾ of the way back to Advanced Base Camp, I caught up to two South African climbers who had departed Camp 1 this morning, an hour and a half ahead of me. I felt good that I had caught up to them but, once I had, all my energy seemed to drained from my body, and I slowed to a crawl. I walked with the South African climbers for the rest of the trip back to Advance Base Camp. As you get close to Camp, the trail becomes a series of small up and down hills that are quite defeating. The funny thing is that, even though today was the day from hell, I feel pretty good right now. It is amazing how fast the human body can recover from such a big exertion.

Recovery at Advanced Base Camp

I WAS recovering well physically on my return to Advanced Base Camp but others were not so lucky. Failure to acclimatize to the extreme altitude was once again at the heart of the difficulties. Retinal hemorrhages, which can lead to permanent eye damage, seemed to be an issue for a member of our team and for several members of the Swiss team. I was getting a real education on the dangers of mountaineering.

I was also getting an education about the psychological challenges of mountaineering. I found it interesting that absolutely exhausting physical challenges, when coupled with successfully achieving a goal could leave me so charged up. On the other hand, large amounts of idle time played negatively on my mind. I dwelled on the people who I missed – my wife, Susan, and my daughter, Amy. I questioned my decision to come, and my commitment to the expedition wavered at times.

This was made worse by my growing doubts about our leader. It appeared to me that he was not really interested in the people he was leading, however he seemed to show a high interest in his own side projects – notably the fixed rope business. My trust in our expedition leadership was rapidly evaporating. This could not be a good thing.

learning in THIN AIR

Learning in Thin Air - Leadership Capacity

Personal capacity, team capacity. It was clear that those things mattered. But in the informal model I was developing in my mind, leadership would be equally critical, particularly if you want to develop into a high performance team.

All teams require a leader and the leader's task will be slightly different depending upon where the team is at in their development. A simple definition of a leader is someone who influences others. This can be done in a positive or a negative way, but hopefully you choose the former rather than the latter.

A leader's job is to oversee the big picture and to be a mentor and a coach. They facilitate meetings, keep the team on track, hold the team and individuals accountable, and remove barriers for success. A great leader is working in front of the team and behind the scenes to ensure a clear path. Ultimately, a leader's job is to make the team look good and to lead them to success.

There has always been a debate whether leadership is an innate quality that you are born with or if it is a learned skill. My belief is that it is a combination of both. Just like a top athlete there is a natural skill that is cultivated through coaching and training over countless years. Without either of these components (the natural skill or the coaching) the athlete will never reach world class performance levels. If you are born with lower levels of natural leadership ability you need to work a little harder, but great leadership can still be attained.

Build a vision of who you want to be as a leader. This vision will present the values, actions, behaviours and characteristics you want to exhibit as a leader. From here you need to create a deliberate development plan and enlist a coach and a mentor.

Camp 1 on Cho Oyu Ridge

learning in THIN AIR

Before the Push

WHEN YOU are on a mountain, there is a small window of opportunity to make a push for the summit. Between waiting for a good weather window and the need for your body to acclimatize, this window of opportunity can take some time to appear. I found these days to be challenging, monotonous, terrifying, lonely and boring — all at the same time.

Journal Entry for April 12 (Day 22) - Rest day; phone update; email from home

Another rest day is drawing near its end. I don't really know what I do, but the days seem to go by. The Swiss team got 12 people to the summit the other day. The ones that did not make it will rest and then give it another try. This is a remarkable feat considering that few, if any of them, have spent time above Camp 1.

I received an email from Susan that was sent to the Swiss team email. It is great to hear what is going on at home. Amy has grown and learned so much. It pains me to read what I am missing considering we are not making much progress on the mountain and we are not forming well as a team.

I spent some time talking to one of the South African climbers today. I was using his solar panel to try to charge our phone as our solar panel is not working. He also has a satellite phone and has said I can use it. His usage fee is only $2.88 per minute which is way less than the $10.00 per minute it will cost to use our phone, assuming we ever get it to work. I think I will make a call home later today or tomorrow. I don't have much new to say but, for the cost, it will just be good to hear Susan's voice.

John, Sarah and Rick are not yet back from their overnight stay at Camp 1. I am anxious to hear how their night was and to see what they did today. They should return any time now.

Journal Entry for April 13 (Day 23) – Rest day at Advanced Base Camp; John, Sarah, Rick, return; Sarah illness; Swiss controversy
Another rest day. Tomorrow will be as well. John, Sarah and Rick came down from Camp 1 about 5:30 pm yesterday. They said they had a tough night. Camp 1, at 6200 m, is in a very desperate place. Located on a very narrow ridge, it sits in a wind tunnel where the wind can rip over the ridge at hurricane force. The tent platform itself is very exposed so if it is windy or snowing, it can be pretty miserable. Also, on either side of the tent platform there is a 700 m drop. There is plenty of room to walk around, but one misstep and you are a goner.

Sarah in particular had a difficult night. Something happened to her eye to cause some impairment of her sight. Her whole face is swollen, but her eyes do not hurt so it is unlikely to be snow blindness. It will likely get better in a few days, but I wonder what will happen as she goes higher.

Looking up the Ridge from Camp 1

There seems to be some controversy brewing here at Camp. The Swiss team says that 12 people made it to the summit, but John says only three made it. I don't really care. What they do and say is up to them, it does not impact me at all. Our leader, however seems to feel it is a big deal. In my opinion he seems to thrive on controversy, confrontation, conflict and embellishment. I never really know how much of any story to believe, but it seems that John is always at the heart of any controversy.

Anyway, I have heard that seven to eight members of the Swiss team got rather bad frostbite on their fingers and toes and that several had retinal hemorrhages. This is a result of their aggressive schedule and lack of acclimatization. They were also attempting the summit early in the season so it was much colder than it will be later in the season. More news as I learn it.

Right now it is snowing; we've had more than 30 cm since lunch. The snow is very wet and heavy. Last night the sky was full of lightning and the thunder roared. Hopefully it will not impact our summit plans. The slopes above Camp 2 and Camp 3 are very avalanche prone so if the snow load is too unstable we will not be able to go for the top. However, with the snow being so wet, if the sun hits it for a day or two, the snow should consolidate quickly and no longer present an avalanche hazard. We'll see what tomorrow brings.

Journal Entry for April 14 (Day 24) - Advance Base Camp rest day; fixed line update

The snow is still falling, but not as hard, although quite a bit has accumulated on the ground. The walls of my tent are sagging from it. The sun is trying to burn through the clouds, but so far with no luck.

We are now the sole owners and controllers of the fixed line from above Camp 1 all the way to the summit. John has said that as any new groups come onto the mountain they will have to pay him if they want to use the rope. It will be interesting to see how this works. Climbers tend to be freedom loving people and don't like to be told what they can and cannot do.

I suspect today will be another day of sitting around. My legs feel like they are wasting away and I fear that I have lost all the conditioning that I had before I came to the mountain. As this is day 24, the trip is starting to get long, but I am only halfway or less through it. It does not feel like we have accomplished much as of yet. We are spending more solitary time away from each other and do not seem to really be bonding as a team. The food is all starting to

Climbing the fixed rope just outside Camp 1

taste the same and I am starting to lose interest in eating it. I know I am losing weight due to the calories I am burning at this altitude and that I need to eat, but it is becoming a more difficult task.

Journal Entry for April 15 (Day 25) - Leaving Advanced Base Camp for Camp 1 Today we will head to Camp 1 for two nights. We plan to make a foray towards Camp 2 as well for the additional acclimatization. I hope I do alright. I am feeling better, but my cough seems to be getting worse. It is all the cold, dry air up here. I have tried to cover my mouth with a bandana so that the air I breathe is warmer and moist, but this makes me feel like I am suffocating. I don't know if it is psychological or real, but I feel like I cannot get enough air. I am also concerned about my overall fitness as we have not done much for a while and I feel as though I have been wasting away. I will fill in the details of these two days when I return to Base Camp.

Breakdown at Camp 1

AS AN experienced mountaineer I did not feel that our team was developing well. I had ample reason to suspect that our leadership was inadequate but I think I was in denial. I did not talk about it, and tried to avoid even thinking about it. It was stressful to live in this world of growing doubt and distrust.

In my opinion we were all withdrawing from our group. I was also starting to see more challenging personal characteristics in our leader. I would be among those targeted for abuse, but I was by no means alone. My perceptions of and reactions to this extreme behaviour, recorded at the time, are, I think, very revealing of human nature. Here I was, a fundamentally competent and self-confident climber, yet I became a victim at the hands of a person in a position of perceived authority which had a damaging effect on my trust, motivation and willingness to contribute.

Journal Entry for April 17 (Day 27) – events for April 15-17
Report on trip to Camp 1, April 15; the blow up

I am now back in my tent at Advance Base Camp. Two days ago (April 15) we went up to Camp 1. I was feeling a little anxious as I did not perform very well on the last trip there. I really wanted to make it, as I knew that, if I did not, my chances of a summit bid would be pretty much eliminated. With this in mind, I asked Rick if he could carry my sleeping bag part of the way for me. I felt that the slight reduction in weight would give me the physical and psychological edge that I needed to get to Camp 1. I did not discuss this plan with John, as I knew he would make a big deal of it and give me a hard time. I am pretty sure, however, he knew of my plan. He either saw me take my bag to Rick, or he spoke with Rick and found out. Regardless, as I was leaving camp he called out and asked if I was OK and if there was anything I needed to tell him. I said no, thinking the question a bit odd, and departed camp with Rick soon to follow. A couple of hours later I arrived at our interim camp and took my sleeping bag back from Rick. The help he gave me was exactly what I needed and I was grateful.

Just then John came bursting over the hill into Half Camp. He came right up to me and stood inches from my face. He asked why I had not told him about my sleeping bag plan. He proceeded to explode in a tirade unlike anything I had witnessed before. As usual it was all about him: "what had he done to fail me;" "why did I not trust him;" "he was busting his butt for me;" "he was doing everything for me and I betrayed him." He went on and on for close to 30 minutes while I just stood there and took it. A small crowd of other climbers had gathered, perhaps thinking they would need to break up a physical fight. If I had pushed back they would have had to. As it was, he made me feel like an idiot that had no right to be on the mountain. He was the professional mountain guide and I was the stupid client. He was right and I was wrong. I had made him look bad in the eyes of everyone else on the mountain. Eventually he ran out of steam and stomped off. I sat for a while to recover from the verbal abuse and then started up the hill towards Camp 1. It was certainly turning out to be an interesting day.

Upon arriving in Camp 1, I learned that I would be sharing a tent with John. I guess he put me in with him so he could keep a close eye on me as he would a delinquent child. Being in the same tent with him was the last thing I wanted to do, but to question him would invite the next explosion and nobody wanted that. The best thing to do was to keep my mouth shut and suck it up.

Practice at Camp 1
Despite the considerable tension that hung over our group, the following day we needed to get down to work if we were going to try for the summit. The job at hand was to familiarize ourselves with working the fixed rope system that would protect us from a fatal fall as we worked our way through several tricky, vertical sections above Camp 1. These were the same ropes that were starting to create friction between our team and others on the mountain.

Fixed rope climbing above Camp 1, April 16
The winds are still high but we decided to go for a short climb above Camp 1 anyway. As we left camp there was a steep drop of about 30 m. We then crossed a small flat section before starting the climb up again. The first section is about 35 degrees of almost perfect snow, the consistency of styrofoam. There are a few sections of black ice, but these are easy to avoid. As the slope got steeper the fixed rope system started.

Although I have been on many mountains I have never used a fixed rope, I have always climbed while tied to my partner. John gave us a quick lesson on how to climb the fixed rope and off we went. About 5 m up the rope my breathing became very laboured as I had failed to pace myself. I thought I would die! Eventually I got my breathing and my pace under control and continued on. We climbed about 50 m up the fixed line while the wind screamed at about 100 kph. We hit a high point at about 6400 m and turned back to Camp 1. I was very tired, but felt pretty good considering. Once back at Camp, I moved into the other tent with Rick and Steve. Sarah was on her way up and she would move into the tent with John.

learning in THIN AIR

Sharing the tent with Rick and Steve was fun but uncomfortable. Our tent was a small two person tent and we are three people so you can do the math yourself. Plus, we had all our gear, sleeping bags, and food in the tent with us; a tight fit all around. Our goal was to stay up until 9:00 pm so we could have a better chance at sleeping through the night. We talked and played cards for a few hours, but eventually exhaustion took over and we retired for the night. I slept about the same as our first night here at Camp 1. It was extremely windy, but I was not cold, only a little uncomfortable due to our tight accommodations.

Back to Advanced Base Camp, April 17
We were planning to go above Camp 1 once again. The wind was still high, but we decided to go as high as we could or until it got too cold. This day I moved much better. I guess I am starting to become better acclimatized. John spent some time coaching Sarah, so Rick, Steve and I moved on ahead. The wind was extremely strong. Every now and then a gust would hit us that would almost knock us over forcing us to brace ourselves. Other than the wind, the sky was clear making for a beautiful day. We could see for hundreds of miles across the Himalayas and the Tibetan plateau. We hit a high point of 6850 m when John called us back as he felt the wind was getting too strong. We were back at Camp 1 in 35 minutes and began to pack to return to Advanced Base Camp. The walk back was quite nice and relaxing. Once back at Advanced Base Camp we sat in the sun for a bit and drank tea. It was a nice way to end a tough few days.

Tragedy at the Swiss and Italian Camps

AS BIG as this mountain is, the established Camps are actually quite small in area and tend to be crowded with several expedition teams huddling in close quarters. The generally tough conditions and shared interests in climbing tend to create a good, collaborative atmosphere. After all, the person you help out today may have the opportunity to return the favour when you most need it.

As in any small community, the closeness can also generate gossip, envy and conflict over limited resources. Whether in positive or negative tones, it is impossible not to take some interest in the human dramas that surround you on the mountain. These next few days provided a glut of drama and controversy.

Journal Excerpt for April 18 (Day 28) - Advanced Base Camp rest day; bath time; Swiss team; traveling salesmen

I think it was a good thing we came down off the mountain when we did. It is snowing quite hard now and it has been snowing every day for over a week. It is cold and windy and the warmer summer weather does not seem to be coming anytime soon. It was warmer and dry when we arrived on the mountain, but things have definitely changed. Today, I can't even see the mountain for the snow in the air.

Today was bath day, I shaved and gave myself a strategic wipe down with baby wipes. I am not much cleaner than when I started and I doubt I smell better, but I feel good to have made the effort. I had hoped to have a shower (sponge bath), wash my hair and do some laundry, but it is far too cold and windy for that. We will be in Advanced Base Camp for a couple more days so I hope that one of them is warm enough.

The Swiss team is now done. Their last few climbers have given up and will not make an attempt on the summit as they are too sick and fatigued. Their

Scott with travelling Tibetans

camp looks like a battle ground with all the frost bitten climbers sitting around with feet and hands covered in bandages. They paid a high price to reach the summit. Some will lose parts of their fingers and toes and others will lose feeling permanently. I am not sure I am willing to pay the same price for the top of a mountain.

A group of Tibetans arrived in Camp and went from team to team like traveling salesmen. They are selling beer, liquor, soft drinks and handmade jewelry. I did not buy anything, but it was fun to look at what they had and to talk with them a bit.

An Italian team arrived in Camp yesterday and I expect we will see many more teams arriving soon. Up until this point we have only had to share the mountain with the Swiss team.

Journal Entry for April 19 (Day 29) - Rest day Advanced Base Camp; Italian crisis

I have had to burst out of my tent it is so hot in there. This mountain is a study in contrasts. It is so cold and yet the sun's rays are so powerful that they turn my tent into a sauna, but when I get out of the tent it is too cold. Last night when I went to bed at 9:00 pm it was -15° C but the night time low was -32° C. I have placed my sleeping bag inside my bivy sack and always bring a hot water bottle to bed. At 7:30 am when I woke up the temperature in my tent had risen to +25° C. I just had to get out. I tried calling home at 8:30 am (10:30 pm home time), but there was no answer. I will try again if I can but our phone is still not working and the South Africans are heading up on the hill for five to six days so their phone will be unavailable.

A **bivy** sack is a waterproof cover that goes over your sleeping bag intended to provide protection when you must sleep without a tent.

There was some excitement with the Italian team that arrived yesterday. They had come from Base Camp to Advanced Base Camp in one day, not stopping at mid-camp to acclimatize. It was a huge elevation jump for them and a very long and hard day. One of their team members was not doing well and had been up with diarrhea most of the night. This morning he was very weak and semicomatose. We took our Pulse Oximeter to him, he had a blood oxygen concentration of 52%. At home he would have been put into the Intensive Care Unit immediately. His team was not very prepared and had

A **Pulse Oximeter** is a small device that when put on the end of your finger measures your heart rate and the percentage of oxygen in your blood.

no emergency oxygen. They had to purchase a bottle of oxygen from the South Africans for $500 and rent a regulator and mask from the Swiss. The team apparently did have a Gamow bag, but the zipper was broken and it did not work. The leader of the Italian team wanted to leave the sick climber for a day to see if he would improve, but others on the mountain felt he would die if he did not descend immediately. Under pressure, the Italian leader agreed to send the climber down. As there were no yaks in camp, two Tibetans were hired for $200 to carry him down to Base Camp. From there he will hire a jeep and go to Tingri and perhaps even all the way back to Kathmandu to the hospital.

A **Gamow bag** is a portable pressure chamber. A sick climber is placed inside and a foot pump is used to increase the interior pressure simulating a drop in altitude.

Besides that, it was quite a nice day. No snow and the warmest it has been in a while. I took my long awaited shower and washed some clothing. The warmth was deceiving as my hair froze as soon as it was wet and my laundry was frozen solid on the line. I and my clothing are now only slightly cleaner than we were at the start of the day.

As the other teams move into Camp they are met by John who informs them that he owns the fixed rope and that if they intend to use it they must pay him $125 per climber. I suspect some people will refuse to pay it and it will be interesting to see what the fall out is.

Journal Entry for April 20 (Day 30) – Advanced Base Camp rest day; more on the rope; the Swiss camp

Today is yet another rest day. John felt that we were not fully recovered from our time up high and that we would need at least 1-2 more rest days before we go up again. I sometimes worry that he loves his rest days so much that we will run out of time for a summit bid. It seems to me that part of John's desire to stay in Advanced Base Camp is to meet the new teams that are coming in every day as this is his opportunity to let them know that if they want to use the fixed rope they must pay him. Apparently there are already about 18 paying customers. I understand that John paid the Swiss about $1400 for the rope and with the 18 people at $125 each he has already recouped his

learning in THIN AIR

investment and now stands to make a pretty good profit. I'm not sure how I feel about this. Firstly, his job here is to help us get to the top, not to make more money for himself and secondly I don't really think it is fair that he turn a profit for others to use the rope. I have no issues with him recovering his investment, but the cost should be split evenly among the users. After all, he did not even expend energy to put the rope up. He purchased it and is now trying to make a buck off it.

I walked up to the Swiss camp today to send an email and I can't believe the change in the landscape. The Swiss camp is surrounded by at least six big new expeditions. Tents, people and yaks are everywhere. I'm glad our spot is somewhat secluded and too small to accommodate any more tents. When I went into the Swiss tent I was even more shocked. It is like a battle zone in there. Several of the climbers were sitting around with their feet in warm water baths to soothe their frostbite and most are on pain killers. The walk back to Base Camp will be excruciating for them.

The oldest member of the Swiss team is 66 years old. He was one of the first people we met when we got here. He is a very nice man but he has already left to make his way to the hospital in Kathmandu. He made it to the summit but I am told his personal Sherpa did not wait for him on the way down. He got off route and took the wrong way. The route was very steep and dangerous, and he almost fell to his death several times. Due to the extended time he spent exposed to the elements he got very badly frost bitten. I am told that when he arrived at the hospital it was also discovered that he had experienced a mild heart attack on the mountain. He has been flown to Delhi to a better hospital where he is now recovering.

Tagging Camp 2

OVER THE next several days we headed up higher on the mountain to continue acclimatizing. On the way, we endured another of our leader's inappropriate rants. Interestingly, I feel that if we'd had open communication within our team, this issue, like the last, would likely not have happened. In my opinion, these actions and behaviours were creating a culture of secrecy and fear where mistrust was rampant, loyalty was non-existent and any problems were hidden. At this time, I felt our team trust and loyalty were at a very low ebb, but our summit goal was enough to keep us moving upward – at the time.

Journal Entry for April 21 (Day 31) - Advanced Base Camp to Camp 1; wind bound

Today the plan was to go up to Camp 1 for a few days and to make it to Camp 2 for at least one night. The trip to Camp 1 was difficult, but not as bad as the last time. The acclimatization is helping. Rick was already in the tent when I got there around 3:30 pm. He had already gotten a big bag of ice for melting into water so we were set for the night. Around 5:00 pm Steve arrived and our little two person tent became a torture chamber. We put everything we absolutely did not need outside to make space, but it was still tight. Sitting around talking or playing cards is not too bad, but lying down to sleep is extremely tight and uncomfortable. Someone was always moving, and then you needed to move to accommodate their new position. It was a chain reaction. To top it all off, we rarely left the tent even to go to the bathroom. Getting out of the tent to pee was too disruptive, too cold and too dangerous. Therefore, we used a pee bottle which is quite challenging in such tight quarters. We all became much closer than perhaps we wanted to. The wind screamed all night long, and none of us got much sleep. The wind was still very high in the morning; all we could do was stay in our torture chamber all day.

Journal Entry for April 22 (Day 32) – Night plan; volcanic eruption; Rick gets sick

The wind was still very strong, but we wanted to start moving uphill regardless. However, John would not let us as he said it was too dangerous in the wind. So we stayed in our tent most of the day and played cards. At about 3:30 pm John informed us that we would move at night as the wind seemed to diminish between 6:00 pm and midnight. Unfortunately my headlamp batteries were dead and I did not have a spare set, and Rick had left his heavy mitts at Advanced Base Camp. Due to these two issues it would not be safe for us to travel at night. John lost his mind when we told him this. For the next one and a half hours we listened to him rant about what a couple of screw ups we were and that he had failed us as a leader because we did not feel that we could speak to him about anything. I think he says things that he does not mean during these tirades, but they are very hurtful and difficult to forgive. He even accused us of climbing the mountain to become famous and that all we wanted to do was climb to get publicity. I asked Rick what he would do when he became famous and he said he thought he would buy a Ferrari. We saw the humour in this, but John apparently did not and it just fed his fire. When he was eventually exhausted from his rant, all I wanted to do was pack my bag and go home. This was a very unpleasant environment and, even though I liked Rick and Steve, I did not even want to be with them. Sarah had pretty much become John's buddy and I felt I could no longer really speak with her about anything. Not a fun way to end the day.

That night Rick started to get sick. He had a fever, shortness of breath, chills, and aches and pains. We gave him a Diamox to help calm his breathing and Tylenol for his fever. I also took a Diamox as I find it can help me sleep better. We all slept pretty well that night.

Journal Entry for April 23 (Day 33) – Above Camp 1; Camp 1 to Advanced Base Camp

Today when Rick awoke he was still sick and decided to head back to Advanced Base Camp. The rest of us decided to head up the hill to try to tag Camp 2. Steve and I put on our one piece down suits and were off around 9:15 am. John and Sarah left about 30 minutes after us, but by that time Steve and I were quite far up. Shortly after she started we saw Sarah turn around and head for Advanced Base Camp as well. Apparently she too was sick. Steve and I kept climbing, but I was not performing well. I was moving slow and felt weak. I figured it was due to the altitude, but I was hoping I too was not getting sick. The wind had dropped and I was getting overheated in my one piece suit. Not far into the climb I suggested to Steve that we turn around, go back to Camp 1, take off our down suits and put on Gore-Tex and give it another try as we would be much more comfortable. Steve felt that to do so would be suicide. As soon as John got a hold of that news he would lay into us once again. He said to suck it up and keep going. It would be easier and less painful that way. Eventually John caught up to us and he too was struggling. He was moving slowly, having a hard time breathing and had lost his voice. I was quite happy about this last development.

I made it to the serac just below Camp 2 but then I was done. John and Steve went up the serac to make sure the fixed rope was anchored properly and to generally check out the route, A **serac** is a block or column of ice formed by intersecting crevasses on a glacier.

but I stayed behind. I did not have the energy to go one more foot. Although the serac is only about 50 m high, at this altitude it is very challenging. I sat alone at the bottom for about an hour as the wind increased to gale force. I was now glad that I had my down suit on. The wind chill was massive, but I hardly felt the cold. While sitting there I started to cough up green phlegm

Serac on way up to Camp 2

and the odd bit of blood. "Not good," I thought. Perhaps my poor performance today has actually been due to the start of a chest infection. This would reduce my oxygen intake and make everything more difficult. It seems everyone is coming down with something.

After about one hour of recovery time I headed down by myself. John and Steve were about 30 minutes behind me. I was so exhausted that even walking down hill I needed to stop and take frequent rests to get my breath back. Rappelling was very difficult. By the time I got to the bottom of the route I was beyond tired and due to the exertion I was totally overheated. I peeled the top half of my suit off, tied it around my waist and started the excruciating trudge up the final hill to our tent located on the highest ridge at Camp 1. This uphill portion is an awful way to end the day. I arrived at my tent at 2:40 pm and collapsed inside with my suit still on and my legs hanging out the door. The plan was to head down to Advanced Base Camp but at that point I seriously doubted that I had the strength or energy left. John and Steve got back to camp at 3:10 pm and said we would head down at 3:30 pm. I took a very long time to get ready to depart and slowly made my way down.

The walk down the scree slope to Half Camp was one of the hardest things I have ever done. Even though it is all downhill, it is covered in snow, loose rock and sand. John and Steve were also very tired taking frequent breaks to absorb the pain and to rest. What normally took 25 minutes took us over an hour. Eventually we made it to Half Camp and began the long marathon to Advanced Base Camp. We were feeling a little better, but still went very slowly. We were all exhausted by the time we made it to Advanced Base Camp.

learning in THIN AIR

I went to the dining tent for dinner, but did not eat a bite. I did, however, drink many cups of tea to try to rehydrate. I started to cough up large hard mucus plugs and was feeling awful. I have decided to start a course of antibiotics to try to cut this off before it gets too bad. This has been one of the most physically strenuous days of my life.

Last Rest Before the Push

WE HAD been on the mountain now for several weeks. The rest days were tedious, the climbing days were grueling, and every day there was altitude sickness to some degree or another. Underlying it all I felt was the constant stress from the poor group dynamics within our team. But I had come this far and I felt I needed to stay the course. Fortunately, at this time in the expedition, something of a plan seemed to emerge.

Learning in Thin Air - Lack of Reflection and Discussion

When I look back upon this now it is obvious to me that the main issue within our team was lack of reflection and discussion which was brought about by the lack of trust. We were not practicing a single part of the Deliberate Success Model (pg. 44). I felt there was no trust within the team and no support, so no one wanted to put themselves in the firing line to bring up the miserable state our team was in.

This is a classic team struggle. When the foundation of the team is not laid well it is open to crack when the pressure starts, and it always starts at some point. When there is no discussion of issues due to conflict and lack of trust, these issues go unresolved and fester becoming even more toxic as time moves on.

This experience was very educational in the eventual development of my Deliberate Success Model, but I had no way of knowing that at the time. At the time, I just felt helpless and hoped that, somehow, everything would work out.

Scott preparing to go to Camp 2

The Final Push
to the Summit

WE RESTED, we climbed. We rested, we climbed. And tensions mounted — there was a lot of stress, and a lot of interesting personal, team and leadership challenges.

Journal Entry for April 24 (Day 34) - Advanced Base Camp rest day; bath; self doubts

I woke this morning at 7:00 am feeling a little better, but mostly awful. When I looked in the mirror the image I saw confirmed how I felt. My eyes were red, swollen and running, I had skin peeling from my nose, cheeks and forehead from sun and wind burn, my lips were dry, burned and cracked and my nose was running. Not a pretty picture. I figured I would shave, wash my face and try to clean up a bit. I got a bowl of warm water from Lhakpa and began my task. While I was at it I washed a few strategic places on my body as well. Not as good as a shower or even a sponge bath, but pretty good considering. When I was done I looked and felt a bit better.

I called home today using the South African team's phone and spoke to Susan for almost 15 minutes. Our phone is still not functional and it appears this will be the case for the rest of the expedition. I am very homesick and can't wait to see Susan and Amy again. Unfortunately, the phone went dead when the battery died and that was the end of my call.

Today is a relatively warm and sunny day. It will do well for our recovery and our spirits. We are now significantly behind schedule due to poor weather and our excessive number of rest days. This puts us in a very bad position. We can still make the summit, but we will need to recover our health and then have eight to nine consecutive days of good weather. We will see what happens. Based on how I felt yesterday, I'm not sure if I have what it will take to make it to the top.

Journal Entry for April 25 (Day 35) - Advanced Base Camp rest day

This morning dawned a beautiful day, the sky is clear, the sun is warm and there is only a slight breeze to make a chill in the air. I had a rough night last night having a difficult time falling asleep and having frequent coughing fits that lasted for several minutes leaving me breathless. Listening to the others in their tents I can tell they had a similar night to mine. I continue to take my antibiotics and hope this sickness will soon pass.

The balance of yesterday turned out to be quite interesting. The near death Italian came back from Base Camp yesterday and from the look of him it was way too soon. John told him to go home and they argued for quite a while. Then a guide from another team came down to talk with John about the use of the fixed rope and they argued for a long time while trading insults back and forth. It will be interesting to see what happens with the rope situation as the season progresses.

As the day wore on, the nice weather went away. The clouds came in, the temperature dropped drastically and it started to snow. As the snow picked

Despite the tension the views were spectacular

learning in THIN AIR

up, the mountain disappeared into the mist. Not a good day to be on the mountain, not a good day to be at Advanced Base Camp either, but it is the lesser of two evils. We will spend two more days here and then head back onto the mountain for our summit bid. It will likely be our only shot at the top.

Journal Entry for April 26 (Day 36) - Advanced Base Camp rest day; the plan; pee bottle

At 8:30 am the day seemed pretty nice. The sun was out, there was little wind, and the temperature had improved a bit. I did not need to put on my long underwear until after lunch. Today will be pretty much like every other day here at Advanced Base Camp. Including today, we have 11 more days before we start our long trek home. If we take today and tomorrow as rest days we should just be able to make it to the top, provided that the weather holds and everything else goes well with our health and with the team.

The plan will be to sleep at Camp 1 on April 28, sleep at Camp 2 on April 29, go back to Camp 1 for a rest day, move to Camp 2 on May 1 then on to Camp 3 on May 2. We will sleep briefly at Camp 3 and then head to the top on May 3. This plan even allows us a couple of extra days in case of bad weather.

Today is now drawing to an end. I will go to dinner soon and then off to bed.

Unfortunately today my pee bottle was stolen from where I had it airing on the rocks outside my tent. I have a couple solutions in mind, but neither is perfect. Some poor guy thinks he found himself a good water bottle, but will soon learn the reality of what he got.

Journal Entry for April 27 (Day 37) - Advanced Base Camp rest day; phone

Today is one of the nicer days we have had on the mountain. It is sunny and warm with very little wind. Overnight it snowed and was very windy. I did not put my ear plugs in so between the constant noise of the wind and my frequent coughing fits I found it difficult to sleep. I finally fell asleep around 2:30 am and slept OK until 7:00 am.

I called Susan this morning. It gets tougher every day. I am quite homesick and am sad that I am missing so much of Amy's development. She is learning to walk and to talk while I am on this cold mountain with a group of people

I don't really want to be with. I could never have predicted this. All my expeditions up to this point have been amazing experiences. Whether we made it to the top or not was of little consequence. The journey along the way was where the true memories came from. What has gone wrong on this mountain? We seemed like such a good group at first. Whenever I call home, I feel guilty that I am robbing myself and my family from time that we will never get back again. I feel very selfish as the purpose for being here sometimes seems lost.

John figured out this morning that we have two less days than we thought. The yaks will come in on May 5 and we head out the next morning. This means that we will need to push a little harder and faster on the mountain and hope for good weather. We now have zero margin for error. All our rest days have caught up to us and we have run out of time. If we get a bad weather day or something else happens to slow us down, we are done, there will be no second chance. I hope we at least get a shot at the top. It is one thing to try and to fail, but it would be very disappointing to have spent all this time on the mountain and to not even get a chance to try for the top.

Rick decided to head up to Camp 1 today. He is tired of sitting around and just wants to get on with it. I decided not to join him in the hopes that one more day at Advanced Base Camp will help my cough get better. Rick will move to Camp 2 the next day while the rest of us move to Camp 1. We will all meet up at Camp 3 and go for the summit from there. I am feeling pretty good about our summit chances. Although I feel that we have not been working well as a team, not really having bonded, I still think we are good enough, being strong and experienced, that we should be okay. I am weaker than I would like to be but, again, I think I am OK. I have lost a lot of weight and find it difficult to eat. The altitude suppresses my appetite and I am getting very sick of the food. Don't get me wrong, Lhakpa and Kami do a great job, but there is only so much you can do with rice, potatoes and pasta. I find I need to force myself to eat as there is no real enjoyment in it any more.

Enough Rope to Hang

THE MATTER of charging other climbers for the use of the fixed ropes became quite an issue. It was a practice that was fundamentally counter to the culture of this type of mountaineering (this has changed a little by 2012, but in 2002 it was rare). I felt it was distracting John from his duties to us, his paying team members. It added to our stress in an already stressful situation and created friction between our climbing team and the others in camp.

Journal Entry for April 27 (Day 37 Continued) - Rope dispute

There was quite a bit of excitement and fireworks at Advanced Base Camp today as John has continued to hound the various teams for the rope money and most are refusing to pay. Most of the exchanges John has with the other leaders end up in a shouting match, sometimes with pushing and threatening. Due to this, our team has now become persona non grata in any other camp. We are confined to our little space on the mountain and I think any cooperation or help we would hope for from the other teams is long gone.

The Sherpa people are devout Buddhists and are not big fans of confrontation and conflict. With all the expedition leaders arguing with John, the Sherpa from each expedition thought they could get together and work this out. The issue was that many people did not believe that John had purchased the rope from the Swiss and that he was just trying to make money from something he had no right to control. A delegation of Sherpa from all the other camps got together and came to consult with Lhakpa and Kami, our team Sherpa, figuring they could get the truth and work out a deal. Kami is one of the senior Sherpa on the mountain and everyone would respect his word. When the delegation of Sherpa arrived at our camp, they asked Kami if John had actually paid the Swiss for the rope and if it was right that everyone pay John to use it. His response was that he did not know what, if any deal, John had made with the Swiss and he could not therefore recommend that the other teams pay for the use. While it is true that Kami had not been involved with the rope negotiations with the Swiss, he was aware of what went on. He was not willing, however, to put his reputation on the line to support John. The Sherpa delegation left with the recommendation to all the expedition leaders that they do not pay for the use of the rope.

This infuriated John which resulted in him lashing out at Kami with a verbal tirade unlike anything any of us had yet to experience. It got so bad that I and pretty much everyone else became embarrassed and uncomfortable with the spectacle and slowly retreated to our personal tents. John had now officially lost control of the rope and the respect of pretty much everyone in camp including his own team members.

This was a very unfortunate way to end the evening and to begin our summit bid.

The Fight for Camp 2

WITH OUR time window rapidly shrinking, we had to get our game on. Over these next few days, we retraced our steps up to our highest point on the mountain and then ventured far beyond. I entered new territory in terms of geography, altitude, physical exertion and emotional strain.

Journal Entry for April 28 (Day 38) - Advanced Base Camp to Camp 1; start of summit bid

Climbing up to Camp 2

This is it, our first and only kick at the can. The weather this morning is pretty good. The wind direction has shifted and is no longer coming from across the Tibetan plateau which is a good thing. It seems that we may have finally passed through the poor weather and entered a more favourable and stable weather window. We only need four to five days of good weather to make it all happen.

We have decided to go for the summit from Camp 2 instead of Camp 3. The rationale for this is that John feels that the effort it will take to establish Camp 3 is greater than the benefit we will gain from the additional acclimatization at Camp 3. I am not sure about this and would rather go to Camp 3, but I have been given no choice. I think that John has lost his commitment to this expedition and just wants it to be over. After all that has gone on I don't think his heart is in it any longer. I almost feel badly for him.

The rest of the day was pretty uneventful compared to the last few days. The trip to Camp 1 was relatively easy for me and I felt pretty good. Steve and I have the Camp 1 tent to ourselves as Rick is up at Camp 2. It was quite a treat to have all the extra room. We had an early dinner and went to sleep to make sure we had the energy we would need for the next day.

Journal Entry for April 30 (Day 40) – Camp 1 to Camp 2; fixed rope on the serac

The trip to Camp 2 was quite strenuous. I had been up the fixed rope before, but never beyond the serac. I was feeling pretty good despite a heavy pack. The serac was challenging, but kind of fun at the same time. It was about 50 m from top to bottom averaging about 70 degrees in steepness. The first part was simple stair step climbing on the ice. I then traversed across a very exposed section that got my heart pumping. Then it was straight up from there. The ice was pure blue glacial ice and as hard as concrete. It took several swings of my ice axe to get the pick stuck in well. I had to pound my feet over and over into the ice to get my crampons to bite.

As I emerged on the top of the serac I was out of breath and feeling weak from the exertion. The fixed rope ended just before the top leaving my final few moves, a 5 m traverse, totally exposed to a several thousand foot fall. Doing this in the condition I was in was unnerving to say the least. Once over the serac I entered the "football field" which is a relatively flat section about 650 m long. Even though it was flat, it drained my energy as I had not yet been to this elevation and was not acclimatized to it. Once across the football field I came to the second serac. Wait a minute! What second serac? Nobody ever mentioned this one before and I'm not sure why. It was a little longer than the first serac but slightly less steep. However, the hardness of the ice, the exposure and the elevation made it just as difficult or maybe even a little more difficult than the first one.

About halfway up I ran into a group of Sherpa coming down who were attempting to install a second fixed rope as a descent line. The line was too short and would not work. The Sherpa are extremely strong climbers, but many do not have the technical skill or experience required for the more complex rope work on the mountain. This was the case with this group. They argued amongst themselves as to what to do and ordered me from one rope to another and from one position to another. Each time I moved I exposed myself to a very dangerous fall. I was getting tired of waiting around as they continued to work on the rope for over 30 minutes, making a complete mess of it. I was now becoming physically and mentally exhausted from hanging out in such an exposed position for so long. Eventually they gave up and left the rope in worse shape than when they had started. I did not really care at this point and just wanted to get up to Camp. I passed the Sherpa team and started to climb once again, but the wait had taken a toll on me.

Once at the top of the serac I started on a long shallow traverse that never seemed to end. The slope was not that steep, but a slip would have meant certain death. There was evidence of several avalanches along the way and I had to actually climb through several sections of avalanche debris. A trail of bamboo wands with flagging tape attached to the top guided me towards Camp. Although I could not see Camp I knew it could not be that far, but it seemed to go on forever. This final section took me almost two hours. I finally made it to Camp 2 six hours after I had departed from Camp 1.

Steve approaching 8000 m on summit attempt

learning in THIN AIR

Camp 2 was located on a flat snow field situated just below a 30-50 degree slope that lead to Camp 3. The Camp was pretty safe from avalanches as it was on a slight rise on an avalanche path that lead away from camp. The area, however, was very exposed. Some teams constructed snow walls around their tents to protect them from the wind. We just tied ours down and hoped for the best. This would not be a fun place to be during a windstorm.

There were about 10 tents at Camp 2. Steve, Rick and I are once again together in a two person tent while John and Sarah were in a second tent about 15 feet away.

Steve and Rick Go for the Summit

THERE WERE several teams gathered at Camp 2, all within striking distance of the summit. Still, there were many factors to consider in deciding when to make a move for the top. Temperature, wind strength, personal energy level and illness were all in the mix, and these last two varied from team to team and from person to person. It is common for teams in this position to split up, or even recombine with other teams, so each person can have their best chance at success. John, Sarah and I thought our best chance would come after a full day of rest at Camp 2. Steve and Rick chose to rest for a few hours and leave for the summit that very night.

Journal Entry for April 30 (Day 40) – Rick and Steve summit bid
Steve and Rick woke at 12:00 am and began their preparations for the summit climb. It took them until 2:30 am to get ready as it was very cold (-35° C) and Rick was not very organized. A total of seven climbers finally set off at 3:00 am. The South African team turned around after about two hours due to the cold, exhaustion and their slow pace. This made it more challenging for the remaining climbers as the South African team Sherpa was the only one who knew the route and he had turned back with his team. The climbers were now going blind and hoping they would find the right route to the top.

The remaining four climbers wasted a lot of time trying to find the route, but eventually were on track and moving well. At 10:00 am I watched the two Austrians top out onto the snow field at 8100 m. About an hour later I saw Steve start to cross the snow field. Rick was sitting on a rock close to the snow field but had not moved for over an hour. At this point the weather was starting to turn bad and they were quickly approaching the turnaround time of 1:00 pm. Rick and Steve were moving too slowly, they were too far from the top, the weather was getting bad, and the turnaround time was too close. Speaking with them through our walkie talkies the difficult decision was made to turn around and to abandon their summit attempt. The two Austrians continued to the summit in white out conditions and said they thought they made it to the top, but they were not sure as they could not really see anything.

Rick and Steve began their long journey back to camp. It was agonizing to watch them. They were so tired that even going downhill they needed to stop and rest every 50 m. They made it back by late afternoon and collapsed in our tent. I had food and water ready for them, but it took them awhile to get the energy to eat and drink. They said the climb had been very exhausting due to the cold, and their lack of rest, food, water and acclimatization. After some food and conversation we all drifted off to sleep. Tomorrow will be my opportunity to go to the top with Sarah and John.

The Expedition is Over

THIS REMAINS one of the most disappointing and emotionally difficult days of my life. The following journal entry accurately captures my feelings around the event.

Journal Entry for May 1 (Day 41) - My summit attempt

Today we were awakened by a radio call from John at about 4:00 am. I was expecting the call to be, "Get your boots on and let's go for the summit," but instead it was, "Sarah is sick and must go down now. The expedition is over." She has a lung infection and had experienced another retinal hemorrhage. John said he personally needed to take her down. Apparently all of this had come about at Camp 1, but Sarah had not told anyone because we were not speaking to each other. She lost close to 70% of her vision and was having difficulty breathing. Rick and Steve were going to Advanced Base Camp anyway, and I suggested that they take Sarah down. John and I could go for the summit together. Unfortunately he said no way, that he was not going to go to the top with me, and that he was going down. The expedition was over.

I was devastated. I was feeling really good and my summit opportunity just vanished right before my eyes. At first, I was very sad and stuck my head *inside my sleeping bag and cried quietly. Then my sadness turned to anger. I felt that I had been wronged. I was not being given the opportunity I had been promised when I signed up with this team. There is no doubt that Sarah needed to go down, but John could still have gone up with me.*

John, Sarah and Steve left camp while Rick and I stayed to break down the tents and clean camp. It was very cold, and my fingers nearly froze, but I did not really care at the time. I had an inner flame of anger keeping me warm. I followed the others about 90 minutes after they departed.

I moved fast downhill with this small nuclear plant inside me and I quickly caught up to John, Sarah and Steve. Sarah was smiling, joking and did not look very sick to me. It pissed me off to no end to know that I had lost my attempt at the summit for, what appeared to me, no good reason. I did not doubt that she was sick, but she did not require all the attention she was getting. The expedition did not need to be called off because of it. I don't think that John really had any intention of making the effort to go to the top, and Sarah gave him the excuse he needed. John said that maybe we would rest for a day and he would go for the top with me, but we both knew this was not true. It would not work and it would not happen. He had no intention of going back up.

I made it back to Camp 1 in just under one hour. The uphill trip yesterday had taken me six hours. I quickly packed my stuff and continued downhill. I was tired when I made it to Advanced Base Camp, but not too bad. I had a drink and something to eat and retired to my tent. This was the end to one of the worst days of my life.

Waiting for the Yaks

ALL THAT remained for me at this point in the expedition was to endure the long, sad trip home and the lingering feelings of bitterness and letdown. These stayed with me for a long time.

Journal Entry for May 2 (Day 42) – Advanced Base Camp; trip over; waiting for yaks
Well, here we are waiting at camp with nothing to do. The yaks are scheduled to arrive on May 5th and we will depart on May 6th. This will be a hard few

days. I just spoke with John to see what opportunities there may be for me to make one final attempt at the top and just as I suspected he has no intention of going up with me.

I called home this morning and it only made things worse. I want to be home so badly. I feel like I have wasted 2 months and a lot of money and worst of all I have missed so much of Amy's development. She won't even know who I am when I get home and it will break my heart. I think I may try another 8000 m peak some day, but it will be under drastically different circumstances. I only hope that I can learn from this awful experience to make the next one better.

Yaks coming to camp to carry our gear back to Base Camp

Learning in Thin Air - Capacities for Success

Whether on a summit climb or in a work environment there are three things you need to be successful: Personal Capacity, Team Capacity, and Leadership Capacity.

learning in THIN AIR

1. **Personal Capacity**: *Those personal technical skills and knowledge sets that are required for the task at hand, including those mindsets and certain "soft skills," such as determination, confidence, etc. which are frequently referred to as emotional intelligence. Studies have indicated that 60-80% of success in life can be directly attributed to emotional intelligence.*

2. **Team Capacity**: *One's own capacity to work well on a team. But also the capacity of the team itself, as a distinct entity, to synergize and work effectively toward a common goal that an individual would have little hope of achieving alone.*

3. **Leadership Capacity**: *The capacity to positively influence people and the results they achieve, beginning with self and extending to those around us. This applies whether or not one is in a formal leadership role or not.*

These capacities do not develop in isolation or even sequentially. There is a lot of overlap. But I think this model gives us a useful breakdown of capacities. Are all levels necessary? There may be some instances where individuals achieve success on their own (or claim to), but this is rare on big projects, rarer still on big mountains. Almost always there is a high performing team involved, and often it is a team of leaders: people who positively influence all those around them.

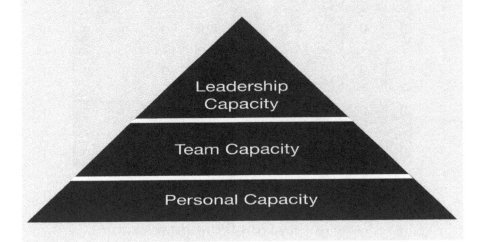

View of Cho Oyu from Base Camp

learning in THIN AIR

Why We Failed

AS YOU can imagine, the expedition took a huge toll on me both physically and emotionally. I had lost close to 25 lbs and most of my fitness was gone. My arms and legs were weak, flabby and covered with loose skin. My face looked gaunt and my hair was falling out. I was certainly not the picture of health. Fortunately, though, I had avoided frostbite and any lingering illness. It would only take time to put the weight back on and get back in shape physically.

The emotional recovery also took time. I had invested a lot of myself in this expedition, and I had taken a beating.

Seven weeks earlier I had thought myself a capable climber on an invincible team. We were all young, strong, talented and experienced, but somewhere along the way, it all went very wrong. The failure on Cho Oyu made me question my very future as a climber, especially my goal of climbing Everest. How could I hope to climb Everest when I had failed this test on Cho Oyu? If I could not perform here, what hope had I of performing on the far more difficult slopes of Mount Everest? I contemplated giving it up all together. Maybe I could swap my crampons for golf shoes, and trade steep, icy, mountain pitches for rolling, green fairways. After all, golf was less expensive, closer to home and done in much warmer weather than mountaineering. If I kept my head up, I had a much smaller chance of dying an early death on a golf course. I knew, however, that this was not who I was.

In retrospect, I see that I went through the classic stages of emotional recovery that are typical after a major loss: denial; anger; acceptance; optimism; and recovery. While I was still on the mountain at Camp 2 and the news filtered in that my summit bid had been called off, I entered denial; surely, I tried to convince myself, there was a way to continue from there. Maybe we would be able to regroup at Base Camp and launch another assault. Anger and resentment were quick to replace denial as it became clear to me that the summit was lost and the expedition had changed. I directed that anger primarily at others, but I saved a decent share for myself. This anger fed me all the way home.

Eventually, though, that anger did subside enough for me to enter a more neutral state. When the emotions had cleared, I was able to accept what had happened and became more objective about the experience. Being more objective, I was able to draw on my knowledge as an educator and employ a familiar model, the Experiential Learning Cycle (pg 20), to the expedition. This was very therapeutic. The very act of trying to draw something positive – the learning – from this experience created a sense of optimism. I could see a future where this experience could serve me well. So, I set about reflecting on the expedition, drawing out the lessons and thinking about how to apply them to my real world.

Learning in Thin Air - Post Expedition Analysis

As I reflected on what went wrong, I was able to identify dozens of ways that I thought we were compromised in our task of climbing Cho Oyu. All of them led back to one fundamental fact: we were not a team.

Right from the start, I felt that we did little to truly form as a team. We somehow just assumed that our vast experience and superior climbing skills were enough. I was just as much to blame as everyone else; I knew what was happening but said nothing. I mistakenly thought that time, alone, would work some kind of magic, and that we would naturally grow closer and stronger together. About four weeks into the expedition, when I looked at our performance, I knew this was not true. Our trust in one another was low, we were unable to confront issues, conflict boiled constantly beneath the surface and meaningful communication was absent. In my opinion, our goals were individual rather than shared, and the plan to achieve them was vague or unknown. We were individually crippled by self doubt and sagging motivation. We were not a team; we were a loose group of individuals stumbling through a dangerous and unforgiving wilderness.

The more I thought about it, the more I am of the opinion that our lack of team cohesion stemmed directly from our leader. Yes, we were all guilty of abdicating personal responsibility to some degree, but the toxic team culture that we endured for nearly seven weeks, I feel was mainly the product of poor leadership. Whether this was intentional leadership strategy or simple incompetence I still don't know, neither is excusable on the mountain. In my mind, our leader not only harboured conflicting priorities, his style was abrasive, authoritarian, condescending and demotivating. I also believe that his extreme temper and selfish behaviour became a huge dark cloud that hung over the entire team. With a constant threat of bullying, I distanced myself first from our leader, then from my other team members. It appeared to me that we all started to avoid personal contact of any kind. We would gather for meals, but we would each disappear into our personal tents as soon as we could.

Effective communication could not thrive in this environment. It was no surprise that, with the threat of an abusive outburst, I would conceal my plans for Rick to carry my sleeping bag to Camp 1 on the first trip. I also felt that other members of the team kept their medical issues to themselves rather than sharing them. Without this information we could do nothing to help each other. An honest, frank discussion was impossible with the constant threat of abuse.

Trust and loyalty also suffered in this environment. There was no transparency. Key information about our expedition plan was guarded. Promises were not met. Our personal and important needs for such simple things as a means to call home were trivialized and went unmet. John reaped the harvest of this when he needed to rely on Kami to vouch for him about owning the fixed ropes. Who will put their own reputation on the line for a leader who has not earned the respect of those that he is supposed to lead? Not Kami.

Ultimately, I feel we had failed as a team because we were not a team. We were a group of individuals pretending to be a team, dragged about on a dangerous mountain by an ineffective and periodically abusive leader.

After reflecting upon all this, I saw four main lessons emerge that I could apply to both future climbs and my business. I felt we had failed because we had: a fractured vision; autonomous actions; ineffective leadership; and a lack of accountability.

It is easy to say these things, but the challenge is to look at what they mean and how they apply to the bigger world beyond mountaineering.

Fractured Vision

A vision describes a future destination; the place or goal you wish to attain. This is the first step in the Deliberate Success Model (pg. 44). Many organizations have a vision, but few unleash the true power of the vision. Most climbing teams don't develop a comprehensive vision because they assume the goal is obvious (get to the summit) and because they believe a vision is relevant only to business organizations. But on a climbing team, just as with any organization, it is important that all team members know from the outset what they are working toward. Their shared vision should describe two main things: 1) What represents success for the team (the ultimate goal or target); and 2) Who they will strive to be as a team while they are trying to achieve success (their collective values and the culture they want to create).

On Cho Oyu, I feel we lacked clarity on both of these visions; success and team. It was not for lack of time. Even before meeting for the first time in

learning in THIN AIR

Kathmandu, we had ample opportunity to discuss what would make our expedition a success to all of us. Would it be for everyone to make it to the top? For at least one member to make it to the top? For everyone to do their best and make it home safely? Or, would it be to summit at all costs? This would have put us on the same page from day one.

We also failed to develop a common team vision or culture. We could have discussed and established our expectations with respect to leadership, communication, information sharing, decision making and so many other things that would have strengthened our relationships and trust. We had days of rest and recovery while on the expedition during which we could have refined and applied our vision of who we would be as a team.

I know now that we greatly underestimated the importance of a common vision. With no vision to guide us, I believe we were wide open to the negative influences of our leader, and the toxic team culture that was created. With no other destination to aim for and no measuring stick to see if we were performing, we were just along for the ride.

Autonomous Actions

On any high performing team, there are times when people must take initiative and act independently. But when they do, they must act on behalf of the team. This is different than being autonomous. When people are autonomous, they act out of self interest. I felt that we were autonomous, each and every one of us.

Due to our ample and highly public personal conflict issues, to me it felt as if we had all cocooned into our own little worlds. We did not get to know one another well enough to bond in an empathetic way, which I believe led to none of us caring about each other's goals or values and not asking one another for emotional support in tough times. Strong personal relationships provide the glue and the foundation for any high performance team. Without a solid foundation built upon trusting and supportive relationships, I felt we were unable to perform adequately when challenge or change arose. We fell apart. In the end, we were not a team at all; we were a group of autonomous individuals.

Ineffective Leadership

I have always believed that leadership is ultimately responsible for team culture. There is no doubt that the team members play a big role, but leadership sets the direction and the tone. I observed this first hand way back in university when I was hired to lead three week canoe expeditions for the third year students. On each trip, there were thirty students, and we would drive from Thunder Bay to Arkansas to paddle the Buffalo River. This drive would take us several days and we would split the students into three passenger vans. Each van had a leader who would also be the river leader for their "pod." I found it fascinating how quickly the individual teams took on the personality of their leader and began to form different team cultures.

One leader was an ex-military man with a very regimented and commanding style. There was little room for discussion in his camp. Precision and structure were a priority. The second leader had also spent time in the military but had since rebelled against the authority, power and structure. His camp seemed to lack structure, clear focus, and discipline. Camp procedures and timelines were treated as "suggestions." I was somewhere in the middle, between these polarities of structure and flexibility.

After only two days, the leadership styles and the team cultures they had formed were becoming evident. We had stopped at a roadside rest stop for lunch and set a departure time of 1:00 pm. We each parked our vans a small distance from one another and began to set up our lunch. At 12:55 pm the first leader was in his van, packed and ready to go. The van was running and his team was seated and belted in. He was looking from his watch to us and back again. His team members were all staring out the window with impatient looks on their faces. They had become their leader. The second team was in the middle of lunch with no real sense of urgency at all. People were happily engaged in conversations, and appeared to be unconcerned about the approaching 1:00 pm departure time. My team was cleaning up from lunch and, while there was a desire and intent to meet the 1:00 pm deadline, we would likely be one or two minutes late.

In a matter of two days, each team had formed its culture, and this culture was an accurate reflection of their leader's style and values. Since that day, I do not underestimate the power of a leader to influence their team.

On Cho Oyu, I believe our leader set the stage for our own unique team culture, one of individualism and fear. Based on our interactions with our leader, I observed each of us acting in a certain way, whether it was consciously or unconsciously. In my opinion we were afraid to communicate openly, we distrusted one another and our leader, and kept to ourselves. We did not deal with conflict or change well and we did not openly support one another, even though we were all emotionally stressed and could have used some support. In fact, the constant stress likely led to some of the sickness we experienced.

Lack of Accountability

Throughout the expedition, in my opinion, we experienced the "elephant in the room" syndrome. We all knew the issue was there, but nobody wanted to acknowledge it or talk about it. In our case, I felt we were not working well together as a team, that we were not communicating effectively and that there was a lack of trust. But no one mentioned it or did anything about it.

At the time, I blamed John for this. I felt that he had created my misery and that I had no control over the situation or the result. This is what it is like to be a victim. You give away power and allow someone else to control what happens to you. Upon reflection, I did not need to be the victim. I could have accepted responsibility for the part I played in creating my reality and acted upon it. There is no doubt in my mind that John had played a huge role in our current situation, but I too had played a role by my inaction. Who knows whether I could have made a difference or not but, by playing the role of the victim, I did not even try.

In the end, Cho Oyu was a huge learning experience for me. I now knew what not to do as a leader. I knew how to set a team up for failure by not attending to vision and culture. I knew how to be a victim. Now I needed to turn it all around and apply it to the biggest challenge of them all – Everest.

Mount

Everest

Mount Everest

Bringing a
Dream to Life

AFTER MY disastrous experience on Cho Oyu in 2001, and after much soul searching as to the reasons for failure, I continued my climbing efforts while building a family and two businesses, Summit Training and Frontier Team Building. Both companies use an experiential approach with a focus on (no surprise here) leadership and team building. I went back to university and received my Masters in Leadership and Training and then started to teach leadership and organizational change at the Executive MBA level. I was able to successfully take the knowledge I had gained through school and climbing and apply it to helping teams and leaders within various organizations reach their full potential.

I also continued to climb going on expeditions to Denali in Alaska, Kilimanjaro in Africa, and Mt. Blanc and the Matterhorn in Europe. I was well on my way to completing my climb of the Seven Summits. But, of course, to accomplish that goal, I would have to summit Mount Everest.

In 2008, everything aligned itself in such a way that this was the year I would attempt Everest. I focused on ramping up my personal strength and capabilities with this big goal firmly set in my mind.

Mount Everest

MOUNT EVEREST is the highest mountain on earth. Like many of the other 8000 m peaks, it is part of the spectacular Himalayan Mountain range. Everest sits right on the border of Nepal and Tibet, and can be climbed from both the north (Tibetan) and south (Nepalese) sides.

With its 8848 m summit rising well into the "death zone," Everest offers climbers the ultimate challenges of extreme weather, high altitude and, of course, dangerous terrain. As if its sheer size and difficulty were not enough, its long history of repelling even the best climbers has secured its legendary status. In 1924, famous British mountaineer George Mallory disappeared on the mountain with fellow climber Andrew Irvine while attempting the first ascent. (Mallory is famous for his poignant reply to the question of why he wanted to climb Mount Everest: "Because it's there.") Mallory's body was found nearly perfectly preserved 75 years later. There are still some who believe Mallory and Irvine may have been the first to stand on the summit, but there is no conclusive evidence to support this.

The first successful ascent of Everest is attributed to Sir Edmund Hillary and Tenzing Norgay, in 1953. His somewhat less famous quote, "We knocked the bastard off," nicely captures the feelings they must have had at the time. Since Hillary and Norgay's climb, over ten thousand people (according to AdventureStats.com) have made the attempt to stand among the giants of the mountaineering world. As of the start of 2012, just over 3,414 people (including guides and Sherpa) have been successful, while over 230 people have died in the attempt.

All these things – the size, difficulty and danger – have made Mount Everest the "holy grail" of mountaineering.

The Dream Never Dies

AS A young man I knew that I should make the most of my life. But, predictably, when the responsibilities of being an adult started to take over, my childhood dreams began to fade.

By the time 2006 had rolled around, I had more responsibilities than could be covered in a day. Susan and I were working hard to develop our businesses, Amy was now 6 and we had a 3 year old son Colin. Twenty four hours were just not enough to get everything done. I was caught up in traffic on the highway of life, just trying to keep pace and stay safely between the white lines. In between all of this, I managed to keep climbing with several major summits under my belt.

I found that I had begun to accept the failure of Cho Oyu and to learn from it. The fact that I had successfully climbed several more summits showed that my resolve was still intact. But it seemed to me as if my dream to climb Everest had slipped back into the shadows. It was the big one. It would take extraordinary planning and effort. I don't mean to sound like Kilimanjaro, the Matterhorn or Denali were like walks in the park – but compared to Everest they were.

Everest was the big one, a life long goal, and I found myself stuck with no traction forward. I had always believed I would not let this happen to me, but there I was caught in the hamster wheel of life. Unfortunately it took a tragic event and a personal scare to get me back on track, to focus on the scope and opportunity of an Everest climb.

One day in 2005 I learned that my father had cancer. He had gone to the hospital emergency room one day complaining of back pain and was quickly diagnosed with a stomach tumor. He never left the hospital. After a few short months he was gone at the young age of 61. All of a sudden my world became a whole lot smaller and life seemed to be much more fragile. My father never got to retire, travel and do many of the things he wanted to do. Losing him taught me an important lesson: life is unpredictable and you never know how much time you have left. The old saying, "Live everyday like it is your last" began to resonate with me. I began to change my habits, but life was still moving way too fast. My children were growing and time was flying by.

Then came a second jolt.

Standing in the bathroom one day, Susan noticed a mole on the right side of my trunk that did not look right. She thought I had better get it checked out by a doctor. A biopsy confirmed that it was melanoma. It was serious, but we had caught it early. I underwent successful surgeries to remove the cancer and some lymph nodes from my armpit, and I am now cancer free.

All this made me look at life differently. I realized that there was never going to be the right time to climb Everest. If I wanted it, I just had to do it. The next challenge was to tell Susan that I wanted to attempt to climb the highest and one of the most deadly mountains in the world.

I agonized about when and how to tell her. Finally one day sitting at a park while our children played I broke the news. She handled it exceptionally well. In her mind it was never a question of if, but when. This is who I am and this is who she had married. I was greatly relieved that my family supported me. Now it was time to bring this dream to life.

Creating a Vision of Success

WHEN I finally made the decision in 2006 to give Everest a go, I had not climbed in the Himalayas since my humbling attempt at Cho Oyu several years earlier. I knew that logistical and task oriented preparations were only part of the equation. Equally important was ensuring the "human" component would be up to the challenge. On Everest, this meant my personal capacities, as well as those of the team of which I would be a part and the leadership in which I would share. I turned to the Deliberate Success Model (pg. 44) that I had created over the years and my previous insights to provide a guideline that I would use over the course of the preparation, the climb itself, and the post climb learning. I would work to create a clear vision of success, actions to get there, and ensure regular reflection to refocus us at every level.

The first step was to clarify my personal vision of what success would look like on this mountain. Then I could work with future teammates to create a common vision of our team and leadership. In terms of the goal, it seemed relatively straightforward. I saw myself standing on the summit of the highest mountain on earth. But it didn't end there. Above all, I saw myself coming home from Everest safely to my family and friends. In other words, preservation of life and limb would trump a "summit at all costs" mentality. Being clear about this to myself was a critical first step because it gave me a framework for future decision making when on the mountain and also when choosing my teammates.

Another part of my personal vision was how I saw myself performing on the mountain and fitting into the team. I envisioned a fit, capable and experienced mountaineer, who could persevere through the changes and challenges that this mountain would certainly throw at me. I also saw myself as a positive, contributing team member, committed to helping everyone achieve success. I knew from previous climbs on high mountains that one's physical fitness was only the "ticket to the show" and that it would be my mental and emotional abilities that would ultimately determine my success. When climbing these big mountains your body is working at the ends of its physical capabilities. Your mind and emotions are what hold it all together. If you lose the mental and emotional challenge the body will be soon to follow.

Regarding personal interactions, I saw myself being open and communicative. I saw myself sharing leadership of the team. Even though I might not be the formal leader, I would exert positive influence, take responsibility and initiative to do what needed to be done, and hold myself accountable for the results. I had seen how poor group dynamics could easily lead to the downfall of a team and the ultimate failure of an expedition.

With that vision of myself in mind, the next few steps were obvious. I needed a fitness regime (which I began immediately), a mountaineering tune up (I began planning for a practice climb on Ama Dablam in the Himalayas) and a team who would share my vision of success.

Team Work and Success

I BELIEVE that the chance of success in almost any large endeavor – and an Everest climb is certainly one of these – can be enhanced by good teamwork. However, as I learned on Cho Oyu, just putting a group of high performance individuals together does not guarantee that good teamwork will occur. If you want to create a high performance team, some deliberate planning and action is required.

One of the best places to start is in selecting the right team members. As Jim Collin's writes in *Good to Great*, "you need to get the right people on the bus and then get them into the right seats." For this task, the right people would have the mountaineering skills and experience to tackle the demanding conditions we would certainly face. But I would deliberately seek out and select people who also had the "soft skills" and commitment necessary to become a true high performing team. I would surround myself with people I could trust and who would trust me. They would be capable of communicating honestly and openly. They would be committed to confronting and resolving issues that arose when they arose. They would freely contribute their opinions, talents and energy to achieve a common vision of success. In short, they would be on my side, and I would be on theirs.

My first few exploratory emails got no interest from my friends. Then I remembered Angus. We had climbed Mount Logan and Mount McKinley (Denali) together. We had lost touch when he and his wife, Sarah, had moved out west. I found an old email address for Sarah and tested the waters by asking if she and Angus were interested in going to Nepal for a climb of Ama Dablam, a 6848 m peak known for its spectacular beauty. Sarah was not available, but she thought Angus would be interested. Angus was indeed interested and after some restructuring of current obligations he was ready to go. As we were planning, Angus asked me why I had chosen Ama Dablam and the truth came out. I told him I was planning to use it as a warm up climb for Everest. Now, that got his attention. But Everest is an entirely different beast from Ama Dablam in terms of resources, cost, time and risk, so he knew he needed to discuss this with Sarah. He cautiously slipped the idea into a conversation and, happily, Sarah thought it was a great idea. With support from home, Angus immediately called me up and asked to put down a deposit. There was no going back.

Angus was on board, but we needed a bigger team. As I researched Everest on the internet, I came across another climber who was just as passionate about it as I was, perhaps even more so. Alan had a website dedicated to mountaineering and, in particular, Everest. Alan had made two previous attempts on Everest and his site was a great source of information. I emailed him and requested a conversation to pick his brain about routes, oxygen and logistics. Over a period of time we spoke often about Everest. One day Alan suggested that he was ready to give Everest one more crack. He was in, and then we were three.

Alan provided contact with Ryan, a mountain guide from Colorado who owns a company called Mountain Professionals. Like Angus and I, Ryan had a long history with Outward Bound. After speaking with Ryan several times we decided that he was the best guy to put together our expedition and provide the leadership to get us to the top and home again. Even though we were experienced climbers, we still needed a skilled leader. A leader's job is to help the team achieve their goals by facilitating meetings, coaching, mentoring and taking care of the behind the scenes logistics so that the team can focus on what has to be done in order to be successful in the climb. Ryan became our fourth team member and our formal expedition leader.

The fifth and last person we added to the team was Al, who was a friend of a friend of someone who knew Ryan. Al had seen a presentation on Everest and

learning in THIN AIR

became hooked on the idea of climbing it one day. He set out to gain the
and experience necessary to put him in a position to go to Everest. He hea_ _ we
were going and contacted Ryan to ask if he could join the team. Al did not have
a lot of climbing experience, but he had proven to be strong and skilled in his
previous climbs. He also appeared to have the personal qualities that we were
looking for. Al was in and our Everest team was now complete.

Plan A

THE BEAUTY of a mountain is that the goal tends to be quite clear to
everyone on the team; the summit. However, there are invariably many options
as to how you will get there. This is true of the actual route selection and for
how the team will work together. We discussed and tested our ideas of good
teamwork and how leadership would be shared while we were assembling the
team and during the task of route selection. This would be a deliberate work in
progress throughout the entire project.

We agreed to climb Everest from the North side in Tibet. We chose this route
for several reasons: the Northeast Ridge is the original route attempted by the
early British explorers; it was the route that George Mallory and Andrew Irvine
were attempting when they disappeared into mountaineering folklore in 1924;
and the route appealed to our climbers' egos. The Northeast Ridge is known
as the climber's route as it presents slightly more technical conditions and a
harsher environment than the route through Nepal. The last factor was the
2008 Summer Olympics in Bejing, China.

The Chinese government had decided to add the summit of Everest to the route
for the International Olympic Torch Relay. Their concerns about potential
protests and interference from other climbers caused them to restrict the
issuing of 2008 climbing permits to just a few small and experienced teams.
This excited us because it was a rare opportunity to experience the Everest of
days gone by, without the congestion of hundreds of tourist climbers in big
expeditions, crowded into the few short weeks when the 200 mile per hour
winds of the jet stream won't rip you off the mountain.

We were fortunate to secure one of the few permits issued in 2008 to climb
Everest via Tibet. Everything appeared ready to go. Ryan set about making the
logistical arrangements while I trained hard, did the practice climbs of Ama
Dablam and Island Peak with Angus, and got all my gear together.

My Everest plan also included sharing the experience with colleagues, friends and family who could not be there with me. I set up a web page on myeverest.com. With the help of friend Paul, I arranged to bring along a satellite phone and handheld PDA (Personal Digital Assistant) so I could connect to the internet from Everest. I planned to make regular postings about life on Everest, particularly about our progress. The system was also set up to accept comments and notes from people who were reading the blog and to send these to me to read. (I recalled the loneliness and isolation I had felt on Cho Oyu years earlier.) I was very cognizant of the powerful positive effect that emotional support can play in stressful situations.

Enter the Dragon

I ESPECIALLY wanted to include my wife, Susan, in the climb. So, we arranged to head off to Nepal a few weeks before my expedition began. With grandparents looking after our children, Amy and Colin, we would fly to Kathmandu and spend several weeks together trekking into Everest Base Camp in Nepal. Then, I would fly into Lhasa, Tibet with the climbing team to begin my expedition while Susan returned home to hold down the fort.

At least, that was the plan. Upon arrival in Kathmandu I learned that, at the last moment, the Chinese government decided to cancel all permits to climb Everest from Tibet for 2008. I can only guess at the reasoning behind this devastating decision. However, it seemed to me that the increasingly disruptive protests that were following the Olympic Torch Relay along its winding journey through other parts of the world had ignited fear in the minds of Chinese officials that climbers might continue the practice on Everest. The best way to avoid negative publicity and potential interference would be to have no climbers. At any rate, the decision was made. There would only be one climbing team on the North Face of Everest in 2008 and that would be the Olympic Torch climbing team.

As Susan and I headed out on our trek, Ryan was in Kathmandu trying to salvage the trip. Not really knowing what would become of my expedition, all we could do was hope for the best.

After a great trek to Base Camp, Susan and I returned to Kathmandu to learn that Ryan had been able to secure a permit for our team to climb Everest via the Southwest Ridge in Nepal. There was a caveat to this however: just because

Amazing views on the trek to Base Camp

we were not climbing in Tibet did not mean that we had escaped the influence of the Chinese government and the Olympic Torch climb. Fearing possible interference from the teams on the south side of the mountain, China and Nepal came to an agreement. The Chinese and Nepali governments jointly drew up the rules and regulations by which we could climb and Nepal would send in the military to oversee the climbing teams (see next page for regulations).

Although we were not happy with the restrictions and conditions put on our permit, we were assured by our local logistics provider that this was all for show. The Chinese government would be appeased, and once we got to Base Camp all would be normal. We could not really do anything about it so our only choice was to carry on as if nothing were happening.

Plan B

BY FAR, the most popular route up Everest is via the Southwest Ridge from Nepal. It is more congested than our first choice, but as it was the only option available to us, we gratefully accepted the opportunity and switched gears.

Everest 2008 Permit Regulations

These Temporary Rules will only apply for the climbing period 1 April-10 May

Issuing of permit and the route for spring 2008 for Everest and Lhotse:

A. The Government of Nepal and the Ministry of Culture, Tourism and Civil Aviation will only issue permits for the South West Ridge Route on Mount Everest for the Spring of 2008. Similarly, for Lhotse, permits will only be granted for the normal route. No other routes will be granted by the ministry such as the West Ridge, Southwest Face and the South Pillar.

B. No Documentary filming permits will be issued for the spring of 2008 on Mount Everest and Lhotse.

Climbing Rules and Regulations:

A. All foreign and Nepali Climbers are permitted to climb from Base Camp to Camp 1, Camp 2 and Camp 3 until May 10th.

B. To Proceed to Camp 4 (South Col) and the Summit will only be allowed after May 10th onwards with the permission from the ministry of Culture Tourism and Civil Aviation. Until then Camp 4 and the Summit climbs will be restricted.

C. Any rope fixing above Camp 3 before May 10th is strictly restricted.

D. All foreign and Nepali climbers will only be allowed to climb from Base Camp to Camp 1 and Camp 2 (through the Khumbu Icefall) from 4 am onwards until 6 pm. This will not apply to any rescue efforts.

E. From Camp 2 to Camp 3 the permitted climbing time will be from 6 am to 6 pm only. This will not apply to rescue efforts.

F. No climbing will be permitted on the mountain after 6 pm. This will not apply to rescue efforts.

G. There will be a climbing liaison officer based at Camp 2 and Camp 3 who will monitor and enforce the temporary rules and regulations. Liaison officers will report to the government of Nepal after the expedition.

Communication:

A. Satellite phones, computers/laptops and mobile phones will be under the supervision of liaison officers. Satellite phones will be available for the use of emergency and rescue. Climbers will be allowed to communicate with their own respective satellite phone to their agents and their families at regular base, under the supervision of the

learning in THIN AIR

liaison officer till May 10th. Weather reports can also be obtained by satellite phone under the supervision of the liaison officer.

B. VHF communication sets will be permitted for use for the duration of the expedition at the frequency set by the Government of Nepal

Photography:

A. No personal video camera will be allowed to be used at Base Camp and above until May 10th. These items will also be under the supervision of the liaison officer.

B. All foreign nationals will not display any flags, banners or stickers that may harm the diplomatic relations between Nepal and its neighboring countries.

C. All Expedition handling agents in Nepal will sign a written agreement with the government of Nepal that they will take full responsibility for any behavior or activities aimed at discrediting Nepal's neighboring countries.

D. There will be a checkpoint established by the Government of Nepal at Gorakshep (5200 m). This checkpoint will be monitored and managed by 3 associations and institutions of Nepal:

    a. Sagarmatha Pollution Control Committee

    b. Sagarmatha National Park

    c. Nepal Army or Police force

E. The above expenses for the checkpoint at Gorakshep will be covered by the Sagarmatha Pollution Control Committee or the Government of Nepal from the Funds that they have raised from the Royalty from the Icefall and the peak Permit.

F. This will apply to all group visitors who wish to trek to Base Camp for a day visit or a night halt. Please note that all the trekking guides who are escorting the group must carry an identity card issued by their company. Failure to show the identity card will result in the Group not being permitted to travel to Base Camp.

Media and Press:

A. Press and Media will only be allowed to visit Base Camp with permission from the Government of Nepal. Liaison officers will have the right to inspect filming permits.

B. The Government of Nepal has the right to inspect all footage for censorship reasons.

Helicopter flights:

A. No helicopters flights will be allowed to land at Base Camp until May 10th except for mountain rescue. These flights will have to be authorized by the Himalayan Rescue Association.

This route involves a flight from Kathmandu to the small mountain village of Lukla, then a ten day trek to Everest Base Camp, retracing the route Susan and I had just walked a few days earlier. From there, the route to the summit threads through the dangerous Khumbu Icefall to Camp 1, continues through the Western Cwm to Camp 2 at the base of Lhotse and then angles sharply up to Camp 3, situated on a tiny ledge high up on the steep Lhotse face. The final camp, Camp 4, is situated on the South Col itself and lies on the doorstep to the death zone. From Camp 4, it is a sustained push from the Col to the summit and back, for camping above this point invites almost certain death. Of course, as in all major expeditions to 8000 m peaks, the trip from Base Camp to the summit typically unfolds over six to eight weeks and involves multiple trips up and down between camps to shuttle gear and facilitate acclimatization. In many ways, the actual methodology of our climb would be similar to that we had planned for on the Northeast route.

Meeting the Team

THOUGH WE had all spent many hours talking and planning together over the two years leading up to the expedition, we had planned to meet face to face

Scott, Al, Ryan, Angus, Alan - The Team

learning in THIN AIR

for the first time as a team in Kathmandu. We were fortunate to be able to do this at the Courtyard Hotel owned and operated by Michelle and Pujan. They were great hosts and provided an ideal and comfortable setting for our first introductions.

Angus I knew well. He was a good friend and climbing partner. Ryan, our leader, made a great first impression. Physically, he's tall, strong and good looking; almost a poster boy for the mountain guide. Most importantly, his behaviours and demeanour matched his appearance. He was very organized and seemed to have everything in control. Alan was very gracious and outgoing and Al seemed strong and determined.

My overall impression of our team was that we were people who were not only physically capable, but had the personal and interpersonal skills to form solid, open and trusting relationships. The raw material was here for us, now we had to mould ourselves deliberately into a high performance team.

Kathmandu to Base Camp

MY EVEREST story begins on April 1, 2008.

Journal Entry for April 1 (Day 1) – Enter the Khumbu

This morning at 4:30 am my Everest expedition officially began. Our Nepal agent, Kili Sherpa of High Altitude Dreams, brought us our climbing permit last night. It was good to have a real permit in hand and to see my name on it.

It was with mixed emotions and a heavy heart that I left Kathmandu. I am very excited to be starting this expedition of a lifetime. I have been dreaming of climbing Everest for over 20 years and planning this climb for over two years. Now that it is here it seems to have come so fast. Am I prepared, is this the right time to go, how will my family handle my time away, how will the businesses do without me? Questions, questions, questions. Many mixed emotions.

I spoke to Amy and Colin last night. That was a difficult conversation for me. I miss them so much that for most of the conversation I was fighting back tears. It was good, however, to speak to them and I plan to make one call a week back home. I also sent a note home with Susan for each of them that they can keep in their room to remind them of me.

Michelle and Pujan owners of the Courtyard Hotel in Kathmandu

Having Susan here was great, but it also made for an emotional departure for me and I know for her as well. She is on a flight home as I write this and will see our children soon.

Pujan and Michelle (the Courtyard Hotel owners) gave us a great send off this morning with a fresh flower lei, a silk kata, and a personal card each. They are great hosts and I would highly recommend their hotel if you are in Kathmandu. After our send off, we drove to the airport. Kathmandu is usually a noisy and bustling city with people, cars, motorbikes, rickshaws, dogs and cows everywhere, however, at 5:00 am the city was just starting to awake and it was quiet and calm.

This calm ended once we got to the airport as there were literally hundreds of trekkers and climbers ready to fly into the mountains. Huge piles of expedition bags were scattered around the departures area as local agents arranged for boarding passes. The departures area was so chaotic that without these local agents it would be difficult for a Westerner to get anywhere.

learning in THIN AIR

We boarded our Canadian built Twin Otter just after 6:00 am and taxied onto the runway. We were now on our way to Everest. Our flight attendant handed out candies to suck on and cotton batten to stuff in our ears for the 45 minute flight to Lukla. It is at Lukla that most trips into the Everest region begin. One can choose to walk in from Jiri, but this adds at least one additional week of walking so most elect to fly to Lukla and start from there.

The flight from Kathmandu to Lukla is truly one of a kind and all adventure seekers should experience it. The flight began as we departed the chaos of Kathmandu and flew into the countryside surrounding the city. The flat valley bottom gave way to rolling hills and farms. Soon the hills were soaring high into the sky and the Himalayan range could be seen off to the left. Towering giants of rock and ice dominated the sky and all on board tried to pick out and name the mountains that had captured their imagination and drawn them to this magical place. After 45 minutes we were almost there. Most landings begin with a slow and gentle descent to the runway, but not so in Lukla. This small village is perched atop a hill surrounded by mountains and valleys. It is not possible to see the landing strip until the plane is almost

Runway in Lukla

on top of it, necessitating a dramatic and steep dive down. The pilot nosed the plane down and gunned the engines. Passengers could see out the front window of the plane through the cockpit as the ground rose up at an alarming speed. Passengers looked at each other with a mix of excitement and fear in their eyes. After all, most planes land safely, especially since the runway was paved, but burned out hulls of crashed planes and helicopters that we saw off to the side of the runway attest to the danger of this landing space.

As the plane was about to strike the runway, the pilot pulled the nose up steeply as the runway was uphill. Once the wheels hit the ground the brakes were jammed on full and the engines roared into reverse. The plane squealed to a stop just before a looming 40 foot rock wall. I landed safely in Lukla one more time.

The plane taxied to a stop and the left engine was shut off to allow the passengers to disembark safely. As soon as we were off the plane the next passengers who were making the return trip to Kathmandu were getting on. Our bags were unceremoniously thrown from the cargo hold and the new bags were jammed in. As we walked from the tarmac the door was closed and the left engine was restarted. The plane was ready for take off with a new load of passengers and cargo less than 5 minutes after it landed. When the weather is good no time is wasted by the pilots who fly in and out of this airport.

We waited around for over an hour for the rest of our bags which were coming in on another flight. Eventually we got tired of waiting and decided to start our walk while our Sirdar (head Sherpa), Lama Babu, stayed behind to make sure our bags caught up with us.

We only had a short walk today to Phadking. I was experiencing some stomach issues so I was glad of the shorter walk. We are staying in the Sunshine Lodge that is quite plush as far as lodges go. I am sharing a double room with Angus. We have a Western style toilet in our room with a sink and a hot shower; quite luxurious.

We had a nice dinner and I am now sitting in bed as I write this. Tomorrow we will be on the trail by 8:00 am and plan to make it to Namche in about five hours.

Lukla to Base Camp

NOW THAT the trek had begun we had a ten day walk in front of us to get to Base Camp. We would hike for four to eight hours each day and stay in various Sherpa villages along the way. The accommodations were quite comfortable at each of the lodges we stayed at and the food was plentiful and excellent.

It was during this ten day walk that I knew we needed to form into a team as, once we got to Base Camp, it was game on. I know from my work with teams and from my previous experience with Cho Oyu that just because you put a group of experienced and skilled people together this does not guarantee they will become a high performance team.

You need to deliberately set out to build a team that will be effective, cohesive and strong. I spent the trekking time walking with different members of the team to get to know them better. I would ask them about themselves, their family, their jobs back home, their past experiences, their goals and dreams. I was, at the same time, sharing this information about myself. The objective here was to build relationships to form a solid foundation for our team. Relationship is the foundation upon which all high performance teams rest. Without this foundation of a supportive and trusting relationship the team will never be able to deal effectively with challenge and change.

Learning in Thin Air - The Stages of Team Development

There were many valuable lessons in the informal discussions and activities we had undertaken. We were going through the classic stages of team formation: Forming, Storming, Norming, and Performing.

Developed by Bruce Tuckman in 1965, this model describes the stages that a team will pass through. These stages are common to all teams whether they be a climbing team, a sports team, a business team or a community team. All teams will pass through these stages on their way to high performance. Some teams, however, will get stuck along the way. Smart leaders recognize the stage their team is in. They know what leadership style to use and what actions to take to move the team forward.

Team Development Stages

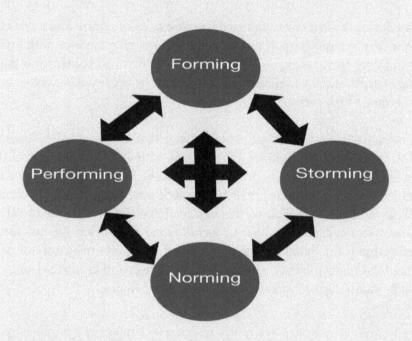

Forming

This is the foundation from which all else will be built. The two most critical factors are vision and relationship. As an individual, a team member, a team, a leader or an organization you need to determine your vision, your mission, your values, your goals, roles, norms and expectations. The expectations must be crystal clear. If this is all done well you will form a strong team built on open, supportive and trusting relationships.

Storming

Storming always happens. It is just the severity that is in question. Nothing ever goes exactly as planned and unexpected things always come your way. If you have done a good job in "forming," the storming phase is a

learning in THIN AIR

great place to clarify anything that was not clear already. If your team is strong, you can deal with stress, change and conflict in a positive fashion. This does not mean that storming will be fun, but it will not be the end of your team.

If, however, you do not have a solid foundation, this is where things get ugly. Trust dissolves, silos develop, communication breaks down and teams fall apart.

Norming
Norming is when you are good. You are not yet great, but you have the potential for greatness if you stay your course. This is where you continue to strengthen your team relationships and focus on skill enhancement and setting standards.

Performing
This is the ultimate goal. This is where life is good. You will not get here without first going through the previous stages. Once here, you need to maintain your focus or you could easily slip backwards. Celebrate your success, but maintain a vigilant focus on results and culture.

This is not a pretty, one way model. You can move back and forth at any given time. You can be high performance one day and then experience a dramatic change that thrusts you back to "storming." You could get a new team leader or a new directive and you are back to square one in "norming." The key is to be consciously aware at all times where you are. This model is your road map for development and just like a road map, you need to have two pieces of information in order for it to be valuable to you. You need to know where you are and where you want to go. Once you know this, you can take the appropriate roads or actions to get there.

Our Everest Team

Getting to Base Camp

The Start of a Long Journey

DURING THESE early days I was, at times, convinced that some of my team members might have thought me a little odd with how much I spoke about the importance of "the team." Yet, I had learned the hard way on Cho Oyu that the development of this foundation was critical. On Cho Oyu we appeared to be a good team until challenge and conflict arose. We had no hope of dealing with these difficulties as we could not even openly communicate or trust one another. This led to a full breakdown of the team and our failure to climb the mountain.

So, on Everest, I undertook a different approach.

After dinner each night we would often have a bit of social time sitting around the lounge or restaurant before bed. During this time I suggested topics of conversation around leadership, communication, change management and conflict resolution. I think at first my teammates thought I was a little obsessive-compulsive about my job back home, but as I began to explain the method behind my madness, they began to understand. I knew that we only had a brief period in which to build our team and that we did not have the luxury of letting our team evolve at a natural pace. If we wanted to be high performance by the time we reached Base Camp, we would need to accelerate our development.

We talked about leadership and what it meant to us. What characteristics we felt were good and bad for leaders to exhibit. What our role as team members was and what we expected of our leader and what he expected of us. We spoke about our communication styles and how we preferred to communicate. We spoke about how we would deal with change and personal conflict.

Our vision of a high performance team was one that was built on a relationship of respect, trust and support with a high level of open and honest communication. We would make sure everyone was in agreement with our plans and we would deal with conflict as soon as it arose. This was our Vision.

To bring this to life we decided we would have two meetings each day. In the morning we would meet to discuss our plan for the day as well as roles and responsibilities. We would then have a second meeting at the end of the day to check in on what we did well, what we did not do so well, how we felt, what we were thinking and what we wanted, if anything, to change. My hope was that by using this deliberate process, we would have a solid foundation from which to build on once we got to Base Camp. We also began to develop our team culture in a focused manner so that we would have the culture that we wanted, not just one that we got. These were our Actions.

We also decided to set aside one meeting a week in which we would discuss how we were doing as a team. We would share what we were thinking, what we were feeling, and any concerns we might have. This was a time for us to check in personally and to measure ourselves against our Vision. This was our Reflection time. (As you can see these are the exact steps in the Deliberate Success Model pg 44)

Our trek continued as day after day we hiked towards Everest Base Camp. The days were as spectacular as they were physically demanding.

Journal Entry for April 2 (Day 2) – Lukla to Namche 3500 m

Today we hiked to Namche and I felt great. No problem on the Namche hill. We are back at the SherpaLand Hotel and everyone is quite happy with the accommodations. It was nice to walk into town. I ran into Ron and Karen who Susan and I met in Deboche a couple weeks ago. They have had a great trek and are headed to Lukla tomorrow to fly out. I have also met up with KC who is the manager of the hotel, Tsedam who runs a gear shop and Pemba who also runs a shop where we bought some Everest Hardware clothing. It makes Namche seem very friendly when I see all these people I know. I almost feel like a local.

We will spend two nights in Namche for acclimatization and then head to Deboche.

The village of Namche Bazaar

The trail today was very busy with trekkers. There is a very visible difference between the number of people here now compared to when Susan and I came in two weeks ago. As we entered the park today I looked at the statistics on the wall. In March of this year there were 3,688 people who came into the park compared to 3,000 in March of 2007. This is the largest March in the last ten years. It appears that this will be a big year for trekkers in the Khumbu valley.

Journal Entry for April 4 (Day 4) - Deboche 3800 m; Ama Dablam Garden Lodge

Thursday was spent in Namche. I walked around town, talked to various people, checked email, ate, and went to sleep.

Today we departed Namche and hiked to Deboche. The day was mostly cloudy so there were no views of any of the big mountains. The walk out of Namche starts quite steeply and then levels off for a long way followed by a big drop to the river, where we had lunch, and then a 75 minute uphill trek to Tengboche. There is a great bakery in Tengboche that serves everything from chocolate cake to apple strudel. From there the walk is only 10 minutes to where we are now. The total walking time today was about four hours.

Upon arrival in Deboche it started to snow with quite a bit accumulating on the ground. I am now in the dining area drinking hot chocolate. It is very hot in here with the wood stove cooking away. Tomorrow we will go to Dingboche for two days. I am feeling good and moving well.

Journal Entry for April 5 (Day 5) - Dingboche 4300 m; monastery nun; Lama blessing; fears of restrictions; Snow Lion Lodge

Today we were up at 7:00 am and on the trail by 8:15 am. I had a cheese omelette and delicious apple fritters for breakfast. As we stepped outside the lodge we were greeted to a winter wonderland as a light dusting of snow covered all the trees and the trail.

Right past our lodge was a monastery for nuns. In this monastery there is a nun who has been walled into her room for 48 years where she meditates and prays. A few of our team members went to her for a blessing. They passed 500 rs (about $9.00) through a hole in the wall and she gave them three small red

Lama Geshe

learning in THIN AIR

pills. We have no idea what they are or what to do with them. They said she looked quite frail and old. I know I could not match her level of dedication.

We walked for about one hour to Pangboche. In Pangboche we went to see Lama Geshe who blesses about 90% of all Everest climbers. We went to his home and sat in the kitchen as he finished blessing some climbers who were there before us. We were given a kata (silk scarf) and told to wrap 100 rs (about $1.75) in it and to hand it to the Lama. We filed into a large room and went one by one to be blessed. As we approached this old man in a monk's habit and a down jacket we bowed our head to have an orange string placed around our neck. This string would be tied and should stay on our necks for the duration of the expedition. We then gave our katas to his assistant, she took the money and placed the scarf around our necks. We all then sat as the Lama prayed for our safe passage on the mountain and back home. He chanted, threw rice, and rang a bell. We were then given a postcard and some rice and told to take them to the summit with us. We were told the card and rice would protect us from bad things such as crevasses and avalanches. It was all quite interesting and we all agreed that we would take any help we could get.

From Pangboche we walked for 45 minutes, had lunch and walked a further 90 minutes to Dingboche. Our lodge is pretty nice with a good selection on the menu. I may try the cheese brugger (exact spelling from the menu). The weather is cold and windy with low visibility due to low lying clouds.

I am a little concerned about the restrictions we will have imposed upon us at the mountain. I can't really say much right here as we are not sure what they will be and I am pretty sure our transmissions are being monitored. There have been rumours that anyone caught doing anything they (China & Nepal) do not like will be deported from the country. We may have very limited or no communication with the outside world once we reach Base Camp. It is all pretty crazy and does not seem real. I'll hope for the best.

Journal Entry for April 6 (Day 6) - Dingboche 4300 m; impressions of crowd; Snow Lion Lodge

Today we once again woke to snow. It has not stopped all day. It is quite cold with low visibility due to the low clouds. We will stay in Dingboche for the day as today is a rest day. After lunch we will walk up to the internet café and I will send this message if it is operational.

There is really not much new today so I will write briefly about the people we have seen along the way.

Everest expeditions are made up of a surprisingly diverse group of people. Gone are the days of the hard core climber who has climbed for 30 years before attempting Everest. Ages range from 20-65 with all walks of life and occupations represented. We have come across two mother-daughter teams, young people, older people, and people of all shapes and sizes. They all aspire to stand atop the world's highest peak.

As a veteran climber, it is difficult not to judge some of these teams. But I have learned a lot from running a marathon this past year. Standing at the starting line you see all ages, shapes and sizes. Some people who I initially think have no chance of finishing, pass me along the way to the finish line. I will likely be pleasantly surprised as some of these folks pass me on the way to the top. Perhaps a bit jealous as well.

Unfortunately, we are still unable to get the satellite phone/PDA dispatch system to work. If this continues, I will only be able to send voice dispatches from today on and will be unable to read all your messages. I will, however, look forward to reading them at the first chance I get.

Journal Entry for April 7 (Day 7) - 5000 m walk to Lobuche; stomach issues; Eco Lodge; rumours of ban

Today we walked from Dingboche to Lobuche in just under four hours. The trail out of Dingboche was fairly steep to start and then up and down to Duglha. Just outside Duglha the trail went up steeply for just over an hour. At the top of the ridge were many stone memorials for climbers who have died on Everest. From this point it was pretty flat to Lobuche.

Lobuche is not a pretty place. It is a way point on the way to Base Camp. It is quite dirty and not somewhere one would want to spend much time. The lodge we are in however, is quite nice. The rooms are big and clean and there is a very nice dining room. I'm not sure of the room charges, but the food is quite expensive. Yak steak and Chicken Kiev is $10 which is a lot by lodge standards.

My walk was a little tough today as I am once again dealing with stomach issues. It seems my digestive system is not designed to handle food and drink in third world countries. Even the Dukoral is not preventing my stomach issues (Dukoral is a drug I took prior to departing for Nepal that is intended to eliminate or reduce travelers' diarrhea). Perhaps, however, it would be a lot worse without the Dukoral.

Tomorrow we will have a two hour walk to Gorak Shep and we will find out what will happen to our communication equipment. There are many rumours from a complete ban and confiscation, to no problem for personal use. We'll see.

Journal Entry for April 8 (Day 8) - Gorak Shep 5200 m; Pyramid Research Station; Yeti Resort

This morning we left Lobuche at 9:00 am. The walk was pretty easy with only two short steep sections. Most of the trail was relatively flat sand or moss. It took us less than two hours.

Along the way we stopped at the Pyramid Research Station. This is a high altitude research station run by Italy. It is a three story glass pyramid with a lodge for eating and sleeping connected to one side. I poked my head in to take a look. Their accommodations seemed a step above the standard trekking lodge. The room was quite warm with comfortable furniture and

Pyramid Research Station

a beer tap on the wall with two selections of draught. The researchers were relaxing watching WWE wrestling on the TV.

As I stepped into the Pyramid to see what was going on, I was met by an Australian researcher. He was at the Research Station studying the effect of various drugs on sleep patterns at altitude. He said he had applied to do this research two years ago and was now here for three weeks. The Italian government covers all living expenses once at the station. There were also researchers examining geology, climatology, and global warming.

After visiting the Pyramid we continued on to Gorak Shep. We are now at the Yeti Resort which is nice but far from a resort. The rest of the team has gone to climb Kala Pathar. I have elected to stay behind as I am still feeling the effects of my stomach bug. I'm getting better but I have a ways to go, plus Susan and I did this climb two weeks ago. If I'm not better by tomorrow morning I will get serious and start a course of antibiotics. Update: after a mad dash to the bathroom I have decided to start a round of Cipro (antibiotic used to treat stomach issues). I have found this drug to be quite effective in the past and hope for similar results this time.

Mount Everest Base Camp

learning in THIN AIR

We have not heard much about communication restrictions which I think is good news. If expeditions were having their communication equipment confiscated I think word would have filtered down the trail. There is no police post here at Gorak Shep and we have not heard of one at Base Camp either. So perhaps we will be allowed to keep our gear. Now I only need to hope that it will work.

If this dispatch goes out it will be a small miracle. I have tried several times every day with no luck. I have not even been able to make a voice call. I'm not sure if the problem is with my system or with the satellite system. Regardless, it has been immensely frustrating. It would be easier to have no system at all than to have one that will not work.

Tomorrow we head to Base Camp. The weather has improved greatly. Today is warm in the sun with a clear blue sky.

Life at Base Camp

WE ARE now at Everest Base Camp, one of the most famous places on earth. We found our camp at the far end of the glacier and started to move in. Acclimatization is critical to success so for the first several days all we did was eat and sleep and allow our bodies to adjust to the extreme altitude.

Journal Entry for April 9 (Day 9) - Everest Base Camp 5350 m
I am now at Everest Base Camp. Our walk this morning took almost two hours over mixed terrain. Some of it was flat and sandy, some of it was on gravel on top of the glacial moraine, and some of it was through huge boulder fields.

I am feeling much better today. I had a difficult night last night but today the Cipro seems to be doing its thing.

It is amazing the difference in Base Camp from when Susan and I were here almost two weeks ago. When we trekked in there were only a few Sherpas here starting to hack tent platforms out of the ice and rock. It looked like a pretty cold and bleak place to spend two months. Today as we walked in it was amazing to see the transformation. Tents are everywhere and there are hundreds of people. It looks like a small city. Our camp is in the suburbs. Each of us has our own North Face VE25 tent with a foam pad floor, a thick sleeping pad and even a pillow. In our camp we have two storage tents that are used mostly for food and equipment, a beautiful dining tent, a stone walled kitchen tent, a shower with on demand hot water, and a toilet tent.

When we first arrived we had lunch in the dining tent. This tent is actually two tents put together end to end. It is about 10 feet wide by 24 feet long. It has an insulated, carpeted floor, is made of a double wall construction for insulation, has compact fluorescent lighting, a propane heater, a long table full of snacks, drinks, and condiments, and plastic patio chairs. It is quite plush.

Our cook is Babaron and our server/assistant cook is Sam (none of us Westerners can pronounce his real name so he just goes by Sam). For lunch we had grilled cheese sandwiches, fried Spam, potato salad, cucumber, carrot and turnip salad and bananas for dessert. I think we will eat well on this trip.

Base Camp Dining and Kitchen Tents

learning in THIN AIR

We also met Lhakpa who will be our Camp 2 cook. We will spend a lot of time at Camp 2 and will use it as an Advanced Base Camp. Whenever we are there, Lhakpa will also be there to make sure we eat well.

We are sharing our camp with a few other people as well. We have three other climbers from High Altitude Dreams and three researchers from Harvard and Brown University. The climbers are Sylvie from Quebec, Mustafa from Jordan (he is a personal friend of the King of Jordan and has been knighted by the King), and the third climber is Ron from North Carolina.

The two Brown researchers are working on a project that began in 1993. They are examining the effects of altitude on specific parts of the brain linked to speech, memory and cognition. They are hoping to use this research to help them better understand and treat Parkinson's disease. I may join their study. The Harvard researcher is here to help the Brown team, but he is also doing a study for NASA on group dynamics based on his work with astronauts. It will be great to talk with him since we both work in a similar field.

Right now I am sitting in my tent relaxing. I have unpacked most of my stuff and arranged my tent, but one bag is yet to arrive. This bag has mostly climbing gear so I don't really need it right now. I am sitting here in my tent with no shirt, socks or shorts and I am way too hot. The radiation from the sun is extreme, but when the sun goes behind a cloud the temperature drops dramatically. I tried to turn on my iPod but due to the extreme altitude it crashed. I will not be able to use it for the remainder of the expedition (I was almost at the end of a great audio book and will now need to wait two months to hear the end).

I have a quick story to tell to end this lengthy dispatch. All of the lodges we have stayed in have a wood/dung fire that is lit every night. This small and inefficient fire is all the heat there is in the common room. Every night the Sherpas stream in to get out of the cold. The funny thing is that every Sherpa who comes in out of the cold leaves the door wide open so all the heat escapes. When one of the climbers or trekkers gets up to close the door they all watch with interest. Then the next Sherpa comes in and leaves the door open once again. This must be a cultural norm as it has happened at every single lodge we have been in. It seems that I do more walking to close the door every night than I do on our trek during the day.

*Our Puja altar with climbing gear and
plenty of refreshments to be blessed*

Puja

THE SHERPA people are devout Buddhists and follow several practices very closely when climbing. As I mentioned earlier the most important of all is the Puja. No Sherpa will set foot on the mountain before the Puja has been performed. The Puja ceremony is conducted to ask the spirits of the mountain to forgive us for trespassing on the sacred mountain and to ask for kindness in weather and mountain conditions. But the Puja is so much more than a mountain ritual.

Before a Puja is performed a Chorten (small rock altar) is built. From the centre of the Chorten rises a tall pole that four strings of prayer flags are attached to. A small mat or carpet is laid on the ground in front of the altar upon which the monk will sit during the ceremony. Branches of juniper are stacked to the side for burning and a small platter with offerings is placed on the other side. The offerings often include five types of grain, butter, and chang (a homemade rice alcohol), but climbers also add ice axes, crampons, harnesses, boots and even chocolate bars and cans of beer to the offerings. The juniper is lit and from this point on the sprigs will be burnt to release the aromatic fragrance whenever

learning in THIN AIR

climbers are on the mountain. As the prayer flags flap in the wind they will carry their prayers to all the corners of the earth. These are the physical basics of the Puja, but the meaning goes much further.

Basically the Puja is an act of giving on the road towards fulfillment, knowledge, enlightenment, and peace. It also acts to cleanse sins accumulated since the last Puja and offers a chance for rebirth to a better life. The ultimate goal for the most devout is to achieve the ability to enter the Buddhist paradise and escape the repeating cycle of rebirth and suffering.

Journal Entry for April 10 (Day 10) - Base Camp Puja
We had our Puja this morning. We were told last night that there was not another auspicious day until Monday and that 7:00 am was the time to start.

We rose at 6:30 am and made our way to the Chorten that the Sherpa had constructed. The sun had not yet hit our camp and it was quite cold. We have the highest camp at Base Camp giving us a beautiful unrestricted view of the Icefall. As the Lama made his preparations we all took seats on foam pads. We had two Lamas, one with a bright orange Winchester hunting cap and ear muffs and the other with a North Face down jacket on. There were also several assistants running about and a group of Sherpa making final preparations for the flag pole.

The Puja ceremony happens on all Himalayan expeditions as the Sherpa will not set foot on the mountain until the Puja has been completed. Each expedition will hold their own. The Puja essentially asks for safe passage on the mountain and apologizes for the damage we will cause to the Mother Goddess of the Earth with our ice axes and crampons.

There was no formal announcement that the Puja had begun, but the Lamas started chanting and the Sherpa got quiet. For about two hours the Lamas chanted while they faced the altar. We were served tea as we watched. Eventually the sun hit us and we warmed quickly. Dry rice was passed around and as the chanting intensified we threw rice into the air. Ryan, our team leader, seemed to have a disproportionate amount of rice aimed at him. Snacks, frozen pop and beer were passed around. We also had a chance to try a local home brew called Chang. It is made of fermented rice with lots of other ingredients thrown in. I think it must be an acquired taste. A bottle of rum was also passed around and everyone took a cap full. Barley flour was passed out and we all took a handful. We stood and the chanting increased once again. Then we all threw our flour into the air, everyone was white as a result. More flour came around and was rubbed on faces with a statement of 'good luck.' This quickly degenerated into an all out flour fight as flour was thrust into faces of unsuspecting victims. The Puja ended with the Sherpa arm in arm, singing and doing a kind of line dance. Slowly people faded away back to their tents to warm up and rest. All this by 10:00 am.

For the remainder of the day I will rest and if we can get the shower unfrozen I may even have a shower. My first in ten days. I am looking forward to it.

I just got word that the shower is broken. I guess it will be a baby wipe bath for now.

I am feeling better as my stomach bug seems to have passed and I feel I am acclimatized to this altitude. I slept very well last night, but I did get a bit cold in the early morning.

Re-enter the Dragon

INITIALLY ALL seemed normal at Base Camp. Apparently the rumours we had heard about the military being at the Camp were just that, rumours. We did not see any military presence at all. I thought about all the regulations and restrictions that had been put into our permits and it seemed that these too were just put in for show.

Then one day I was out for a walk around Camp and I ran into another climber who was quite agitated. He told me that the military had just arrived and they were starting camp to camp and tent to tent searches. I was told they were confiscating satellite phones and video cameras. They were also looking for Tibetan flags and any 'Free Tibet' paraphernalia. He said to me, "hide your phones now or they're gone." I ran back to my camp, but I was too late. The military was there. They spoke with our head Sherpa and our expedition leader Ryan and were just about to depart. I was told that we had been given one day to comply with the orders or we would be searched. Any person caught with a banned item would be arrested and deported from the country and their team would also be sent home. I now realized that the government really did mean business.

We called a team meeting to discuss our options. In the end we decided to comply with the military rules, as it appeared that we really had no choice. Although we felt the rules were unjust and uncalled for we did not think they were worth risking our whole expedition over.

With some grumbling we brought our satellite phones to the next meeting and sealed them into a barrel that would be taken to the military camp.

Our 'happy' barrel which held our phones

Learning in Thin Air - Communication

It really didn't take us long as a team to come to the conclusion that we should comply with what the military wanted. That's because we had, by this point, established very effective team communications.

As quoted from Dictionary.com 'communication' is defined as "the exchange of thoughts, messages, or information, by speech, signals, writing, or behavior."

For us, as an expedition team, communication was critical to our functioning. Being on a climbing expedition for two months with a team is unlike any other team scenario. We were with each other for pretty much 24 hours a day. We worked, ate and slept together, frequently side by side. Petty differences and annoying habits can be magnified in such close quarters, especially when you add in sleep deprivation, food stress, and physical weariness. The result can lead to people isolating themselves from the team (like silos in an organization) or to personal conflict. In order to keep us working smoothly together in a dangerous and constantly changing world, communication was critical. Good communication was part of our common vision of who we would be as a team and, to achieve it, we employed a simple model that I drew from my training programs. This model breaks communication into four essential components: sending, receiving, understanding and follow through.

Four Stage Communication Model

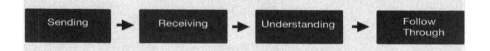

Sending: When sending a message, the sender must attend to both the content and the method. In terms of content we needed absolute transparency, honesty and clarity about how we were each doing health wise, about potential dangers around us and about information coming in. Nothing else would do. In terms of methods, we had few choices on the mountain: face to face or through walkie-talkie. However, we could still base our communication methods to some extent on our partner's preferences for receiving information through visual or auditory channels. Of course, in office settings the choices vary widely and we must be careful not to simply choose the option that is most convenient or comfortable for us.

Receiving: For communication to occur, a message must be received. On the mountain it was usually easy to verify this stage, at least among our own team members. But we did, during planning, experience those same challenges of messages being lost in cyberspace or accidentally deleted from voice mail. Getting and giving confirmation of the message is an important precaution in any context.

Understanding: Once we know the message has been received, we must ensure it has been clearly understood and not misinterpreted. This can be challenging in any situation. On the mountain we often had to make important decisions based on our understanding of weather conditions, climbing hazards, the physical condition of our teammates and many other factors. Sometimes these messages were garbled through walkie-talkies, swept away by the wind or muffled by oxygen masks. This called into play our skills in active listening, questioning, and paraphrasing. We would always summarize our understanding and ensuing actions to be sure everyone was on the same page and knew what to expect next.

Follow through: This is not micromanaging, but letting people know you remember and checking to see if an agreed upon action has been completed. This must be done carefully so as not to imply lack of trust, but rather accountability and importance. This step became increasingly important the higher we climbed on Everest because our brains simply could not function well on their ration of oxygen.

As a team we spoke about our vision of great communication. We practiced all four stages and when it was clear and everyone was agreement we committed to the vision. In a business environment this may include the signing of a written document that expresses your communication vision, but for us it was a verbal commitment.

Once we had committed to this communication vision we needed to live it on a daily basis. The vision became our measuring stick and if we were not living it, we needed to give each other permission to coach one another.

Upper Everest

It's All Up Hill From Here

PLACING OUR satellite phone under lock and key was annoying, but we did not feel that it was too great a hardship. Up until recent history satellite phones did not even exist, and making a phone call home was not even an option. We would hand in our phones and get on with the climb.

We were told that we would be allowed by the military to make a call home provided that we did it in the presence of a military officer and if we said anything that could "harm the bilateral relationship between Nepal and China" that our phone call would be terminated and we would be removed from Base Camp. I asked about making internet dispatches and was told I could do this provided that my writing was read and censored by the military if necessary. I was told that there was government teams monitoring web sites and if any unauthorized information appeared on a web site, the offending person would be ejected from the mountain and banned from the country.

We tried to put this behind us and started our climb. The only problem was that the route up the Icefall to Camp 1 was not ready and seemed to be taking longer than usual to establish.

The Icefall

THE ICEFALL is the first section of the mountain that needs to be climbed in order to ascend the mountain via the Southwest Ridge. This notorious section of the climb is easily one of the most dangerous sections on the route and by the spring of 2012 it had claimed over 50 lives.

What makes this section of the climb so dangerous is that you need to negotiate your way up a moving river of broken ice blocks. As the glacier descends off Everest, it is squeezed between Everest and Nuptse then drops over a steep cliff. As the glacier moves over this steep section it begins to break up into pieces. Imagine a river of water flowing down a gentle grade and then dropping over a steep waterfall. As the water moves over the edge of the fall it breaks up into rapids. It is the same on Everest, but the water is frozen so the rapids materialize as large broken ice blocks. These blocks can range in size from that of a small car to a small apartment building.

What makes this area so dangerous is that the glacier is flowing at a rate of three feet per day downhill. As the glacier is pulled down hill by the force of gravity, the big blocks of ice roll and slide. If a climber is in the wrong place at the wrong time as one of these blocks decides to roll they are crushed to death.

If this is not enough, the Icefall is flanked by huge and massively steep rock faces on both sides. These faces collect snow and ice that frequently avalanche into the Icefall often right across the climbers' route. Being caught in the Icefall during an avalanche a climber most likely will die as there is no hope of outrunning it.

Looking down into one of the crevasses in the Icefall

learning in THIN AIR

One of the keys to safety in the Icefall is speed. The challenge is that moving across such uneven and broken ground at altitude is anything but fast. The solution is to install aluminum ladders over the cracks and crevasses and up the steep ice faces to help speed the passage. Recently this task has been taken over by a group of entrepreneurial Sherpas, a brave and hard working group affectionately named the "Icefall Doctors." This group of Sherpas, who are paid by the government of Nepal via our permit fees, establish and maintain the route from Base Camp to Camp 2 every season.

In 2008 there were over 40 ladder crossings that needed to be negotiated in order to get to Camp 2. As the glacier is constantly moving, the Icefall Doctors enter the Icefall every morning to fix any damage that has been caused through the night and adjust the route accordingly. This allows the climbers to make it through this dangerous section much faster thus reducing the chance of being caught in a collapse or an avalanche. Since the Icefall Doctors have taken over the establishment and maintenance of this route the death rate has dropped drastically.

To further increase the safety margin while climbing through the Icefall, climbers leave in the early hours of the morning, setting out anywhere between 2:00 am and 5:00 am, climbing by headlamp. The theory behind this is to move through the Icefall while everything is still frozen from the cold night air. If the ice is frozen in place it is less likely to move or avalanche.

An additional bonus of the early morning starts is to avoid the hottest part of the day. You may think that cold is the biggest challenge on Everest, but it is actually heat. At these extreme altitudes there is little atmosphere to filter the sun's rays thus making the sun much stronger than it is at sea level. Exposed skin will burn in minutes requiring climbers to keep their skin covered at all times.

This section of the climb at the top of the Icefall that leads to Camp 2 is called the Western Cwm. Cwm is a Welsh word meaning valley, which was exactly what we were in. The valley is surrounded by the steep walls of Everest, Lhotse and Nuptse. The extreme heat along with very little wind turns the area into a giant reflector oven. The heat is so oppressive that movement slows to a crawl and dehydration becomes a huge concern. The early morning starts through the Icefall helps to alleviate this challenge, as any climber caught in the valley at mid day would be baked alive.

We did not need to worry about the danger of the Icefall immediately because the route to Camp 1 was not ready. When we spoke with the Icefall Doctors we were told that the route was very difficult this year and therefore taking longer than usual to establish. This was the official story anyway. The unofficial story was that the Icefall Doctors had been told by the military to slow down their work. The objective here was to slow climbers down in their acclimatization process and the establishment of camps. The result would be a lower chance of one of us climbing beyond the control of the military and making a break to the north side of the mountain to interfere with the Olympic torch climb.

This increased the stress level around Camp because everyone knew what was really going on. People began to challenge the military and small skirmishes broke out daily. The stress level also started to cause challenges between and within teams. There was a huge amount of pent up energy and desire at Camp as we were being restricted from doing what we had come for.

As a team we stuck to our vision of keeping a high level of communication and we talked about the situation and our feelings around it. We determined that this was beyond our control and that we needed to focus on keeping our team in a good place and hope the situation on the mountain worked itself out soon.

Ladder crossing in the Icefall

learning in THIN AIR

We decided that for us it was now time to start to climb and to begin our advanced acclimatization. We made a plan to make our first trip into the Icefall. The plan was to go as far as the route of ladders was established. We would not need to start quite as early for this climb and would plan to be back in Camp before lunch.

Journal Entry for April 12 (Day 12) - Icefall

Today was our first day in the famous Icefall. We had breakfast at 8:00 am and headed out at 9:00 am. We had to think carefully about what to wear and what to take. We had to bring all our technical climbing gear and be prepared for a variety of weather. It started out cloudy which was great as the UV exposure can be extreme in the Icefall. I wore light climbing pants with no long underwear underneath, a light coloured base layer top, a windstopper vest, a buff around my neck, a sun hat, and my sunglasses. I also applied lots of sun protection.

The walk to the start of the trail is about five minutes from our campsite. By the time we got there I was already over heated. Taking off my vest, I applied more sunscreen, pulled my buff up to protect my face and drank a lot of water. I already had my harness on so I put on my crampons and took my ice axe off my pack.

The start of the Icefall trail winds up and down and back and forth. After about 15 minutes we reached the roped up section where we clipped onto the fixed line for protection from a potential crevasse fall. In steep sections and when crossing the longer ladders we also attached a jumar.

Jumar is a cramming device that will slide one way on the rope but will lock in place in the event of a fall.

For the most part the Icefall is a series of short steep sections followed by flatter sections and slight inclines, up and down. I have never been in the Icefall before, but I am told that there are fewer ladders this year compared to previous years and that the route is safer. That sounds good to me.

We had done some ladder practice yesterday so when we got to the first ladder it was not too bad. The first couple of ladders were only one section of 12 foot ladder over relatively shallow crevasses. After about 90 minutes we came to our first double ladder over a crevasse so deep I could not see the bottom.

When you cross a ladder you clip your carabineer to a rope on one side and your jumar to a rope on the other side. You pull back on the ropes to give yourself support and take the first tentative step. I found a big mental difference between the single and double ladders.

There are two ways to walk across the ladders. The first is to have your front crampon points on one ladder rung and your back crampon points on the rung behind. Sometimes I walked one rung at a time and sometimes I walked on alternate rungs depending upon how scared I was. The other way to walk across the ladder is to step with your crampon straddling the rung. This way is less stable, but much faster.

We continued up the Icefall for about 2 1/2 hours with 7-8 ladder crossings. We topped out around 5600 m which is a 300 m altitude gain from Base Camp. This is just below a section that is called 'popcorn' because the jumble of ice blocks resemble popcorn.

Multiple ladders are used to cross wider crevasses

learning in THIN AIR

I alternated between having a nice walk and gasping for breath. I found that at the top of a steep section I was breathing really hard from the exertion and at the end of a ladder I was also breathing quite hard. I did not find the ladders too scary, but I did find that I was holding my breath as I crossed.

For the most part I was sweltering hot which sapped a lot of my energy. The next time we go up we will go all the way to Camp 1 but we will start earlier to beat the heat.

I am happy with my performance so far, but did find today a little harder than I would have hoped. I had a great sleep last night (taking 125 mg of Diamox just before bed really helps), and am not feeling sick at all. I have a slight cough (the famous Khumbu cough) but it is not too bad and calms down fast once I am at rest.

First Trip to Camp 1
Crazy Times on the Mountain

WE SPENT the next few days resting at Base Camp as our next trip onto the mountain we would climb to Camp 1 and stay overnight. This would be my first big test and I was anxious about how I would do.

By this time the military was firmly in control of Base Camp. They had our satellite phones and all communication from the mountain was now being monitored and censored if they felt it necessary. We tried to continue our climb as normal, but the atmosphere was strained and stress filled.

Journal Entries for April 18 to April 20 (Days 18-20) - Base Camp to Camp 1 overnight; the action suit; traffic jam; inexperienced climbers; popcorn; Western Cwm; Camp 1 welcome; first night at Camp 1; descent; pack search

This message was read and approved by the Nepal military.

On Friday we made our first trip to Camp 1. The night before an early morning climb, I sleep in my "action suit." This is all the clothing that I would wear for the climb the next day. I was sleeping in, and would climb in, my expedition long underwear, my climbing pants, my grey base layer top and my windstopper vest. In the pockets of my vest and pants I had sunscreen, candies and toilet paper. The idea is to sleep in what you will wear for a quick departure in the morning. It also saves getting dressed in the cold dark of early morning. I would also take with me my sleeping pads, my high altitude gloves, my balaclava, my Gore-Tex jacket, my warm hat, my sun hat, my buff, my cup and spoon and all my climbing gear. Much of this would be left at Camp 1 ready to be moved higher up the mountain.

We had breakfast at 5:15 am and were on the trail by 6:15 am. There were already many people on the trail ahead of us. This was the first day that the Icefall had been fully opened to Camp 1 and many people were anxious to get up high for acclimatization and to escape the boredom of Base Camp.

We reached our previous high point 30 minutes faster than last time, but this is where the speedy ascent ended. We were met by a barrage of Sherpa descending the route. At some of the technical sections we would wait 15-20 minutes for our turn. We also ran into exceptionally slow climbers. Some of these climbers appeared to have little to no climbing experience. One guide was clipping and unclipping every rope for his client. The client would just stand there with his hands out of the way and the guide would do all the work. When they got to technical sections it was almost unbearable to watch as the guide explained what the jumar was, hooked it onto the rope for the client and then showed him how to use it. The client then moved upwards at a snail's pace. They did let us pass eventually, only to get stuck behind another slow climber who appeared to have no system at all. Every time he got to a vertical section, he had to search his harness for the gear he needed, decide how to use it and then move forward. As a climber, you develop a system. There is a place for everything on your harness and you know exactly where to find it and where to put it back. This makes all transitions much faster.

We did eventually pass this group as well, but it is unbelievable the lack of skill, experience and fitness on this mountain.

The route itself was spectacular. The scenery staggeringly beautiful, and the climbing unlike anything else I had done before. The ladder crossings were exhilarating, the multi-ladder ascents were literally breathtaking and the brilliant turquoise blue ice we saw within the 'popcorn' section was amazing.

Vertical ladder assent

I wandered in and around huge blocks of ice and stepped over bottomless crevasses. It is a wonder that the Sherpa can find a route through this maze. It does appear, however, that the route does not change too much from year to year as we could see old ropes and anchors not too far off the trail we were on.

Above the 'popcorn' are a series of huge ladder assents (4-5 ladders tied end to end) and several large flat areas. After a final huge vertical ladder climb, we emerged into the Western Cwm, the massive valley that leads to Camp 1, Camp 2 and the Lhotse Face.

It was quite hot in the Cwm, but overall the weather for the day had treated us quite well. I was rarely too hot or too cold. We walked for another 20 minutes over slightly rising ground until we spotted the tents of Camp 1. We stopped at the first set of tents hoping they were ours, but they were not. We had to drop into a big valley and climb out the other side to get to our

Relaxing at Camp 1

tents. Overall, the trip to Camp 1 took seven hours. Without the slowdowns we encountered I think our time could have been closer to five hours.

Our camp was made of four North Face tents lashed to the snow and ice with ropes. When we arrived, the two Lamas (Babu and Thame) were there to greet us with hot juice. We drank, ate some food and moved into our tents.

Angus and I shared a tent and spent the first bit of time unpacking and getting settled. We did not have much, but it would do. For the rest of the afternoon we ate and drank and talked. At 5:00 pm Lama brought us a dinner of noodles and soup and that was it for the night. We took some Diamox and settled in for a very long night.

At first the tent was quite hot due to the sun, but once the sun dropped the temperature went down fast. I still found it quite warm and lay in my sleeping

learning in THIN AIR

bag with the zipper undone and my jacket undone as well. I had brought a lighter sleeping bag with the intention of sleeping in my down suit inside my sleeping bag, but it just seemed too warm.

Neither of us had carried up a book or cards so we talked and dozed until it was 8:00 pm when we felt it was late enough to try to go to sleep for the night.

I woke at midnight to find that it was cold enough in the tent to require me to zip up my sleeping bag. I also zipped up my vest which I was sleeping in.

Due to the huge amount of liquid I had consumed I quickly filled my pee bottle. At 4:00 am I woke and needed to dump my bottle out the back of my tent before refilling it. It was at this point that the deep cold of the night struck. It was extremely windy, but my ear plugs had enabled me to sleep over the freight train noise.

Climbing in the Icefall

It was so cold that I pulled my down suit into my sleeping bag with me (I should have just put it on, but that seemed like too much work), put on another hat and down jacket and settled down for the rest of a cold night. I did not sleep much after this probably due to the cold and to the fact that I had already slept for 8-10 hours.

We started to move at 7:30 am on Saturday morning. The wind was still howling, but once the sun hit the tent at 8:05 am it warmed quickly. I had some tea and a Mars bar for breakfast and got dressed for the descent. I packed a bag which I would leave in the tent and hope it did not get blown off the mountain, or stolen.

At 8:30 am I was outside and ready to go; our designated departure time. No one else was ready however. I stood in the wind outside the tents for a while and then moved into the adjacent valley hoping to get out of the wind. No such luck. It was a wind tunnel. I climbed to the other side to wait. Fortunately it was not too cold by this time. I estimate -15° C with the wind chill. Eventually, the rest of the team joined me and we started down.

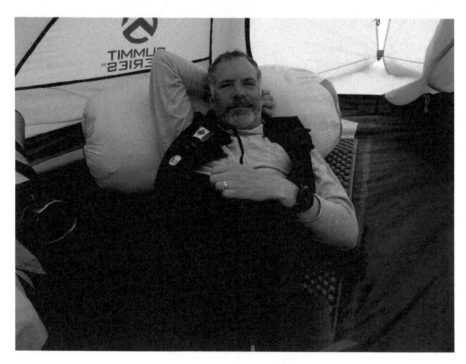

Relaxing in my tent at Camp 2

learning in THIN AIR

Immediately we ran into a ton of Sherpa coming up which impeded our progress. We then ran into a ton of climbers also coming up. Some people are not very patient and butted into line for a rappel, or pushed past on small trails. It is all kind of silly. Some get so mad at each other and start yelling back and forth. It is what it is. It is Everest. If you don't like it, go somewhere else.

The trip down was slow, but not too bad. Once we passed the halfway point we met very little traffic up or down. It did, however, get very hot which sapped my energy. We made it back to our Base Camp just in time for lunch.

Since then I have mostly hung out in my tent. Al, Alan, and Angus had showers. I will have a shower tomorrow. I will also wander down to the military tent tomorrow to call home and to try to send a dispatch. Not sure what will happen.

That reminds me that I was told that several climbers were stopped in the Icefall by the military and had their packs searched for sat phones. Just when you thought it was ridiculous enough something else happens.

Back to Base Camp

OUR FIRST round of acclimatization was now complete. Our bodies were adapting well to the reduced availability of oxygen and the low pressure. No one on the team was showing the effects of high altitude pulmonary edema (HAPE) or high altitude cerebral edema (HACE). Our plan was to continue this routine of climb high, sleep low all the way to Camp 3 which would be our highest acclimatization point. Most scientists and climbers believe that the human body cannot acclimatize over 7300 m (the height of Camp 3) and there is therefore no point in climbing above this height in preparation for the summit. The only result would be increased fatigue.

The following few days were spent recovering and resting at Base Camp. During this time relations with the Military started to get a bit strained. Here, in this relatively small, crowded space were crammed several hundred climbers from all over the world, on time sensitive missions and facing physically demanding conditions. Most had grown up in countries where certain "rights" and "freedoms," particularly the right to free speech, were taken for granted. Facing the climbers was a military with little appreciation for human rights, and who had just impounded indefinitely all means to communicate with colleagues, families and friends. Tension was high.

Journal Entry for April 21 (Day 21) - Base Camp; rest day; phone challenges; protest; military clampdown

Well this was a rest day, but a lot went on today. It started when Al and I went down to the military camp to use the phone. Al's wife was leaving on a trip and he wanted to talk to her before she left. When we got there we were told we could not use the phone as they had decided only to have open hours from 1:00 pm - 3:00 pm. This was quite different from what they had originally said; 6:00 am - 12:00 am. I looked at the soldier and said that was unacceptable and that Al needed to speak to his wife. He said no, they had already turned away lots of people. I said I did not care and that we were going to use the phone and I went and stood by the tent that housed our "Happy Barrel" and said I wanted our team barrel.

After staring at me they came over to the tent and got out the barrel. While Al was making his call I went over to talk to two of the soldiers. I said that 1:00 pm - 3:00 pm would not work as that was the middle of the night for my family and I could not call at that time. They ignored me, said something in Nepali to each other and laughed. I looked at them and said that the restrictions placed on calls allowed us to use the phone at any time during the day. They did not respond. I said because of your changing the rules I cannot speak to my children and my wife. They finally looked at me, laughed in my face and said "I don't care." I looked at them stunned with their attitude and turned away before I said or did something that would jeopardize my time here at Everest.

Al finished his call and I retrieved my email. I put the phone back in the barrel and walked away without saying another word to the soldiers or looking at them. Not that they cared. I fumed all the way back to Base Camp. I had sent a dispatch yesterday, and it now looked like our rights were being infringed upon even more.

Once back at the camp our Liaison Officer heard of the story and asked to talk to me. He listened and said he would see what he could do. He also told me that two people had been expelled from Base Camp today. An American climber had unfurled a banner at Camp 1 that read FREE TIBET F&@#

CHINA. A Sherpa took down the banner, carried it to the military camp and turned in the climber. The climber was then promptly escorted from Camp by the military and will be deported. Apparently the government has offered financial rewards to Sherpas who turn in climbers for infringements of the Nepal based, Chinese led restrictions.

Another Italian climber was caught in Base Camp with a satellite phone and he apparently refused to give it up. He too was escorted from Camp. This is a pretty crazy place this year. Freedom of speech is not acceptable, communication to people outside Camp is not acceptable, and they have even restricted our ability to climb by enforcing climbing restrictions and not allowing the Sherpa onto the mountain to fix the route or establish camps. As a Canadian I never thought I would experience this. People talk about leaving Camp to protest the way we are being treated, but nobody has yet gone through with it. The military knows that people have too much time and money invested to protest and they are using this against us.

Our plan right now is to head up to Camp 1 on the 24th, to Camp 2 on the 25th and to spend 3-4 days at Camp 2 acclimatizing. We are hoping that we will be allowed to go above Camp 2 to acclimatize, but we are not sure. With the military rule in Camp and a few climbers doing things to anger them I'm not sure what will happen.

Camp 2

BY THIS point we had now been on Everest for almost a month. We had been up to Camp 1 and were now on our way to acclimatizing. Life on Everest in the spring of 2008 was nowhere near normal, but we were doing well. We were ready to make the first trip up to Camp 2 from Base Camp where we had been recovering.

Journal Entry for April 27 (Day 27) - Camp 2, 6400 m
We left Camp 1 around 9:00 am taking two hours to walk up to Camp 2, which was much faster than I had expected. Camp 2 is built on the left side (as you are walking uphill) of the Western Cwm on top of a huge pile of glacial debris. It is a very unwelcoming place, although the Sherpa have done an amazing job of hacking out tent platforms and setting up a cook and dining tent.

Camp 2 in the Western Cwm

Within the Western Cwm is a huge glacier that flows from the base of the Lhotse face to the top of the Icefall where it continues sharply downhill. As you look up from Camp 1 towards Camp 2 the glacier unfolds in front of you. It resembles the gently rolling meadows of farm country back home. The glacier flows in gently rolling hills all the way to Camp 2. There are many small crevasses along the way that we just step over but there are a few huge ones that require ladders. Even though the trail is relatively easy it is still quite tiring. This is, I suspect, because we cross over into the mid 6000 m's. The final 30 minutes was quite slow for me (as it seemed for most people).

Once in Camp 2 I unpacked my pack, organized my tent and went for lunch. Lunch was mushroom soup, chapattis, cheese and fresh made coleslaw.

Camp 2 is a beautiful place. From here I can see the Lhotse face (steep and scary), the trail to Camp 3 (looks hard), the trail to the Yellow Band, the Geneva Spur and almost to the South Col. Despite the natural beauty of the mountain, Camp 2 is also an ugly place with the remnants of old camps and garbage littered everywhere.

learning in THIN AIR

After a nice mac n' cheese dinner I got ready for bed. The last time I slept on the mountain I was a little cold; this time I slept in my one piece down suit. As I prepared for sleep I put on my suit and fluffed up my sleeping bag. I would sleep in my suit with my bag pulled over me like a duvet. Unfortunately for the first few hours I had to sleep with the suit pulled down to my waist and the sleeping bag pulled to the side because it was so hot. When I woke at midnight it was cold enough that I needed to put the suit on my upper body and pull my bag up a bit. By 2:00 am I zipped the suit up and actually got into my sleeping bag. Overall it was a pretty comfortable night.

**Looking up at the Lhotse face
from the top of Camp 2 6600 m**

Learning in Thin Air — How Team Development Connects to Resiliency

Just as I had on Cho Oyu, I sat back and reflected upon our team performance and development. My lessons from Cho Oyu had given me the idea to accelerate the development of our Everest team through a focused and deliberate strategy. The question was, had it worked?

I feel quite confident in saying that, yes, it had worked. We had stuck to our developmental plan and kept up our meeting schedule which helped us to evolve nicely as a team. The few times that things seemed to be going off the rails we called a team meeting to talk it out and to make a plan. This was a good feeling as things were about to change. The stress levels on Everest were already high due to the challenges at Base Camp with the military, but they were about to go through the roof.

I felt fortunate that we had made a deliberate focus on building our team because when I looked around and spoke to other teams they were not fairing quite so well.

Many teams, in fact most teams, on Everest these days are not made up of a tight knit group of experienced climbers. Most are commercial teams comprised of climbers from around the world with different experience levels, skill sets and personalities. The big challenge when you have a team such as this is that there is little personal connection between the climbers and the guides. This can have a dramatic impact on support systems, such as the willingness of a climber to help others.

Once upon a time climbers lived by the code called the "brotherhood of the rope." Similar to the sailor's code, it requires any climber to help another climber regardless of how it impacts their personal climb. When you have a tight knit group of climbers on a team this is often automatic. However, when there is no solid foundation of relationship there is a reduction in supportive behavior and people are less willing to lay their climb on the line to help others. Now extend this to people outside your immediate team members and the willingness to support and help goes down dramatically.

Not only does this lack of supportive relationships impact safety and rescue missions, but it reduces the individual's ability to withstand pressure and to deal with change. When I looked around Base Camp there were many teams that had obviously not placed much emphasis on team development and they were now paying the price.

Team members on these lower performance teams were unhappy and often had a pessimistic outlook on daily events. They were quicker to become emotional when reacting to an event and their impulse control (the ability to delay the time between action and reaction) was impaired, resulting in a heightened number of confrontations among team members and with others outside their teams.

It became obvious to me that the 'forming' stage in team development was critical. With it you build resilience within the team. Without it, the team is rife with potential cracks that could burst open under the slightest pressure.

*Looking up the Western Cwm from Camp 1
with the Lhotse face centre back*

P-A-A-R-R-T-T-Y!

LIFE ON the mountain was about to get very interesting!

Journal Entry for April 28 (Day 28) - Camp 2, 6400 m; high winds; restless night; sign in the snow; snipers
Today I woke to the sound of a freight train passing over Camp 2. All day the wind has been raging. Fortunately it is up high and only lighter winds and the odd gust hit our camp. The wind up high is easily 100 mph or more. I don't think the Olympic torch will summit today.

Last night I was in my tent around 8:00 pm. I read for a bit, but not for long as my eyes were tired. After I shut off my headlamp I laid awake for a very long time. I was hot in my suit, but I did not want to take it off. I was also very restless. You may have heard of restless leg syndrome, well I had restless body syndrome. I could not stay still. I could not get comfortable. My whole body had a mild ache from exertion and altitude. I think I finally drifted off around 10:00 pm and slept well until 1:30 am. At that point I woke up a little cold. I zipped up my suit, pulled up my bag and went back to sleep until 6:30 am. Overall not a bad night at 6400 m.

After breakfast we went for a walk to the top of Camp 2. The 100 m climb took about 20 minutes. Overall I felt I was moving quite well, but I was breathing pretty hard. Several people were stopped and hunched over on the side of the trail gasping for breath. To regulate my breathing and my walking I breathe in on the first step and then breathe out on the next. If I am moving fast or going up a steep incline, I will take a breath for each step I take.

When we got to the top of Camp 2 we were rewarded with an amazing view of the Lhotse face and the route to the South Col. The route up the Lhotse face looks pretty spectacular. It also looks very exhausting. I look forward to putting my crampons on the face, but also know that it will be extremely challenging physically. Some people will start to use oxygen at the base of the face, but I will not use it until sleeping at Camp 3 and at a low flow from Camp 3 to Camp 4. I know this will make it more difficult, but I also believe it will help me acclimatize better. I can see where Camp 3 will be placed, it looks quite exhilarating but also scary. It will be great to spend a night there to acclimatize, but it will also be nice to move on.

There were two other things we found at the top of Camp 2: the military and a sign. The army had dug in, setting up camp, drawing their line in the snow. The sign read "Dear climbers, all of you are not allowed to go forward from this point till 10 May 2008. Thank you for your cooperation." This date had been chosen because it was the day that the Olympic torch climbing team said they would summit Everest. However no one can really predict what day they will summit as there are too many factors involved. As climbers we were afraid that if they did not make it on the 10th they would just cross out the 10 and put in a 15. If they did not then summit by the 15th they would cross that out and put in a 20.

This did not make anyone very happy! To add to the stress, the army has posted a sniper at the top of Camp. He has apparently been given the orders to shoot to kill. Anyone who tries to climb above Camp 2 before the Olympic torch has summited will be shot. Hopefully it will all work out and it will just be a good story.

As we were at the sign we were joking about the sniper and daring each other to make a run for the Lhotse face. We all thought it was quite funny and ridiculous. Then as we were walking back to our camp we saw two soldiers in blue down jackets. One of them was carrying a very scary looking, high powered, sniper rifle with a scope. I'm sure they don't want to use it, but given all that has gone on I think they would if some fool decided to make a dash for the higher camps.

High Stress

STRESS LEVELS were now very high, not so much for our team, but for many of the other teams. Everyone on the mountain was stopped dead in their tracks at the top of Camp 2. The concerns were real, our summit dreams could

Everest closed for business

be over for this season. Since Everest has such a small summit window many people were concerned that if the climbing ban was not lifted in time we would run out of time to climb the mountain. Our permits were set to expire June 1 and we were not going to be allowed to climb above Camp 2 until May 10, at the earliest. Given the potential for bad weather, this small window of opportunity seemed even smaller. Due to the route blockade we were also not able to climb to Camp 3 to acclimatize, to lay the fixed rope necessary for the climb, or to stock the upper camps with oxygen, tents, food, and all the other gear required for a summit attempt. Some people were predicting that this blockade could cause catastrophic results on the mountain. If people were not allowed to acclimatize at Camp 3 they would be much more susceptible to cerebral and pulmonary edema.

When climbing above 8000 m you are walking a very thin line between life and death and if everything goes well you will likely survive to tell the tale, but if something goes wrong, a storm rolls in, you get injured, or your oxygen system malfunctions, you stand a very good chance of dying. Many people were fearful that even though the climbers would not be fully acclimatized, the route would not be prepared and the safety net would not be in place, that summit fever would take over and the climbers would go for the top regardless. If the slightest thing went wrong there could be massive deaths on Everest in the spring of 2008.

Naturally all these factors combined to jack the stress level at Camp sky high. Teams were starting to fall apart and people were abandoning the climb.

Closed For Business

WE WERE now told that the mountain above Base Camp would be closed from May 1-10 to all climbers. This was a pretty nice way to ramp up the stress level another notch.

It was not only this additional stress that was taking a toll on the climbers, it was the actual climb itself. As Everest is such a long climb there is a huge attrition rate from those that show up at Base Camp to those that actually make it through to the end. Due to the altitude the immune system is weakened and many climbers get sick. Antibiotics do not really work at this altitude so if a climber does get sick their recovery takes a lot longer than normal. Something as simple as a small cut can take weeks to heal as cells do not regenerate as quickly.

There was a high rate of attrition all around us with climbers dropping out due to illness, injury, fatigue and just plain stress. Our team had been immune to this up until now.

Journal Entry for April 29 to April 30 (Days 29-30) - Camp 2 to Base Camp; Al's trouble in the Icefall
This morning I woke after a pretty good sleep. I am getting used to sleeping in my one piece down suit.

Last night we got word that the mountain would be closed from May 1 to 10. Our plan is to go back to Base Camp today and spend several rest/waiting days there. We will then head back up the mountain going directly to Camp 2, skipping Camp 1, spending two nights at Camp 2 and then climb to Camp 3 for a one night sleep. We will then descend all the way to Base Camp, rest and be ready to go for the summit. Our first summit window will be around May 14-16. This is, of course, weather and health dependent. That will leave us with an additional two weeks for summit attempts if necessary.

It was a drag that we did not get to sleep at Camp 3 on this past foray up the mountain. That would have saved us an additional trip through the Icefall and saved some energy as well. As much as I would rather have gone to Camp 3 on this past trip, I do think this new schedule will produce greater acclimatization. This, I hope, will translate into better summit success.

The walk down was pretty easy as I have become quite familiar with the ground. We did not meet many people coming up as everyone will be kicked off the mountain in a day. There was also a steady stream of Sherpa heading down, but this did not cause us to slow down very much.

The trip from Camp 2 to Camp 1 only took 45 minutes. Once we got to Camp 1 a very strong wind picked up. It only lasted for about 10 minutes, but was strong enough to push us around. I even found it made it a little difficult to breathe.

About halfway down from Camp 1 there is this one ladder bridge that is particularly unnerving. For the most part I am used to the ladder crossings and while I always go slowly and move cautiously, they are not a big deal. This one, however, is another story. It slopes up hill on about a 20 degree angle with a slight lean to one side and a good bit of wiggle from side to side. It is stable, but seems far from it. Going up it is intense, but not too bad. Going down on the return trip is another story. The first time I went down I crawled backwards on my hands and knees. It felt stable, but I'm sure I looked a little silly. Regardless of how I looked, I felt safe. I watched other climbers walk down it forward and backwards, always very shaky and with a slight look of terror in their eyes.

On this trip through, it appeared that the crossing would be a bit better. Two very tight hand rails had been added to make the crossing less precarious. As I approached the ladder I took a look at the snow stake on the uphill side. This was the primary anchor for the one hand rail and it was tensioned as tight as a piano wire. It was so tight that it had twisted and bent the aluminum snow stake. The anchor looked very scary. At no other time in my life would I consider using an anchor of this dubious quality. However, it was just a hand line, and I guess a safety line if I fell, but there were two of them and I felt it was an acceptable risk. I clipped onto both safety lines, backed onto the ladder and slowly walked backwards. Soon enough I was across to the other side.

Scary ladder crossing for Al

Al was coming next. I stood safely on the other side and shouted to Al to turn around and walk across backwards as that would be the most stable way. He began to turn around and as he did so he grabbed the super high tension hand line. It was then that with his additional leverage, the anchor decided to let loose. The anchor shot out like it had been fired from a cross bow. The aluminum snow stake smashed into Al's forearm and he buckled over in pain. In the process of reacting to the pain he bent over sharply and smashed his head on a piece of ice and went down. Lama Babu was right behind him and came to help. All I could do was watch from the other side of the crevasse. Faster than I would have, Al stood up and prepared to cross the ladder. I think he was running mostly on adrenaline at this point. Once across we continued down as a team to a safe spot.

We gathered at the football field (a large flat spot in the Icefall) and as the adrenaline wore off the pain hit Al and he buckled over once again. As Al got the pain under control, he sat down and Ryan took off his jacket to look at his arm. There was no blood and there was no obvious deformation from a break. His hand was swelling up quickly, but it appeared to be better than I had feared. After applying a tensor bandage and taking some pain killers, Al continued the descent. He went amazingly fast and handled the ladders

learning in THIN AIR

and ropes exceptionally well with one hand. He was even the first one back to Base Camp.

Once back at camp he applied ice and the swelling began to go down. As of this morning he was moving his hand with some pain, but it appears to be getting better exceptionally fast. If it had hit me, I'm not so sure I could have handled it as well as Al.

We are now back at Base Camp. We had a nice dinner last night and watched the DVD, LOST. At 9:30 pm, before I went to bed, I checked my email where I found four messages waiting for me. It was great to receive them. I heard all about Amy's first communion which made me happy and sad. I'm sure she looked beautiful and did a great job with her reading, but it made me sad to know that I had missed it.

At least things here are going well. We have had to deal with a very unpredictable schedule, but it has not been too bad as it has not affected our chance of success too much yet. As a team we are getting along pretty well.

Our kitchen team kept us well fed.

I have heard that the Nepal officials may be changing some of the regulations once again, but it is only a rumour at this point. However, it would not surprise me if they did.

The Rumor Mill

WE WERE now back at Base Camp and all appears to be going pretty well for us although the stress level due to the military presence was high. There was not much that we could do about all the restrictions that had been put in place and the constantly changing rules and regulations. Little did we know! Our team was about to be tested in our ability to cope with rapidly changing circumstances. My journal entries reflect why, as rumors of change, and change itself, began to affect our careful planning. The interesting thing about rumours is that they are a direct result of lack of communication. When communications are not flowing, people will take tidbits of information and add to it, simpy making up the rest.

Journal Entry for April 30 (cont'd) - Consolidation of rumors
The changes and the rumors are fast and furious around here.

- *We have heard that the Olympic torch has made it to the summit, but that the torch blew out at or close to the top. What this means to us I don't know. It has not made any real changes in what we can and cannot do on the South side. I have heard that there is a big press conference on the 8th on the North side and they do not want us up on the mountain until that is over. The fear is that we will jump over the ridge and cause trouble for them.*

- *A few days ago several government officials had a big meeting. They flew into Base Camp in a helicopter to have a look around and tell us what we can (more can't) do. I was not at the meeting but was talking to someone who observed it. Apparently they spread out a big map and looked at the route. They were very animated and quite adamant that no climbers be allowed on the mountain because they said we would jump over the ridge and cause trouble for the Olympic torch climb. This is basically impossible to do, but this does not play into their decision making.*

- *One of the things that made things so difficult for us was the banner boy who put up the "FREE TIBET F&@# CHINA" banner at Camp 1.*

learning in THIN AIR

Apparently he is a minor celebrity back home, has done several interviews and been in Sports Illustrated online. Here at Base Camp he is also a celebrity, but the difference is everyone wants to beat him. I'm not sure what he accomplished as far as a political statement, but all he did here was make life more difficult for us. Before his demonstration things were starting to ease up a bit for us. The military saw that we were cooperating and were not a real big threat so they were letting us use phones and even send dispatches. There were talks about easing off on some of the climbing restrictions as well. Then once this stunt was pulled the military dropped the hammer. Tents were searched, people evicted from Camp, phone restrictions increased and climbing privileges revoked. He was lucky he left Base Camp under guard.

- *I was over talking to the Base Camp doctor the other day and he was telling me that most of the Liaison Officers want out. He said they come to see him once a day to see if they are sick enough to go home. They all want a letter to excuse them from their role at Base Camp. While I was there a bunch of soldiers came over. He said they come every day to have their blood pressure and oxygen saturation level checked. When they got there he asked how they were feeling and they all said "very sick today" and he said OK come on in.*

- *He also told of a Liaison Officer who wanted to go home because he had heart burn. The Doctor gave him Rolaids and said he would be OK. The problem was that the Rolaids were expired. Many of the drugs at the clinic are donated or are samples, some are even past their expiry date. This Liaison Officer was not happy to get expired Rolaids so he told the Base Camp Commander. The Commander and five other top soldiers came to the clinic to examine their practices and told the Doctor that they would now be required to be under military supervision. What made the problem worse was that Luanne who is the founder of the Base Camp clinic was quoted by the BBC saying that what the military and Ministry of Tourism were doing at Base Camp would cost climbers their lives. While this may be true, the military was not too happy to be accused of this in the national media.*

- *I was speaking to a climber who witnessed another climber being arrested at gunpoint at Camp 2. Apparently he was using a professional video camera when no video cameras were allowed. Some people discreetly use small video cameras, but to pull out a full size model and walk around filming is not too smart. When this climber saw him he was on his knees at gunpoint while the soldiers searched his pack. He was then taken away.*

- *I just heard this morning that one expedition's website has been identified by the Chinese as one of the, if not the, most offensive to their cause. They are apparently watching him closely. It will be interesting to get home and read what is on his site.*

- *I also heard this morning that the Adventure Consultants owner has been quoted in the press as saying that his team is being extorted at Base Camp. Apparently the military are making them pay for food, lodging and bribes. Who knows?*

- *When the climbing ban was imposed, the military also evicted all non-climbers from Base Camp. This included support staff, trekkers, and even team doctors. This, as with most decisions, made no sense. What threat do these people pose? I think the Chinese government wanted to kick everyone out, but they could not convince Nepal to do this so they compromised and had Nepal throw out all non-climbers.*

- *I did hear that at the beginning of the season that China wanted to buy out all the climbing permits from Nepal and close the mountain completely. This obviously did not happen, but they tried.*

So with all of this going on we felt that the best thing for us to do would be to have a party.

Staying Grounded
Finding the Circle of Influence

AS A team we had a meeting to discuss what to do. Ultimately, there was very little we could do. We could not climb any higher so our only choice was to stay in Base Camp, focus on our team and have a party!

We called it our "Free Everest 2008" party. We sent out invitations to other teams, made popcorn, got beer brought up from lower in the valley, plugged

Free Everest Party

our iPods into speakers and got ready for a great time. Some other teams were looking at us critically thinking that we were being a bit juvenile. After all we were in a very serious situation. We were being blocked from climbing the mountain, there were snipers ready to shoot us and people were being arrested and deported from the country. Yes all of this was true, but it was also true that we could not control most of this and therefore could only focus on what we could control and that was us and our immediate environment.

This idea stems from a model from Stephen Covey that examines our Circle of Influence and our Circle of Concern. The Circle of Concern are all those things that impact our world, but that we can do nothing about. On the mountain this was represented by the military restrictions, satellite phone confiscations, climbing bans, and all the various rules and regulations. All of these things were impacting our world and our ability to climb the mountain, but we could not do anything to control them. We could not get the military or the government to change their policies and decisions and if we tried to get around them we were in for a world of trouble.

The Circle of Influence on the other hand represents all those things that we can control and influence. For us this was represented by ourselves, our immediate team, our attitude and how we chose to respond to the situation.

We as a team chose to live in the Circle of Influence whereas others decided to live in the Circle of Concern. We were responding to the environment and others were reacting to it.

Those teams that were existing in the Circle of Concern were starting to unravel even more. They were fighting with each other and arguing with the military, and overall starting to fall apart. Having spent some time talking with the Base Camp doctor he was telling me about the various illnesses around Camp and it became very clear that the teams that were living in the Circle of Concern, and therefore had increased stress levels, were also the teams that were sick. Countless studies have revealed that when our stress levels increase our immune system is negatively affected making us more susceptible to illness.

Conversely, having chosen to live in the Circle of Influence (and some other teams had as well) we were enjoying relatively low levels of stress and not experiencing the same levels of illness. We were living in the same environment but we were not getting sick. The cause and effect relationship was amazingly clear. We often are told how stress impacts health, but when you see it so clearly it is difficult to ignore.

The interesting thing about stress is that it is a choice. We often think that stress is forced upon us, but in reality it is a choice. We were all experiencing the same events we were just choosing to respond to these events differently.

Post climb, I would do a very informal survey to see what impact stress levels played in the ultimate success of reaching the summit. When I looked at the teams that were living in the Circle of Concern they experienced about a 9% success rate whereas those living in the Circle of Influence experienced about an 80% success rate. Granted there are many factors that play into success and failure

Party at 5300 m!

learning in THIN AIR

on Mount Everest, but it seemed to me that where people chose to place their energy had a huge impact on success.

Those that expended tons of energy in the Circle of Concern reduced their overall health and energy. I believe that their desire was beat out of them so when it came time to go for the summit they just did not have the energy or the heart left to do it.

Learning in Thin Air - Managing Change

The previous journal entries indicate that everyone at Base Camp was struggling with the potential for dramatic change in their plans. How did our team respond to this situation? By throwing a party! As a team, we had figured out a way to deal with the challenge of change. There's a lot to be learned on how we came to the decision, in such difficult circumstances, to do something that simply might not seem rational.

In our personal and business lives, change is the only constant and those that cannot adjust to change will be left behind. On Everest we had to deal with change every day. Sometimes it was weather and the mountain conditions, sometimes it was military and political decisions, and sometimes it was within our team or with other teams. Regardless of what the change was, the part that led us towards success or failure was how we dealt with the change.

What helped us to deal with the change? In large part, it was our ability to focus on our Circle of Influence and to let go of the things that existed in our Circle of Concern.

This model is a perfect one to use when you come up against change. Although reality is never perfect, when facing change you should examine what you have influence over and what you don't. If you do not have influence over it, try not to focus all your attention and energy on it. If you do, all you will accomplish is to stress yourself. Very little if any headway will be made. However, if you place your attention and energy towards things that you do have influence over you will find that you have much greater success and that your Circle of Influence will actually grow.

Avalanches can occur at any time
due to changing weather conditions

Back on Track

AS ANYONE who has ever had a party knows, there's always the morning after.

In our case, we were soon to have great news. True to their word, once the torch made it to the top the military packed up and left. In fact, I think they were just as happy to go as we were to see them go. They were not overly happy with the job they had been made to do and they knew they were not well liked within camp.

Once the military left it was pretty much business as usual on Everest. We got our satellite phones back and plans were made to resume climbing. However, for some teams it was too little too late.

Journal Entry for May 8 (Day 38) - Base Camp; Chinese make the summit; restrictions lifted

I woke this morning to the sound of jets flying over the summit of Everest. This was a promising sound as the Chinese were reported to have planned another summit attempt for this morning.

After breakfast our Base Camp manager, Chering, came over to us and said he had just been told the Chinese have made the summit. He said the military was packing up at Camp 2 and at Base Camp and will be out of here in a few days. They may maintain a small presence just to make sure we continue to play nice. We have been told that we must still maintain friendly relations with the Chinese government until we leave Nepal.

This is excellent news as we should now be able to do what we want. There are rumours of many FREE TIBET flags going to the summit. The Chinese government has not made any friends here in Base Camp.

As usual there is controversy over the reported summit. Looking up at the summit of Everest from Base Camp today is not a pretty sight. The winds appear to be ferocious. Some people in camp have been reading internet reports that say the winds are way too high on the summit for the Torch climbing team to have made it. Therefore, some are saying the summit is a fake. I doubt we will ever know the truth or be 100% confident that the Torch truly made it to the top. However, all that really matters to me right now is that I can climb this mountain, and in a few days I should have my phone back. I will still write with caution, but I will be able to write.

Conga Line Through the Icefall

WE WERE now on our way back up the mountain to go to Camp 3 for our final acclimatization round. The problem, however, was that due to the climbing restrictions everyone else was doing the same thing. Usually over a two month expedition, the various teams get on slightly different schedules. This helps to spread out the mass of climbers onto different days and makes the route not so crowded. We did not have this luxury in 2008 and would need to contend with a conga line of climbers ascending the mountain.

Journal Entry for Friday May 9 (Day 39) – Base Camp; Camp 1; Camp 2 at 6400 m; delays through the Icefall; fatigue; tent explosion
We made our break for Camp 2 today. It was a bit of a death march. By the time we got to Camp 1 I was a bit of a zombie, and by Camp 2, I was the walking dead. Actually I did get a second wind by Camp 2 so it was not too bad.

We departed at 5:30 am as planned which in retrospect was a little late. Next time I would vote for starting about an hour earlier. I don't think I slept one minute last night. I did not doze at all. I went to bed at 9:00 pm and quickly overheated. Once I am too hot it takes me a long time to cool down. I think this, combined with the early start, worked against me for sleep.

I heard our cook rattling pots at 3:15 am and the generator starting at 4:00 am. Breakfast was milk tea (tea made with milk instead of water with sugar and spices; it is a Sherpa specialty) and oatmeal. We were then on our way.

We were all dragging our butts a little today. We had nine rest days before we came back up and I'm sure we lost some fitness during this time. We moved slowly through the Icefall, but quickly caught up with the line. It seems we were not the only ones moving slowly.

The Icefall had changed over the last nine days. With the constant motion of the ice and the warming temperatures there were a lot of changes. New routes were in place in some sections and new ladders spanned newly opened gaps in the ice. Overall I think there were fewer ladders than the last time we went through.

We were making pretty good time (faster than last time despite our lengthy rest) until we got to the unstable ladder I wrote about last time. It was creating quite a traffic jam. Just above this ladder is another vertical one that is also a

Long line of climbers move through the Icefall

little tricky. Not only were there many people going slowly across the ladder (I counted about 25 in line), but there were also about 20 Sherpa trying to come down. One would think that the best thing to do would be to alternate, but the challenge is, once you let one Sherpa in, they all file through.

Eventually we got over the ladder and got in line for the next one. Once again there was a large queue with fast moving Sherpa trying to work the line. There is a rappel station to help ease congestion on the ladder, but most Sherpa will not use it. Some don't know how to rappel but many just find it too scary and refuse to do it.

With all these slowdowns we lost more than an hour. By the time we wound our way into Camp 1 the sun was on us full force and this slowed our pace to a crawl. We took a break at Camp 1 having some food and drink. It had taken us almost five hours to get here.

After our break we set out for Camp 2. The heat was almost unbearable. We stumbled along the trail like everyone else. The rolling hills of the Western Cwm did not seem so beautiful this time. All I could do was put one foot in front of the other. Camp 2 could be seen from a very long distance away, but the distance was misleading. It looked so close, but there was at least another two hours before you get there. It was also very important to apply copious amounts of sun block frequently, as any exposed skin would burn in minutes.

Halfway to Camp 2 the clouds came in and partly blocked the sun. The air temperature dropped dramatically and some light snow started to fall. This change gave me the energy I needed to make it to Camp. It was still very tiring, but the last hour was not too bad. In all it took seven hours to go from Base Camp to Camp 2. I do not look forward to the next time.

Everyone was quite tired as we enjoyed our lunch of popcorn and tomato ginger soup. We were sitting on the floor of the dining tent, relaxing, when all of a sudden the tent fly (the outside layer) spontaneously exploded and shredded to pieces. I guess it was this fly's time to go. With the constant hot/cold temperature fluctuation and the extreme UV exposure, the fabric does not last long up here. It went with a loud pop and the sound of breaking poles. When we stepped outside to have a look, the damage was extensive. A blue tarp was used to make the repairs for now as almost the entire fly had been destroyed. Fortunately, the tent itself was still usable.

learning in THIN AIR

Camp 2

Right now it is 5:30 pm and I am lying in my tent waiting for dinner. Soon the cold will come and I will crawl into my down suit for the evening.

Tomorrow will be a much needed rest day and then we will tackle the Lhotse face to Camp 3. This will be extremely difficult, and a big step in our preparation for the summit.

On to Camp 3

OUR NEXT plan was to go to Camp 3 for a night of acclimatization. There were different opinions about this as I wrote on May 10.

Journal Entry for Saturday May 10 (Day 40) – Acclimatization
Our plan is to depart Camp 2 tomorrow around 5:00 am. We figure it will take two hours to get to the base of the Lhotse face and an additional three hours to reach Camp 3. I am looking forward to getting there, but I know the trip there will be a real test physically. We will carry up the absolute minimum to spend the night in reasonable comfort, but it will still be a long night. I do not expect to get much sleep.

There are various philosophies regarding Camp 3, about 50% of the climbers will spend the night there, while the other 50% will just touch the Camp and go back down. The Sherpa will not sleep at Camp 3 as they think it is too scary a place and they don't need it for acclimatization. There is a debate if spending a night at Camp 3 gives you more acclimatization than just touching it and going down. Some say the ability to acclimatize above 7300 m is questionable. We have decided to sleep there because we feel it will give us some additional acclimatization.

Journal Entry for May 11 (day 41) – Depart Camp 2; crowds on the mountain; travel on fixed line; Camp 3 at 7200 m; view of Cho Oyu; plan for tomorrow

At the moment, it is 2:00 pm and I am sitting in my tent at Camp 3. It is quite amazing just to be here. This is such a famous camp. I feel that if I can make it here without too much trouble I should be able to make it to Camp 4. From there it is a whole new ball game.

I am sharing a North Face VE 25 with Angus and Al. Ryan and Alan are in another tent not more than 2 feet from us. Our two doors face one another for easy communication, to pass food and water back and forth, and because this is all the space we have on our tiny ledge.

Here's an account of the day:

We woke at 5:00 am this morning and packed our bags. Breakfast was porridge and eggs at 5:30 am. It was difficult to eat much at this hour, but it was necessary for the day. I managed to choke down one egg and a hot chocolate.

We were on the trail by 6:10 am, making pretty good time, and faster than our walk the previous day. I felt stronger and less tired. We stopped after one hour for a water break. I could see up onto the Lhotse face and counted at least 100 climbers. (With climbers before and after us I estimated that around 250 people made their way to Camp 3 today.) Many of these were Sherpa who did not spend the night and many were climbers who just touched camp, rested a while, and then descended. Probably somewhere around 75 people will actually spend the night here.

learning in THIN AIR

It took us two hours to reach the base of the face. We immediately clipped our jumars onto the fixed rope and did not unclip until four hours later when we reached our tents.

The route starts out steep and stays that way. The first section had some snow cover so it was not too difficult to gain good footing. Shortly thereafter the route got much steeper and turned to pure hard glacier ice. Footing became trickier and more strenuous. In some sections it was so steep we had to front point (this is when only the two front points of your crampons are biting into the ice and your entire body weight is suspended on these small pieces of metal).

About every 30 m or so (longer if the terrain was less steep) we came to an anchor point. These anchors were made of ice screws, snow stakes, or V-threads (two holes placed in the ice with ice screws to create a V which a piece of rope is looped through). Some of these anchors looked a little scary, but most were quite solid. Most were made of multiple anchor points, but

Steep climbing on our way to Camp 3

some were just a single anchor point. Back home I always made sure I had at least two anchors and usually three. While it is not uncommon to use a single anchor point in an alpine setting, the scary part about the single anchor here is that there may be 30 people hanging off it.

At the anchor point you had to clip your safety line above the anchor before you took your jumar off and moved it above the anchor. If you did not do it in this order and lost your balance while you were unclipped you would take the express train to the bottom of the Lhotse face. Many climbers have died in this exact manner. I was very careful in these transitions.

There were about 20 of these transitions on the way to our tent site. Some people chose to pass at these anchors, but mostly people just stayed in line as passing was too dangerous. There was an up and a down line. Some people chose to pass using the down line, but there were usually people coming down so this caused problems. For the most part there was little passing as passing consumes a ton of energy.

The face was, for the most part unrelenting, but there were a couple of semi flat sections that could be used as a rest stop. Mostly once you started you didn't stop.

When we first got on the face we were in the shade and it was quite cold. This was the coldest I had been on this expedition so far. At one point my hands were very cold and had gone numb. At 8:45 am the sun hit the face and it warmed up considerably. We had to make sure we had our sunglasses on (if not we would go snowblind in a very short time) and put on a generous coating of sun block. Even with the sun block we all got some level of sunburn. The sun also started to warm my hands and I experienced great pain as they thawed out.

The sun was hot, but we had some cloud cover for most of the day so it was not unbearable. It was quite strenuous, but I did not find it too bad as we were moving fairly slowly. This was good because any increase in speed would have left me breathless in mere seconds. I found that I needed to set a pace for myself in order to be comfortable. I settled on one step for four breaths. I would take a step and then breathe, breathe, breathe, breathe, and then take another step. This may sound very slow, but was actually a pretty

learning in THIN AIR

good pace. I was able to keep at the front of the line (there were several lines spread out on the route) so no one passed me.

Every now and then I would come to the bottom of a short steep section. Looking up at it, I would mutter a curse and know it was going to be a killer. The four breath pace would go out the window and I would do whatever I needed to do. This usually involved lots of stops and heavy breathing. At the top of the section I needed to deep breathe for a minute or so to get my breathing under control. Often I would cough and cough and cough from the exertion. At the top of one steep section I came across a climber laying spread eagle in the snow. I asked if he was OK and he gasped yes. I knew he only needed recovery time so I moved on.

The final 25 m are always the toughest for me, I could see my destination, but I knew that I was still 15 minutes away.

As I arrived at Camp 3 it started to snow. After five hours of climbing from Camp 2 (three hours from the bottom of the face) I had reached the first section of tents. There are three tiers of tents this year. These take advantage of three relatively flat areas on the face. As I did not see our tents on the first tier, I muttered another profanity to myself (this occurred frequently today), dug in and kept going. After another agonizing steep section I could see our tents directly below a huge ice wall. Upon reaching our tent, I sat down to rest.

Our tent platform is less than 2 metres wide. We need to be clipped into a rope whenever we are outside our tent as one slip and it would all be over. Surviving a fall from here would be impossible. We will stay in our tents for 99% of our time at Camp 3. The only reason to get out of the tent would be to get snow for melting into water or if you are unfortunate enough to have to go #2. Peeing is done in our pee bottles and dumped out the back of the tent. Modesty is thrown out.

We had a lot to drink since we got here and had a small snack, which I proceeded to throw up. My throat is a little sensitive and the hot pepper salami did not go over very well. I am doing well now, drinking lots and resting. Dinner was noodle soup with cheese and salami. It was pretty spicy, but not too bad.

Tents covered in snow at Camp 3

At 5:45 pm it was still sunny. It was pretty warm in the tent, but I knew it would drop drastically once the sun went down. However, I didn't feel it would get too cold as there were three of us in the tent.

Outside our tent was an amazing view. I could see down the Cwm to Camp 2 (it looked very far away), I could see up the west shoulder of Everest where it dips down to the Geneva Spur and the South Col (but I couldn't actually see the Spur or the Col from our camp), I could see the scary ridge that leads to the summit of Nuptse, I could see the pyramid summit of Pumori (it looked small from here), and I could see Cho Oyu in the distance. The clouds in the valley below us made for a spectacular sun set, but once the sun set I retreated to the tent again as it got very cold.

We have just made our plan for the morning; we will rise at 8:00 am, have breakfast and depart at 9:00 am. The sun should hit our tent around 8:00 am so we will be able to pack and descend in the heat of the sun. I just hope it is not too hot.

learning in THIN AIR

It is 6:45 pm and time for bed. The sun has just dipped behind the horizon. We will spend around 13 hours in bed, but will not sleep that long. If I am lucky I will sleep well until midnight and then it will be off and on until morning.

Retreat From Camp 3

Journal Entry for May 12 (Day 42) - Camp 3; description of night's sleep; O2; wet sleeping bag lesson; cold windy descent; rappels and passing; waiting for team; storm sets in; unplanned descent to Base Camp

Today was a very exciting day. Very exciting is not something one usually looks for on Mount Everest. Our trip motto is "No Drama." I'll tell you more about it in a moment, but first let me sum up last evening.

We had a pretty good night. We went to bed early (not much else to do and we were tired from the day). I slept well considering the altitude and the comfort rating of the glacier. Our tent platform was quite flat compared to others I have spoken with. I did not get cold and found that breathing was no problem. Some people will sleep on a low flow (0.5 litre/minute) of oxygen at Camp 3, but I did not and did not feel it was necessary. Maybe on the summit push I will, just to give me a boost. I have not decided yet.

I fell asleep around 9:00 pm and slept off and on for most of the night. Even though the VE25 is a good sized 3 person tent it fills up fast with three guys and our gear. A strong wind picked up during the night and shook our tent violently. The noise made it difficult to sleep (I should have put in my ear plugs), but the biggest issue was from the blowing snow. In the tent there are several vents to help bring the fresh air in and to allow condensation from breathing to escape. Two of these vents have mesh and two are open under the outer fly. We had all four vents open. The strong wind picked up spindrift snow and blew it under our tent fly and right into the tent through the open vents. None of us realized this until we opened our eyes in the morning. It was not too bad, but my sleeping bag had a good covering of snow on it which proceeded to melt. Fortunately we were heading down so I could dry my bag out. A wet down sleeping bag is not much good at Camp 4. Lesson learned. I will be more careful next time.

Now, here is the exciting part: Our planned departure time was 9:00 am. The wind was still howling as we were getting ready to head downhill. It did not seem too bad in the tent as we packed our bags, but as soon as I stepped outside it was a different story. The wind and the blowing snow along with the fact that our tent was still in the shade made it quite cold out. By the time I had my crampons on my fingers were numb. I stood there for a moment waiting for the others and then said that I was going downhill about 100 m to get to the sun and warm up. I clipped onto the rope and started to make my way towards the sun. Once I got there it was no better. If anything, the wind was even stronger, which made it feel even colder. Angus came down to meet me and we decided to move to a flat spot to wait for the rest of the team. We stood at an anchor point looking down at the two ropes (one up and one down). Both had climbers coming up on them. Standing there freezing, waiting for a free rope, and waiting for the rest of my team was not pleasant, but I held my tongue. Eventually the rest of the team arrived at our waiting spot. I looked at the team and said I was going down as I was frozen to the bone.

I hooked my figure 8 onto the line and started to rappel. The wind was blowing so strong at times that it blew me across the face. Once I got to the next anchor point I looked up and did not see anyone from my team, but I did see two other climbers starting down the rope I was on. I had to keep going to get out of their way. I also did not want to stop for long as my hands were getting colder and colder. The rest of my body was fine, but I was losing dexterity in my hands and I was afraid of making a mistake. Some of the sections were less steep and I did what we call a Sherpa rappel. You keep your harness clipped to the rope, but instead of using a rappel device you just wrap the rope around your arm and use this friction to control your descent. For the steeper sections I used my figure 8 which is a device I attach to my harness and to the rope that allows me to control the speed of my descent.

Looking back up the mountain was quite amazing. It was a classic Mount Everest scene. The sun was reflecting off the ice creating a beautiful view, the snow was swirling around and there were climbers scattered everywhere hunkered down against the wind. When the snow hit my face it stung with the force. It was a beautiful if not somewhat scary scene. This is what mountaineering is all about. I took the odd photo, stopped every now and then to wait for my group, but mostly I just kept going.

I stopped when I got to a flatter section and waited for the rest of my team, but I never saw them. Sitting at an anchor point was not a pleasant experience on this day so I did not linger too long. The feeling was coming back to my hands and I did not want to lose the feeling in them again.

When you get to an anchor point you need to clip from the high side to the low side in order to keep going. At no time do you ever want to be completely unclipped from the rope. A fall would be fatal. Therefore, I had one leash attached to my harness with two carabineers. When I got to an anchor point I would first find a stable stance, I would leave my upper carabineer attached, connect my lower carabineer below the anchor and then unclip the upper carabineer. If I was using my figure 8 to rappel the next section, I would connect it to the rope before I unclipped my upper carabineer. I was then ready to keep going. With numb hands this process became much more difficult and the chance of error became greater. I would not say that I was afraid at any time, but all my senses were on high alert.

Regardless of which rope I was on, as I was going down I would invariably meet up with other climbers coming up. There was some confusion as to which rope was the up rope and which was the down rope. Most often these were pleasant experiences as both me and the other climbers were looking for human contact, and a reason to stop for a moment. The upward bound climber would see me coming towards them and I would wave to them and tell them I would pass them once I got to them. Usually they just stared at me and nodded their heads while gasping for breath. Once I reached them we would exchange a few words as I clipped around them the same way I would an anchor. As I was ready to go, we would say good bye and pat each other on the back. This human contact seemed important, especially on a day such as this.

I continued down the mountain like this from one anchor to the next, passing one up bound climber after another. It was not really that hard, it was not really that cold, but it was fairly intense.

At times I would stop to catch my breath, snap a photo, look up hill, admire the view and keep going. As I got closer to the bottom the snow started to accumulate on the lower angle sections. In places I was rappelling through snow halfway up my calf. I made it to the bottom in one hour. It had taken me four hours to go up the day before.

Once down, I made my way across the glacier looking for a place out of the wind to rest and wait for the rest of the team. All in all it was quite an exciting descent. It had all the classic elements of a real mountaineering experience; steep ice with huge potential for danger, very strong winds, and blowing snow; quite the experience.

Approaching storm forces us back down the mountain

As I was walking across the glacier I came across Lama Babu and Lhakpa waiting for us. They had hot juice which was quite excellent. I had not eaten or drunk anything since leaving the tents and had expended quite a bit of energy. The plan was to take a break along the way, but the conditions did not permit this. From this spot on the glacier we watched for Ryan, Angus, Alan and Al. They had some crampon challenges and had gotten behind some slower climbers so they were quite far behind me. I felt bad that I was not with my team, but at the time I had no way of knowing how far behind me they were plus there was no where I could comfortably wait for them on the face.

learning in THIN AIR

I could see them high on the face making their way down, but all I could do was watch. As I was waiting, the wind was raging even stronger around me. Other climbers were making their way up to the face to make their shot at Camp 3. Some of these climbers were agonizingly slow. Our team is not the fastest on the mountain, but we are far from the slowest. I observed many of these climbers make it to the face and start up, only to turn around and come back down. The conditions were too harsh for them. Going up is much harder than going down.

My team made it down to where I was, we had a drink and then we started out for Camp 2. The snow had stopped, but the wind remained high. When we got back to Camp 2 the excitement continued. We heard that several people had gotten frostbite on their way down from Camp 3. All of our team was fine, and it did not really seem cold enough to get frostbite. The only way this could happen, in my opinion, was that people either had inadequate gloves, or took their gloves off for some reason. It could also be that these reports were exaggerated.

The other news we heard back at Camp 2 was that everyone was abandoning ship. The weather forecast was calling for three to four more days of heavy snow and people were afraid that if they did not get back to Base Camp now, they may not be able to do so for several days. The issue was that if the trail down was covered with snow it would be very difficult to find the way down. This was exacerbated by the fact that it had started snowing again, the clouds were low, we only had 60 - 150 m of visibility and the wind was quickly helping to bury the trail. An additional fear was that if the seracs in the Icefall got loaded with heavy snow it could force them to topple over without warning. With this information we too decided to 'get the heck out of Dodge' while we still could.

We had a quick lunch, packed our bags and were off. Visibility was extremely poor and we had to follow the partially filled in trail towards Camp 1. We had wanted to stay a night at Camp 2 to recover, but we had to dig deep into our reserves to make it down. At no point were we in danger of losing the trail, but the conditions were far from perfect.

As we got closer to Camp 1 we started to come across a lot of drift snow. This made the walk extra tiring. Ryan was out front doing a great job of finding the trail and breaking through the snow.

Once we got to the Icefall it was not as bad as the route is fixed with rope from top to bottom. The snow slowed down and the sun periodically poked through the clouds. We were making good time, but I was getting very tired. At one point the sun came out and the temperature went way up. This acted to sap almost all my strength. I trudged on, slowly making my way down. The majority of our journey through the Icefall was downhill, but there were a few uphill sections which were quite tiring. The worst part of the Icefall for me, from a physical point of view, was the bottom 30 minutes. This is where the ropes stop, but you continue to walk along the glacier towards camp. The bottom part becomes like rolling waves, up and down, up and down. Even if you are acclimatized, up hills are still tough, especially when you are running on the last of your energy reserves. I was severely dragging my butt near the bottom. After another 4.5 hours we made it back to Base Camp. It was great to be there, and our trip to Camp 3 had been amazing.

Learning in Thin Air - Leadership and Emotional Intelligence

By this point in time, all of us were being tested — on a personal level, as a team, and with our ability to work with our team leader. But we were also being tested in our ability to stretch and redefine the concept of leadership, one in which all of us could take on a leadership role within the team.

Leadership is critical to the success of any team or project. A leader has tremendous influence over the formation of team culture and the ultimate success of the team. Having a leader who possesses what is called "emotional intelligence" is a huge asset.

Emotional intelligence is a set of emotional and social skills that collectively establish how well we: perceive and express ourselves; develop and maintain social relationships; cope with challenges; and use emotional information in a constructive way. It can be broken down into: how we see and understand ourselves (intrapersonal realm); how we connect with and understand others (interpersonal realm); how we deal with stress (stress management realm); how we deal with change (adaptability); and our overall enjoyment of life (general mood).

learning in THIN AIR

Studies into leadership success have revealed that between 60-80% of leadership success is directly connected to emotional intelligence. This is not surprising since people with greater emotional intelligence can generally connect and interact with others more effectively. They are also better at dealing with the stress and pressures of work and life.

Our expedition leader, Ryan, had a high level of emotional intelligence. He could connect with each of us on a personal level and help us to create a meaningful, collective vision of success, particularly as we took on this far more challenging part of the climb.

But more than that, he recognized that we all wanted and needed to take a leadership role on Everest. The team culture that he helped us create was one of shared leadership. He knew, as we all did, that if you see yourself as a leader you will do things differently than if you see yourself as a follower.

On Everest, those climbers that had high levels of emotional intelligence stood a much greater chance of success than those with low levels of emotional intelligence. The climbers that were able to withstand the stress and pressure and interact effectively with themselves and others had a greater chance of maintaining their physical and emotional strength. They were in a better state to be able to endure the severe punishment, both physically and mentally, on summit day and have a greater chance of reaching the summit.

Steep climb as we leave Camp 3

The Summit Push

ALL OF this training — the constant up and down, up and down — meant that we were now ready for our summit push. The only thing now was to wait for the weather window to open.

Journal Entry for May 17 (Day 47) – Summit plans

And now the news you have all been waiting for — summit plans. We had a meeting this morning and provided the weather forecast does not change, we will head up on the 17th to Camp 2, take a rest day at Camp 2 on the 18th, go to Camp 3 on the 19th, go to Camp 4 on the 20th, and summit (if all goes well) on the 21st. This is the perfect scenario but we all know that many factors could impact this plan.

At this point, ropes are fixed to the South Col and gear will be there within a few days. There are at least two groups that we know of that are planning to go for a May 17th summit. This would be excellent as they would break the trail and set the ropes from the Col to the top.

As a team we are doing very well. We are all healthy and moving strong. From a group dynamic perspective all is going well and Ryan is a good leader. We travel at a similar pace and our goal will be to all stand on top together. This is a lofty goal, but I believe within our reach.

The Summit Push - Camp 4

THE TIME at Base Camp passed quickly. We were soon on our way back up the mountain for our summit attempt. I chose not to carry my satellite phone as we would all share one. I did carry my pocket PDA, but did not pull it out until I made it to Camp 4.

Journal Entry for May 20 (Day 50) – Camp 3 departure; O2; route description; Yellow Band; Geneva Spur; South Col; Camp 4 description; garbage; plan for summit; 7900 m
We have made it to the South Col and Camp 4. One of the most, if not the most, famous camps in the world.

Here's the way it went: Last night at Camp 3 was a very good night. It was quite warm in our tent with the three of us. I did not even zip up my sleeping bag all the way. I slept pretty well, but woke frequently. We were up at 4:30 am to start to pack and get hot water for breakfast. Everything always takes longer than we think. We did not set off at 5:00 am as planned, but were on the trail just after 6:00 am.

We all had our down suits on, but it was not that cold. I could have gone with my standard climbing suit. We were also wearing oxygen for the first time. This was my first time ever climbing with oxygen and the benefit is not immediately apparent. It actually seemed to hamper my breathing at first.

Right out of Camp 3 is a 10 m vertical ice wall. Standing at the bottom of this vertical wall it did not look too bad, but at this altitude everything is always more strenuous than you think. I clipped my jumar onto the fixed rope and began to heave. After I got to the top of the wall I collapsed on my knees gasping for breath. I thought the oxygen was very ineffective at best. I tore the mask off my face feeling I was suffocating. This was, of course, the wrong thing to do. After realizing that it was worse without the mask, I put the mask back on and took several deep breaths. That did the trick and I kept climbing.

I found the oxygen to be amazing! I was running at a flow of 1 litre per minute but it was like magic. Not only did it give me the oxygen my body was craving, but it also helped to reduce my cough. As I breathed into my mask

Oxygen can be amazing at 7200 m!

it would warm and moisten the air I breathed in. This soothed my throat. Without the constant coughing, I was much stronger and faster.

The route up the remainder of the Lhotse face was unrelenting. Up, up, up, at a constant angle of 45-60 degrees. Near the top of the face we made a big traverse to the left. Looking across the face it did not look too bad. At the end of this traverse is the Yellow Band, a prominent band of limestone that bisects the face. The Yellow Band looked daunting, but turned out to be not too bad. About 20 m of crampons scraping on rock and I was on top. After some more upward gain we had another traverse. This one was much longer than the last. Over an hour later I was still crossing it. Distances are deceiving when you are moving so slowly. At the end of this traverse I came to the Geneva Spur. This is a large band of black rock that is the final barrier to the South Col. I took a long rest at the bottom of the spur and let Ryan, Angus, and Al catch up. I had been in the lead most of the day and had not seen them for hours. By the time they got there I was getting cold. I did a quick check in and hit the trail. Angus did not break for long and was soon behind me.

The Geneva Spur was pure rock this year, no snow to be seen. Our crampons became more of a hindrance than a benefit. We took them off and stashed them in our packs, walking the rest of the way to Camp 4 without them.

The Geneva Spur was pretty straight forward and we were on the top of it in about 40 minutes. At the top of the Geneva Spur I lifted my head and was struck with the sight of Everest's upper pyramid for the first time. It almost knocked me off balance; it was such a powerful sight. Somewhere up there is a Sherpa team fixing line to the south summit. I was just told by Kala that they are continuing to fix all the way to the summit if possible. From here it was just a long traverse on broken rock to the South Col and Camp 4.

Camp 4 is situated on a large, flat expanse of broken rock. The first thing you notice as you walk into camp is the vast amount of garbage left over from past expeditions. Most of the garbage consists of ruined tents, broken tent poles, fuel canisters, batteries, and food packages. There are no used oxygen bottles as they retrieve a deposit when brought down.

Camp 4 7900 m

learning in THIN AIR

We located our tent and moved in. Kala Sherpa, who will climb with us to the summit, is in the tent with us and has been feeding us drinks. I am a little tired from the climb, but feel surprisingly good. I have been off oxygen since I got here with no ill effects. Ryan, Al, Angus, and Alan also seem to be doing well. Overall it was a beautiful day. The views were amazing and the temperatures were pretty good.

The next several hours will be spent getting ready for the summit. We will try to sleep, but will not get much. We will depart around 9:00 pm. It should take us around 12 hours to get to the summit. After my performance today I feel pretty positive, but would not guarantee the top. I will do my best and that is all I can do. It will be brutally tough, that I know.

Summit Day

MAY 20TH at around 9:30 pm we set out for the summit. I did not have a phone with me, but Alan had his and we were all planning to share it to make a call from the summit. This ultimately did not work as planned and there was quite a long time when I was not in contact with the outside world.

For Susan, my children, and the rest of my family and friends, this was the most stressful time as summit day is when most things can go wrong. Of those that die on Everest many of them die on summit day. With no news coming off the mountain all that the people back home could do was wait and hope that everything was going well.

My wife Susan and Angus' wife Sarah found support in each other, even though they were on opposite sides of the country. They emailed back and forth and spoke several times as they scoured the internet for news. My friend Paul in Australia also became part of this informal group. I was using Paul's web site, myeverest.com, to post my dispatches, so he too had been following our climb closely. Paul was also scouring the internet and between the three of them they found what meager news there was about our summit attempt.

Finally after almost 36 hours of silence from us on the mountain I made a call from Camp 4 to Susan to tell her I had made it to the summit. I got voice mail. It was quite depressing to hear my own voice asking me to leave a message. Susan got the news and posted the following message on the web site:

Note on website from Susan:

"Angus and Scott made the summit of Mount Everest!!! This is Susan here. I was out with Colin at swimming lessons and missed a call from Scott. He reported that he, Angus and Al made the summit and more importantly they are back at Camp 4 on the South Col safe and sound. Scott said "it was good, it was really hard but it was good." Despite the fact that he sounded exhausted he also sounded very happy and excited. They are heading down to Camp 2 tomorrow and I am sure he will post then. Thank you all so much for your support....it obviously helped!!

Susan"

Scott at the top of the world!

learning in THIN AIR

Journal Entry for May 21 (Day 51) – Camp 4 to summit to Camp 4; Camp 4 elevation 7900 m - summit elevation 8848 m - total gain 950 m (just over 3000 ft)

WE KNOCKED THE BASTARD OFF! These famous words were spoken, off the cuff, by Sir Edmund Hillary after he and Tenzing Norgay climbed Mount Everest for the first time in 1953. Those words would haunt him for the rest of his life. Mountaineering is supposed to be a gentleman's sport and gentlemen do not speak that way. However, having just climbed the thing I am inclined to agree with Sir Ed.

This is as far as I got after my summit. I was exhausted and my eyes were burning. So I put my PDA away, put drops in my eyes and lay in a prone position until the following morning.

Journal Entry for May 22 (Day 52) - Camp 2 6400 m

Angus and I are back at Camp 2. It is cold and snowing, but we got in before the worst of it. We are both quite tired, but are safe and healthy. I will tell the tale of our summit now:

I wore, from the inside out, my long underwear base layer (top and bottom), my Gore-Tex bib pants, my windstopper vest, and my one piece down suit. On my hands I wore my big high altitude mitts, on my feet I had my Millet Everest boots, liner socks and mountaineering socks, and on my head I wore a balaclava, a North Face windstopper hat, my headlamp, and my oxygen mask.

In my backpack I carried one four litre oxygen bottle, one litre of water in an insulator, my down sweater in case I got cold, my goggles, and that's it.

Inside my various pockets I had snack food, a one litre water bottle, my camera, sun glasses, photos of my family, and sunblock.

Pacing and Oxygen

A quick note about oxygen and pacing. I LOVE bottled oxygen. I think I may even use it at sea level. Climbing Everest is extremely difficult, but doing it without oxygen would be near impossible for me. I found the oxygen gave me tons of energy and really soothed my cough. It was amazing.

Pacing was critical, at least for me. As I have stated in previous posts I use a slow and methodical breathing and stepping approach. Many other people use a sprint and gasp method. They take seven to ten fast steps and then stop, bend over and gasp for breath for a minute or two. The challenge is that these two approaches are not compatible. All the Sherpa seem to use the sprint and gasp method, and about 70% of climbers do as well so that was the pace for the summit bid. I needed to use my pace to keep my breathing under control, but I always ended up with some sprinter gasping at my back. I would also run into the sprinter ahead of me when they were in their gasping phase. It was a pain in the butt let me tell you.

Leaving the South Col

We left Camp 4 on the South Col on a beautiful night, the stars were shining, the full moon was lighting our way and it was warm; too warm actually. I was prepared for the mean Everest. This was the nice Everest and I started to overheat in about three minutes.

Out of camp we walked on broken rock for about five minutes and then we hit the snow. The snow slope started out pretty gentle. As it gets a little steeper

Looking down on Camp 4

learning in THIN AIR

a fixed line appeared. We were walking on glacial ice with a thin covering of snow. In places there was no snow and the ice shone blue in my headlamp. The ice was also as hard as concrete and my crampons barely scratched the surface.

We started to head straight up the glacier at this point. This initial slope was not too steep (25 degrees or so), but it felt much steeper. I used my jumar to help with the upward ascent. The easiest way to do this was to straddle the rope, push the jumar forward, grip the handle with one hand, put the other hand on top of the first and pull while stepping up hill at the same time. This method helped to spread the exertion between my legs and my arms. I was often walking with both feet pointed away from each other at about 45 degrees from center. This provided good traction on the snow and ice, but became uncomfortable after many hours of doing it.

We were going up this initial slope for approximately two to three hours — it was difficult to keep track of time. The pace was pretty slow due to the big line of climbers ahead of me. Even though we had left camp early there were many others who had left before us. Often these were the climbers who thought they would be slow and needed extra time. And they were right, as we caught up to them pretty quickly. It seemed there was always someone moving slowly at the head of the line and this slowed us all down. There was only one rope and passing was nearly impossible, not to mention very dangerous. When the slow person at the head of the line thankfully pulled over for a rest it seemed there was always another slow person ready to take their place. Sometimes a group of the fast people would make a big presentation of passing, only to then become the slow people because they expended so much energy passing that they were reduced to a crawl once they took over the head of the line.

At about hour three, or maybe it was two, we hit the rock. Nobody ever told me about this. It was a slab of shale, on a slight angle, covered with broken shale like gravel. Let me tell you, this was far less than fun. When I would take a step forward I would either skid around on the shale or sink in the gravel and slide backwards. And the high steps were even more fun. Every so often (quite frequently actually) there would be a step I would have to surmount. The step was always just a little too high to be comfortable, and foreshadowed what was to come later. At these steps I would need to look for the best foot placement, hike my foot up, hoping my crampons would gain purchase, grab my jumar with both hands and give it all I had. At the top of the step I would gasp for air.

This loose rock continued for 90 minutes or so, and then I hit the steep rock wall. It was about 20 m of pain. This shale was at about a 45 degree angle, sloping in all directions, with uneven stepping and not made for crampons. What this meant was that you jumarred with all your might, skidding around, and gasping for breath from the exertion.

Eventually getting to the top of this rock band, I was met with the next snow band, which carried on for 60 minutes or so to The Balcony. This snow slope was more to my liking. I was better able to pace myself on this slope and I regained some energy here.

From what I understand, this was a low snow year. Much of the rock I had encountered thus far was often under snow, and therefore much easier to travel across. Too bad for me.

Equipment Issues

I forgot to mention that five minutes after I left camp my headlamp died. Fortunately there was a full moon to light my way. At each anchor transition I would turn my lamp on and it would last for all of about five minutes and then shut off. It was atop of the aforementioned rock band that I replaced my headlamp batteries that worked fabulously for about 30 minutes until it once again died.

Additionally, I absolutely hated my new, expensive, fabulous, high altitude gloves. They were super warm, but had no dexterity at all. Knowing this I decided to wear liner gloves inside them so I could take my big mitts off at transitions, and switch lines with my liner gloves. The problem was that once my liners got a little damp with sweat, they were like Velcro with the mitt. Every time I tried to remove my mitts the liner gloves would get pulled inside out. This was a huge pain so I took off my liners and did the switching with bare hands. Fortunately it was not a very cold night so frostbite was not an issue. If it were cold I may have been forced to turn around or risk the possibility of losing fingers to the cold.

The Balcony

The Balcony is one famous piece of real estate on Mount Everest. It has been the location of many epics in past years and may be this year again. However, one does not just show up at The Balcony. You have to earn it. It took me five and a half hours to earn it and was one of the toughest things I have ever done. The Balcony can be easily identified because it is one of the only substantial flat spaces on the summit push. It can also be identified by a prominent big rock, an abundance of used and waiting to be used oxygen bottles, and by the stunned and exhausted climbers that are standing around in a daze. This spot is used to eat and drink what you can, switch to a new oxygen cylinder (thus the piles of empty and full bottles), and to regain energy for the continued push. I do not know what the statistics are, but I would bet that the majority of

Knife edge ridge looking at the true Summit

people who turn around on summit day do so at The Balcony. It is hard won and demands such a great physical price. I was spent while there, but The Balcony is also tantalizingly close to the summit. It is slightly more than half way.

Pulling up onto The Balcony is excruciating for many climbers, most flop down on the snow to rest just as I did. Although the rest is wonderful it is also a curse. Anyone who has done any long distance endurance running or walking knows that restarting from a rest is very tough. The old physics principle plays true here. A body in motion stays in motion and a body at rest stays at rest. Breaking the momentum of this stop is quite difficult. This is where some climbers find it is just too difficult and daunting to keep going and they turn around.

Even though I was physically exhausted I knew I could not stop. I had to dig down and keep going. I decided that if the weather remained good (it was amazing) and I did not have an equipment malfunction, I would not stop. I would find the energy reserves necessary. This energy came from a mantra I would repeat to myself every time I wanted to stop, every time I thought I could not go another step. This mantra was: Susan, Amy, Colin, Susan, Amy, Colin; my wife and children. This may sound a little sappy, but every climber has their motivator and this was mine. When I would repeat those names in my head my world would shrink, the pain would fade, and I would focus on the task at hand. I would find the energy for the next push.

The South Summit

Leaving The Balcony we had a nice stroll along a gentle slope for about 200 m before starting up a ridge towards the south summit. The ridge started up from The Balcony and then made a hard right and got steeper. It was mostly snow and not too bad going, but it was very long and again demanded a big physical price. However, the cost of admission to the south summit was a long band of rock near the top of the ridge.

The sun started to rise as I was on this ridge. It was amazingly beautiful, but I was really too tired to care at the moment. The full moon was shining brightly to my left and the sky was starting to lighten to my right. For as far as I could see there were mountains. It was a post card. I tried to care, but I just couldn't.

The sun came up just as I was nearing this rock band. As climbers we stood in cue and waited for our turn at torture. The snow up to the start of the rock climb was weak and continually gave way under our feet, causing us to expend even more energy. Once at the face, I looked at the array of old, faded and frayed rope and clipped onto what seemed to be the best rope and heaved myself up one step, then another. I gasped for breath regardless of my supplemental oxygen. I went as fast as I could so as to not delay the climbers

Looking up from the South Summit towards the
Hillary Step and the Summit Ridge

*behind me, but my pace was quite slow. Several times I would rest my head
on my arms and repeat my mantra just to keep going. After a while the angle
eased off and the going became better.*

*At this point the sun broke the horizon and it was truly beautiful. I grabbed
my sunglasses and stuck them on my face. Going snowblind is a huge concern
up here. Basically, without protection the sun will burn your eyes and you will
temporarily lose your sight. This happened to me while climbing in Ecuador.
It is scary and very painful. I did not want it to happen again.*

When I put my sunglasses on, the combination of my body heat, my sweat, and my moist heavy breathing into my mask, acted to instantly fog my glasses. I could hardly see a thing. Think of looking in the mirror when you get out of the shower. You can sort of see, but not much. This was my vision climbing to the south summit. I was forced to pull my glasses slightly away from my face so I could look down and see where I was going. This allowed sunlight in the bottom of my glasses and left my eyes exposed. I knew I was taking a chance here, but I really had no choice. This gap would also allow in any wind to clear the lenses, but it was such a beautiful day there was no wind. Here I was, praying for wind on Everest.

I slowly made my way up the ridge and eventually made it to the south summit. From here I could see the rest of the route laid out before me. It was stunning, one of the most beautiful visions I have ever seen. I sat down to rest and take in the view. I was exhausted, but too close to stop. I could see the Hillary Step and the heavily corniced summit ridge. In this great weather it looked benign, almost fun, but in bad weather this place is a killer. In this area in 1996 many climbers lost their lives, including Rob Hall, Andy Harris and Doug Hanson.

Looking up at the Hilary Step 8790 m

learning in THIN AIR

I gathered my strength and started down. Yes I said down. This is the only time on the push to the summit that you have to go down. There is a beautiful snow slope that leads from the south summit to the final Summit Ridge.

I stumbled down this slope. Reaching the bottom of the snow slope I was overtaken by exhaustion, relief, and anxiety, causing me to have a breathing issue. I felt like I had run out of oxygen, I gasped frantically for breath. I became scared as I could not catch my breath and rescue was not an option. It felt like I had a plastic bag over my head. I tore my mask from my face gasping for what little air was available in the thin atmosphere. I had to concentrate and relax, focus on my breathing. This was all in my mind. Fairly quickly I got my breathing under control and continued up, but this little spell had cost me dearly. My energy reserves were almost gone.

The Hillary Step

To get to the Hillary Step I crossed a long line of sharply sloping limestone that was like a skating rink for my crampons. In years with more snow I imagine this to be an easier traverse, but for me it was painfully difficult.

Finally I was looking up at the Hillary Step. It was only about 12 m high and looked like nothing compared to the rock I had already climbed. The most difficult part about the step was to determine which rope to clip onto.

The main rope used up to Camp 4 and a bit above is what is called 'Korean.' I suppose this is because this is where it is manufactured, but I am not sure. It is a braided polypropylene rope of about 9 mm. This is the type of rope you would buy at the hardware store to tie up your boat, or to secure something to the roof of your car. It is not something any climber would ever associate with climbing, except that is, in the Himalayas. I have been on four Himalayan peaks and it is standard issue. It is very strong and tough and cheap. It is replaced every season so it is considered disposable.

The other type of rope that is used above Camp 4 and in a few other locations is a 5-6 mm accessory cord. This is a smaller version of a real climbing rope. This rope is used high on the mountain and in areas that are considered more dangerous. It is light to carry and has a reasonable strength, but it is a little disconcerting when you are looking at a 1500 m fall and all that is holding you up (and many others at the same time) is a 5-6 mm cord (about the thickness of a pencil). Again, this would never be done in other parts of the world, but is standard on the biggest and most dangerous mountains in the world.

So these are the ropes that hung in front of me on the Hillary Step. There must have been 20 or more of them. I chose the one that looked the newest and the least faded and clipped on. The other ropes, while a hindrance on the way down, helped on the way up by providing hand holds. I grabbed a handful of rope, hoisted my foot up high and began to climb the Hillary Step. There was very little snow so it was mostly a rock climb. A moment later I was gasping for air having just climbed the Hillary Step.

The Summit

At the top of the step there was a tricky move over a slanted rock to a narrow ledge. The move over this was far from pretty and I smeared myself across it. Once on the ledge I moved towards the true Summit Ridge. The Summit Ridge is a beautiful ridge that slopes on a 45 degree angle on one side and 90 degrees on the other. The one side falls away about 2000 m into Nepal while the other side falls away 3500 m into Tibet. Not a place to slip. From here I could see the summit, but it was still agonizingly far away due to my slow speed of ascent.

After about another 15 minutes I took the last steps to the summit of Mount Everest. I was standing on the top of the world. It was 8:15 am on May 21st.

What did I do when I got there? I threw my hands up in the air in a gesture of victory and then sat down in the snow and cried. So many emotions were flooding through me at that time. I had just achieved a lifetime goal. Unfortunately I was too exhausted to really appreciate my accomplishment. I hoisted my camera over my head and took some random shots. I took a personal photo and had my Sherpa climbing partner, Kala, take a few summit photos of me. The photos were not the best, but at the time, I did not really have the energy to care. I regret that now, but at the time, it was what it was. I was sitting about 3 m below the true summit where there are flags marking the top. I wanted to go to the top for a photo, but there was a big group there sitting, talking and taking photos. When I approached, their Sherpa said not to interrupt his group and would not allow others to the top. They hogged the summit for close to 30 minutes. By the time they left, my energy level was very low. I stepped up to the top, but took no photo. I was too anxious to start down.

It had taken me just over 11 hours to get there. Angus arrived about 20 minutes before me, and Al arrived about 15 minutes after me. I stayed on the top for about 30-40 minutes and all too soon it was time to go. It would be a long journey down.

Summiting on May 21 2008
was an overwhelming feeling

Learning in Thin Air - Inspiring Vision

I had achieved my goal — the vision that formed in my mind so many years ago had been achieved.

At least, partially. I still had to get myself safely down the mountain — that was a key part of my vision.

While on the mountain I often thought about the Deliberate Success Model (pg. 44) that I had developed for use in my business. To achieve success you need to have a vision, determine the actions and then reflect often. Whether it is in business or on a mountain, having a vision is more important than almost anything else. Your visions are your foundation from which everything else will flow. It is difficult for you to expect others to live up to your expectations if they do not know what they are. It is not enough just to say that we will be a 'high performance team.' What does that really mean? If you cannot define it, you cannot measure it. If you cannot measure it, you don't know whether you are achieving it or not.

Each person will define the vision differently based on their personal values. Therefore, you must develop a vision based on the collective team values. This will provide direction and can be used as a measuring stick. A great vision is inspiring and can be used to make almost any decision. Most organizations have a vision printed on a plaque and hung on the wall somewhere, but few people know what it is. If a vision is not known or memorable it is useless. A vision needs to be simple and striking at the same time.

It is critical to spend time to develop the appropriate vision and to make sure everyone understands it and commits to it. Once the vision is in place you need to figure out what actions will bring this vision to life. These actions can encompass a mission statement, tasks, roles and responsibilities as well as operational norms or a code of conduct. It is crucial that everyone knows how their role contributes to bringing the vision to life.

learning in THIN AIR

The last part of creating a successful vision is to reflect upon it frequently. For us on Everest we would have weekly reflection meetings just to be introspective and to check in on how we were doing. This would provide a time for open and honest communication and any course corrections if necessary.

It was during our 10 day trek to Base Camp that we really developed our vision and laid out the actions that would bring this vision to life. In a business environment you may have a little more time than we did on Everest, but it is no less important. Make sure to take the time to lay a solid foundation consisting of relationship and vision and then develop the actions to bring it all to life. These simple steps will give you a much greater chance at developing into a high performance team and will allow you to more easily deal with change and stress.

View from the top of the world May 21 2008

Coming Down

I WAS now at the summit, but needed to get down. Ed Viesters, the first American to climb all fourteen 8000 m peaks without oxygen always says "getting to the summit is optional, getting back to Base Camp is mandatory." I was now in the mandatory part.

Departing the Summit

Journal Entry for May 21 (Day 51) - The descent to Camp 4; leaving the summit; zombie climber; stuck at Hillary Step; The Balcony and Al; O2 issue; Camp 4

The views at the summit were spectacular, but I was not really in a state of mind to appreciate it. I sat around for a while at 8848 m without my mask on and started to feel the effects of the lack of oxygen. I had a difficult time breathing and walking around and my memory was not very good.

It did not really feel real. I thought it was a dream. Did I really do this? It is such a huge project and commitment and so few people actually make it. It has still not really sunk in. Susan did some research and it appears that Angus and I are (give or take a number or two) the 50th and 51st Canadians to have summited Mount Everest.

Eventually I decided it was time to go. I was so tired I was a little concerned about getting down safely, as 80% of fatalities on Mount Everest happen on the descent.

People are working at the extent of their physical and mental abilities. They are exhausted from being awake for over 36 hours and from having burned way more calories than they have taken in. I have been told that climbers burn 1000 calories per hour on summit day and can easily burn 20-30,000 calories during the summit push. These reasons combine to create a deadly mix causing climbers to lose their focus and make mistakes.

Ultimately I think success has a huge part to play in the accidents that happen on the way down from the summit. There is the saying that "nothing fails like success" and this is so true on Everest. Many people blow all their energy to get to the top and have next to nothing left for the way down. Their adrenaline levels drop because they have reached their goal and things start to go downhill from there. I have seen climbers on the summit who appear to be in good shape only to see them 10 minutes later near death as cerebral edema, pulmonary edema or physical exhaustion takes over. I had no desire to join this group so I started down slowly and methodically. I asked Kala to turn up my oxygen to a flow rate of 3 litres per minute so I could move better.

The first few steps were painful, but I forced my body to keep going. The view was amazing. I had not really taken the time to appreciate it on the way up. It was just keep your head down and put one foot in front of the other. Now I noticed the array of mountains spread out before me. The sky was almost cloudless so I could see for hundreds of miles in any direction. There was nothing that could block my view. I could even see what appeared to be the curvature of the earth from where I was. I watched Angus slip off ahead of me and disappear down the Hillary Step. At the top of the Hillary Step my progress ground to a stop.

As we were some of the first climbers to reach the summit, there were many, many climbers coming up the Step as we were trying to go down. In many cases, common courtesy is thrown out on Everest. The obvious thing to do is to allow a few people to come up and a few people to go down. Take turns. Well, this is not what happened. The climbers kept coming up with no break. I was standing on a narrow ledge, hooked to a safety line and could not see the bottom of the Step and how many people were there.

As the climbers passed us they had to unclip from the safety line, walk around us and clip back in on the other side. This was a daunting prospect at best as a slip while unclipped would mean a fall of about 900 m. As the climbers

learning in THIN AIR

Line of climbers going up and down

unclipped to go around me I would make myself as small as possible to give them space and give them my hand to help them past. Although scary, it worked.

One climber decided that he would not unclip. He looked at me and just started walking. I guess he thought he would go through me somehow. His tether was clipped to the same rope as mine so as he got closer his line started to move across my body. He pushed harder and started to bend me backwards. Soon his tether reached my neck and he kept pushing. I could not breathe, but he did not care. He was determined to somehow pass right through me. Several people saw what was happening and they jumped on him. They pushed him back and physically unclipped him from the rope. He said nothing, but just kept going. He was in some sort of trance. He was not in the same world with the rest of us. Was it summit fever or hypoxia? I'll never know. All I know is that it was strange.

I have modified a saying to help explain the weird stuff that goes on here at Everest. I recently watched the movie Blood Diamond and in that movie a lot of bad and weird things happen. They explain it by saying TIA - This

Is Africa. I have changed it to TIE - This Is Everest. It does not make things right, it just means it is a different world up here.

After the strangling incident I still stood at the top of the Hillary Step waiting. The line of people coming up did not stop. Finally I looked down to a climber approaching the Step and yelled "You, in the blue, STOP" and I waved my hand in an emphatic stop gesture. He stared at me and stopped, took a few more steps, looked up at me once again and sat down in the snow. The line in front of that person kept going until it ran out and we could finally descend. We had stood at the top of the Hillary Step for 90 minutes. It was crazy. At this height we were living on borrowed time as so many things could have gone wrong in those 90 minutes. I got to the top of the Step, skittered over the angled rock and looked at the mess of ropes to climb down. I grabbed a handful of rope and started to lower myself down the face. My crampons became entangled in the rope and I started to invert. It took all my energy to stop myself and correct my descent. Several years ago a climber died in exactly this same way. He got caught in the ropes on the Hillary Step, ended up upside down and alone. He could not free himself from the rope and died. I made it to the base of the Step safely and worked my way around the waiting climbers towards the South Summit.

To make it to the South Summit I had to go up the slope I had previously gone down. Going up was very tough. I made it to the top of the South Summit and sat down for a rest. Al showed up with Lama Tame Sherpa and sat down. Lama Tame looked at him and said "no rest, too late in the day, go down now." Al looked at him and reluctantly said OK. I too started down. I was so exhausted that I had to sit down and rest every 60-90 m. I knew I was tired when I had to rest going downhill. I crossed the rock at the base of the South Summit and slumped in the snow. I would then move a little further down the hill and sit down in the snow. I found as I would sit down I would involuntarily moan out loud. I have heard people doing this on mountains before and found it strange, but never understood it. Now I was doing it. I was exhausted and in physical pain from every movement.

I continued down and told Kala that we would stop and take a break at The Balcony. I was beyond exhausted stopping every 30 m to take a break, but the thought of that break kept me going. Eventually I made it to The Balcony and collapsed in the snow.

learning in THIN AIR

I pulled out my water and a snack to eat. I lay in the snow and stared at the sky. Eventually I had enough energy to keep going and grabbed my pack to put it on. I looked at my oxygen regulator to turn it up a bit because I was feeling so bad. When I looked at it I saw that it was set at 0.5 liters per minute. I couldn't believe my eyes.

On the way up I was running at 2-2.5 litres per minute. When I got to the top I was exhausted using this flow. After my rest on the top, I asked Kala to turn me back on for the descent. I wanted it at 3 litres per minute, but I guess he wanted to conserve oxygen so he set it at 0.5. As a result, I was way more tired than I needed to be. Once we reached The Balcony, I realized how low it was and I was shocked. I cranked it to 3 and moved down hill.

The difference was amazing. I was a whole new person. I moved ahead of Kala and left him in my dust. I was a little upset that I had suffered so badly when a little more oxygen could have solved my problem and made the descent way more comfortable.

After a four hour descent I walked into Camp 4. I was tired, but not too bad. Ryan met me with a cup of juice and we talked for a few minutes. Ryan had problems with his regulator during the summit bid as he was not getting a clear flow of oxygen. He was essentially climbing without oxygen which is extremely difficult. The oxygen also helps to keep climbers warm. Just above The Balcony Ryan decided he was too cold and moving too slow and turned around. Alan also returned to Camp 4 after climbing to The Balcony. I have not spoken to Alan and do not know exactly what happened. I do know that making it to The Balcony takes a huge toll on a person physically and mentally.

Once in camp, I took off my climbing gear and slid into the tent. Angus was already there resting. He did not have the same hold up at the Hillary Step so he made it down much faster than I did. Kala soon arrived and we made water and soup. The next thing we did was to strap our oxygen masks to our face and go to sleep.

Alan had already descended to Camp 2 with Lama Babu Sherpa before I returned to Camp 4 and Al arrived in camp about two hours after me. Ryan decided to make a second attempt that night. I thought it was a good idea at

Scott and climbing partner Angus arrive safely at Camp 4

the time, but was concerned about his energy level, his lack of rest, and that he would go alone. Ryan started for the top around 8:00 pm as Angus and I went to sleep. I slept amazingly well that night and woke the next morning feeling refreshed.

Rumours of Death

Journal Entry for May 22 (Day 52) - Descent from Camp 4 to Camp 2; rumours of death, the body; Scott Fischer
After a good night's sleep it was time to leave Camp 4. I know that Camp 4 can be a very hostile place, but while I was there it was a pretty nice place. It was warm with no wind and the views were spectacular.

Even though I had a great summit night, the night was not without tragedy. Reports of several deaths were in the air. Rumours were saying that three had died, but this was unconfirmed. I could not understand how anyone could

learning in THIN AIR

have died on such a beautiful night. Two of the people I personally talked to during the summit push were reported to be dead.

When I got out of my tent in the morning there was a body wrapped in a tent fly not far from me so it was true that at least one person had died. The other two turned out to still be alive — barely. They had spent a night out at The Balcony and had somehow survived. As far as I know they are still alive, but I do not know their condition or where they are on the mountain.

As I was descending from the summit I also came across another body not too far above Camp 4. As I was rappelling just below The Balcony I saw some colour in the snow just off to my left. As I got closer I could see it was a person, but the person was not moving. As I got closer yet I saw that it was the body of a climber who had died on the mountain. From the faded clothing I could tell that he was not recently dead, but he was still perfectly preserved. It was almost as if he had sat down for a rest and would get up any minute. It is so cold and dry up here that bodies are pretty much flash frozen and little to no decomposition occurs. Later I was told that the body was Scott Fischer and having read the book "Into Thin Air" about the 1996 tragedy on Everest when Scott Fischer died I feel that it could actually be him. The location that he was reported to have died was exactly where I saw this body. I was told the body was usually covered with snow, but since this was a low snow year the body had come to the surface. Usually the bodies are interred in a crevasse or pushed over a cliff, but in this location there were no options.

It was kind of surreal to see a dead person laying there. In all my years of climbing this was the first time I had come across a dead body. I don't really know what I felt. In some ways it was

Most Deadliest Year

1996 was the deadliest in Everest history with 15 people losing their lives. On May 10-11 eight climbers lost their lives including two of the most experienced guides in the world; Rob Hall and Scott Fischer. There are many factors that led to this tragedy and much learning has resulted. Ultimately it was the storm that killed these climbers, but it was a breakdown in leadership, teamwork, communication, and personal accountability that put them in this vulnerable position.

kind of interesting because I was seeing a part of Everest history but it was sad at the same time. No person, regardless of how much they love climbing, wants to die on the mountain. Scott Fischer was so young and had so much life in front of him. Everest is a very dangerous place, but for some reason Everest smiled upon me.

Descent from Camp 4

Journal Entry for May 22 (Day 52) – Leaving Camp; oxygen issue; snow blind climber; Geneva Spur and Yellow Band; injured climber; Camp 3; rap down Lhotse Face; Camp 2

Angus and I had spent the night at Camp 4. Just after my arrival in camp from the summit I had a lot to drink and some food to eat and then I laid down to rest. I had my oxygen mask on at a flow rate of 0.5 litres per minute and I slept like a stone. I woke up around 7:00 am and went to the bathroom for the first time in about 20 hours. I guess I was a little dehydrated. We

Descending the Yellow Band after our summit

learning in THIN AIR

then prepared some food and water and started to pack up for our descent to Camp 2.

Angus and I set out from Camp 4 around 9:00 am. Before we departed Angus and I had both run out of oxygen. I searched through a pile of oxygen bottles to try to find a couple of full ones. I was able to find a full one, but Angus kept looking. After a few minutes he declared that he did not need the oxygen and that he was sick of looking so he would just go without. A few moments later I found him a bottle, but he did not want it. He had put his mask and regulator away and was a little grumpy about it. He was tired and the lack of oxygen was starting to play with his mind. He was in no mood for argument so I just shrugged my shoulders and said "your choice" as we left camp.

I was wearing oxygen and Angus was not. The difference in our level of performance and speed became immediately obvious. After only about 150 m Angus looked at me and said that perhaps he had made a mistake in not taking the oxygen. We should have just gone back and got the bottle, but the effort seemed too monumental at the time so we elected to keep going downhill slowly. When his breathing became too laboured, we would stop and I would remove the mask from my face and give it to Angus. We were buddy breathing just like we would if we were SCUBA diving. After a few moments of rest and a lot of deep breathing I would put the mask back on and we would keep going.

There was a bit of a slow down at the top of the Geneva Spur as a climber who was snow blind was being helped down. This would not be a fun way to leave Camp 4, but I suspect it is not that uncommon.

Angus and I descended the Geneva Spur with no problem and started the traverse across the Lhotse face towards the Yellow Band. Part way across the traverse we saw a climber being lowered from the Lhotse high camp. The climber could not walk and was being belayed down the face. We stopped and I offered them my oxygen, but they declined. I have no idea what was wrong with the injured climber as their English was not good enough to explain it to us. The situation seemed to be well in hand so we moved on. It would be a long and hard descent for the pair.

It was a glorious day as we continued our descent. As we got lower Angus felt better in the thicker air and our need to buddy breathe soon became unnecessary. We got to our Camp 3 and took a break. I was very hot in my down suit so I changed out of it into my standard climbing gear. I continued to use oxygen down the Lhotse face as it just made me feel so good. Most people take their oxygen off at this point, but I figured that if I was going to carry it I might as well use it. And besides, I loved the extra boost it gave me.

Our four hour descent to Camp 2 was spectacular. I loved it! It was a great mountaineering experience to rappel down the Lhotse face heading back to Camp 2. After reaching the base of the Lhotse face we started the walk to Camp 2 arriving around 1:00 pm. I spent the rest of the day resting, eating and drinking.

Descent to Base Camp

WE WOKE this morning to three pieces of bad news: 1) it was snowing and windy, not looking too good for our descent, 2) Lama Tame could not see due to being snowblind, and 3) Ryan was not doing well at Camp 4.

Ryan was extremely tired from his summit and was experiencing some health issues. I was not there so I cannot say exactly what was going on, but we were all quite worried.

We gave Lama Tame some eye drops and told him to stay in a tent with his eyes closed, we could not really do much else for him. He would just need time to recover (usually 24 hours). He would be well looked after by the rest of the Sherpa team.

The weather was getting worse so we had to go. Ryan was in radio contact with the camp and was slowly making his way down.

Journal Entry for May 23 (Day 53) - Descent to Base Camp; through the Icefall; Ryan in trouble
Angus, Al and I left Camp 2 around 10:00 am. It was snowing and blowing, but not too bad. We were all pretty tired from our summit and our climb down to Camp 2, but we only had to make it to Base Camp for our summit to

**Celebrating our summit success
and our last trip through the Icefall**

be official (in my mind at least). It was a relatively warm day so the snow was wet and stuck to our faces and clothing. The trail was fairly easy to follow which was good because as the snow intensified and the wind picked up, visibility became about 30 m or less. I loved it. This is what mountaineering is all about; a small team of climbers making their way through the mountain wilderness. Few other people were on the trail so we pretty much had the route to ourselves. We made it to Camp 1 no problem and headed for the Icefall.

The Icefall was beautiful. There was a coating of fresh snow and no people to be seen. We started down in the silence and worked together to get through the Icefall safely.

Because of all the fresh snow there were quite a few avalanches as we proceeded through the area. Mostly they were far away, but a few sounded too close for comfort. I was not too worried however, as the route descends down the middle of the Icefall and there are tons of cracks everywhere to absorb an avalanche before it would ever reach us.

The snow stopped as we continued to walk. I really enjoyed my last trip through the Icefall. Perhaps exactly because it was my LAST TRIP THROUGH THE ICEFALL.

As we got close to the bottom we were met by Chering and some of our other Base Camp Sherpa. They had come out to meet us, congratulate us and to give us juice and beer. It was a nice welcome, but we were all anxious to get to Base Camp. We downed our drinks and finished the walk to camp.

Once in Base Camp we changed out of our climbing clothing. Mine were incredibly stinky. I had been wearing the same clothing (all layers) for a week. I walked in them, ate in them, and slept in them. My Gore-Tex pants proved to be quite an odour barrier as I did not think I was too smelly until I took them off. Then I realized it was bad. I gave myself a baby wipe bath in my tent and put on different (not necessarily clean) clothing. We then had a big lunch.

After lunch the tension in camp increased greatly. Ryan was not doing well and was sitting in Camp 3 in need of help. He was suspected of being severely dehydrated and having the start of HAPE. It was very bad news. Our friend, Phil, was at Camp 2 and started up with Sherpa, oxygen, medication and drinks. There were a tense few hours as we waited to see what would happen.

There were also apparently many other teams in trouble on the mountain. Bad weather had moved in higher on the mountain and it was becoming a survival situation up there.

Partly due to the lack of acclimatization, people were having a hard time dealing with the bad weather. Many people had not fully acclimatized due to the climbing restrictions imposed by the Olympic Torch carry. It turned out the storm was not too bad and that Ryan made it to Camp 2 without too much trouble. Before we went to bed we were told he was sleeping on oxygen at Camp 2 and taking medication for his condition. He was not out of the woods yet, but was doing much better. A crazy few days.

Update on Mountain Safety and Rescue

Since I left the South Col the weather has been far from perfect. Coming down in the wind, snow, and whiteout conditions was actually quite fun for

learning in THIN AIR

me. This is what mountaineering is all about. However, going up in these conditions is a different story and people with different levels of experience will react differently.

There have been multiple reports of frostbite by many climbers, and Angus and I saw a climber being lowered from the Lhotse high camp. This climber could not walk for a reason unknown to me. I suspect the climber may have had frostbite. Angus and I could not really offer much help, but I did offer them my oxygen which they declined.

Many people are probably wondering about Ryan. I don't have any details right now but it seems Ryan had a rough summit and may have suffered some health issues. He spent last night at Camp 2 with many people and is on his way down to Base Camp now. He is not in danger.

One of our Sherpa, Lama Tame, suffered severe snow blindness on the way from Camp 4 to Camp 2. Why he was not wearing eye protection I do not know. He lost his vision and was in severe pain in Camp 2. We left him in the care of his fellow Sherpa yesterday as we made our way back to Base Camp. I was just told that he is doing much better today and will start his descent later in the day.

Mount Everest

Reflections on the Climb

AND SO ends my journal of Everest. This adventure is over and I achieved my goal.

From this point, we returned to civilization. I was met at the airport at home by my wife and wonderful children. I started to live a life in which I was a member of a very small club within the human race to have summited the highest mountain on earth. I feel very fortunate to have made the summit on my first attempt, something that only about 15% of climbers do.

Now that the expedition is over it is amazing to look back upon this journey. I would love to come back to Everest one day, but having achieved my goal I know that I don't need to.

Angus and Scott with their Yeti foot

Up until recently every Everest team who summited would go to the Rum Doodle restaruant in Kathamndu and have their personalized Yeti foot put onto the wall.

Learning in Thin Air - Being Personally Accountable

What was perhaps the most important lesson from my successful summit of Everest?

Perhaps it is personal accountability.

When I look at the role that we play as an individual in success and failure I see that we can play one of two parts; to be accountable — or to be the victim.

learning in THIN AIR

Playing the victim is easy; it implies that someone else has done something to us. Victims can make excuses: "It was not my fault!" "I had no control over the results."

Being accountable is far scarier, as it means that we played a role in our failure, and that we could have altered the results through our own actions.

On Everest there were many people who did not make it to the summit, and some would say they failed. Others who did not make it to the summit did succeed, though, because they were accountable for everything they did — including a wise decision, in the light of extreme circumstances, that it would not be a 'smart thing' to continue on.

So perhaps we can't judge success with Everest as to whether one has reached the top or not. The ultimate is whether one has succeeded in being personally accountable to their own true selves.

There are many reasons for failure on Everest; lack of physical fitness, bad weather, lack of technical skills — the list is endless. But true failure comes from those who play the victim and blame these external forces — not their own selves — for their results. They become too focused on the Circle of Concern - not the Circle of Influence.

On the other hand, those who succeed — regardless of whether they achieve the summit or not — have focused on their Circle of Influence. They've come to realize that if they own the role they played in their attempt (i.e. their accountability), then they have the power to make the best decisions for their long term growth as a person.

Circle of Concern. Circle of Influence. It's a powerful choice, and is one of the most important lessons from my summit experience.

YOUR ATTITUDE DETERMINES YOUR ALTITUDE!

Fried Spam, Scott's high altitude treat!

Learning from
the Mountain

I LOVED my Everest expedition — every part of it.

In my mind, I vividly remember distinct sections and elements to what was truly a very long journey.

Base Camp was great. It was a fun and enjoyable place to spend almost two months. Not quite Club Med, but great none the less. Our Base Camp Sherpa team was amazing. The food was plentiful and high in quality. This is so important on an Everest expedition. Without high quality and high calorie food, climbers quickly lose weight and strength and have very little chance for success. The social aspect of Base Camp was also fun; even for an introvert like me. With my team we played cards, Monopoly and watched a lot of DVD movies. I would wander over to other camps during the day and visit with other climbers that I knew and meet new ones. And then there were the parties. I think we had the most active party camp on Everest in 2008. Not that we were being silly frat boys and girls, but we were having a good time and doing our best to create a good environment within which to live.

The Icefall was beautiful and scary at the same time. It was a challenge every time I went through it, but the physical exertion made me stronger for the summit. The absolute beauty of the Icefall is without comparison and its danger is unmistakable. I think it is the combination of the beauty and the danger that made it such an appealing place for me. The absolute white of the snow contrasted with the turquoise blue of the ice to create a beautiful physical environment. The route was complex and ever changing. The ladder crossings were exciting and scary at the same time. I loved to stop in the middle of a long crossing and just enjoy my situation. I mean, how many people ever get to do this in their lives?

Camp 1 was really just a waypoint on the way to Camp 2. We only spent 2 nights at Camp 1 throughout the expedition. Once we were acclimatized it was better to push past Camp 1 and go directly to Camp 2 from Base Camp.

Camp 2 was not the most comfortable place in the world, but it was amazing to be in the Western Cwm. The huge valley had such a contrast in temperatures from scorching hot in the day to freezing cold in the night. Fortunately we had a good sized communal tent that we could congregate in for meals and conversations. We had a permanent cook staff at Camp 2 who provided us with good, nutritious food. Not the same variety as at Base Camp, but pretty good. One complaint about Camp 2 was that our cook was not very skilled at preparing one of Angus and my favourite snacks; fried Spam. This may not sound appealing, and at sea level I don't even really like it, but at high altitude it is rich and creamy and fatty and salty and delicious. The key is in how it is cooked. It must be sliced thin and fried until crispy. If it is just warmed up and mushy it is hard to swallow.

Many people do not like Camp 3 and most of the Sherpa will not even spend the night there. I loved it. It was an amazing and beautiful place. I spent a couple great nights there and we had fun as a team. The views from our tent were spectacular. I could look down on Pimori and see out across the Himalaya to Cho Oyu and many other amazing mountains.

The Lhotse face was challenging but exciting. My first trip up was a test for me and I felt if I could get up the Lhotse face without too much trouble I had a reasonable chance at the summit. I felt that I had at least earned a shot at the top. As I progressed further up the face towards Camp 4 I crossed the Yellow Band. Crossing rock with crampons is not always fun, but it is exciting in a painful kind of way. Camp 3 was also where I started to use oxygen for the first time. I was skeptical at first, but quickly came to love the gas I take for granted at sea level.

Camp 4, the death zone, was spectacular. There is so much rich history here. If only these rocks could talk. Camp 4 can be hell on earth, but when I was there it seemed warm, gentle and inviting. I strolled around to explore a bit,

learning in THIN AIR

but strolling is not all that easy in the death zone. I could not help but think about the saga that played out here in 1996 with so many people dying and being injured.

The summit push was immensely challenging, but I loved it because of that. There were so many challenges that I did not expect. Even though I had studied the route and read numerous accounts of the summit route, so much seemed unknown to me. Perhaps it was due to the low amount of snow on the mountain this year that made it so different. Watching the sun rise from just below the South Summit was spectacular.

Standing on the summit of Mount Everest was a dream come true. What an amazing journey I have been on. I could see for hundreds of miles in any direction and I felt pretty good considering where I was and what I had done.

Learning in Thin Air — C.L.I.M.B.

What is it that I have taken from all of this? George Mallory had an interesting take on this exact question back in 1922. He said "The first question which you will ask and which I must try to answer is this, "What is the use of climbing Mount Everest?" and my answer must at once be, "It is no use." There is not the slightest prospect of any gain whatsoever. Oh, we may learn a little about the behaviour of the human body at high altitudes, and possibly medical men may turn our observation to some account for the purposes of aviation. But otherwise nothing will come of it. We shall not bring back a single bit of gold or silver, not a gem, nor any coal or iron. We shall not find a single foot of earth that can be planted with crops to raise food. It's no use. So, if you cannot understand that there is something in man which responds to the challenge of this mountain and goes out to meet it, that the struggle is the struggle of life itself upward and forever upward, then you won't see why we go. What we get from this adventure is just sheer joy. And joy is, after all, the end of life. We do not live to eat and make money. We eat and make money to be able to enjoy life. That is what life means and what life is for."

Climbing for me is about living life, but it does not stop there. When I reflect on the Everest expedition I am amazed at our success, especially given the complex political challenges that were layered onto an already extreme undertaking. The politics of the climb were not really what I planned for, but in the end they turned out to be a blessing of sorts. Not only did we need to deal with the standard challenges of climbing Mount Everest (high altitude sickness, avalanches, crevasse falls, the Icefall, physical exhaustion, etc), but we had to deal with political challenges unlike anything ever seen on Everest before. This created such a rich learning environment for me. I was able to examine teamwork, leadership, communication, and change management in a non-stop, high stress challenging environment.

I find it even more striking when I compare it with my climb of Cho Oyu years earlier. Everest is so much bigger, more challenging and more dangerous. Our Everest climbing team was considerably older and likely less fit and yet we were extremely successful.

What had created the difference between success and failure on these two peaks?

By the time of the Everest climb, I was well underway in applying the lessons of my climbing experiences to the world of business. I was deep in thought and reflection on the elements of climbing — what might make for success, and what had led to failure? Remember, by the time of Everest, I had summited dozens of peaks throughout the world — and was busy teaching, leading team and leadership development sessions, and applying my unique mountain lessons to the world of business.

During my Everest expedition I took the time to talk to my teammates about those lessons. I attribute our success to making the deliberate effort to develop our team using the Deliberate Success Model (pg. 44) — something we had been practicing from the earliest moments of the expedition!

What did it help us to achieve? We created a common team vision of success. Not just the goal of reaching the summit (results), but also how we would behave and interact as a high performance team (culture). We took

learning in THIN AIR

deliberate actions all along the way to lead to that vision, and we reflected together and often on how we were doing.

Through the Deliberate Success Model, we attended to five main factors that were at play. These conveniently fit into the acronym C.L.I.M.B., a great way to help to remember the key elements.

We spoke of these things right from the start and throughout the expedition. I believe that, had we not placed emphasis on these five factors, we would not have been successful. This belief is reinforced by my observations of other teams that failed to focus on these five areas and, not surprisingly, fell apart before they could achieve success.

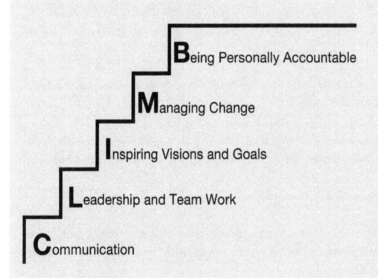

Being Personally Accountable

Managing Change

Inspiring Visions and Goals

Leadership and Team Work

Communication

Communication

As an expedition team, communication was critical to our functioning, whether it was discussing our options with respect to the military restrictions, or the constantly changing weather conditions. Being part of a climbing team is unlike the typical day to day business world; however, just as good communication was critical for our team, so too, is it critical to any business environment.

As a team we discussed and reviewed what our vision of a great team communication plan would consist of — we agreed that we would have to provide for a lot of structured communication on top of the regular unstructured communication we might have.

Once we agreed on what the vision was we put this into action by establishing two formal communication touch points each day. We would have a morning meeting where we would discuss our plans for the day, the role we would play, the resources we would need and we would answer any questions.

At the end of the day we would meet to review the day; what went well, what did not go so well, what we had learned, and what we needed to do to prepare for the next day. These two daily meetings provided a formal opportunity for communication and assured that we were all on the same page.

Obviously, we would have several informal communication touch points throughout the day as well.

Overall, the key was to create a culture of communication — one that was open and honest, supported through trusting and supportive relationships.

Leadership and Teamwork

Leadership is critical to the success of any team or project as the leader has tremendous influence over the formation of team culture and the ultimate success of the team.

A good leader also has a high level of 'emotional intelligence.' They have the ability to connect and interact with others more effectively and deal well with the pressures and stresses of work and life. I also believe that a good leader has a personal vision of who they want to be. This vision guides their development and how they interact with others in various situations.

We were very fortunate that our expedition leader had a personal vision and a high level of emotional intelligence. He saw that we all wanted, and needed, to take a leadership role on Everest. He was able to lead and share the lead therefore making for a successful climb.

His ability to focus on and change what we could rather than focusing on things we could not change helped all of us to deal with the stresses of the expedition. I often compare his role and skill as a leader with our leader on Cho Oyu. The contrast couldn't be more extreme.

Inspiring Vision and Goals

Successful business organizations have a clear vision and goals; so too must an expedition. In this case our vision was two fold: 1) to climb Mount Everest; and 2) the vision of the team we wanted to be. The culture vision may seem soft and fluffy to some, but it is so critical in the development of a high performance team. While teaching at the University of Edinburgh I heard a great quote, "Bad culture will eat great strategy for breakfast and everything else by tea time." Once the vision is clear, goals will help you stay focused.

The setting of multiple goals for our expedition was also critical for us to succeed. For me it started way before I ever got to Everest. I had my big dream vision, to climb Everest, but there were countless goals that kept me focused along the way. If you are anything like me, you work better when focused on a goal.

I set climbing goals and fitness goals and these led me on my track to Everest. These goals changed along the way and sometimes I faltered, but having my Everest goals always brought me back to where I needed to be. I have learned that personally I am lost without a goal. When I have no goal I get lazy and my creativity drops. It even affects my general mood and enjoyment in life. I have learned that for me goal setting is critical in success and overall life enjoyment.

Clearly when our team arrived at Everest we were focused on the big vision. But when we arrived and looked at the summit so far above, we decided to focus on smaller interim goals first. We were preparing for the summit, but that was not our immediate goal. We focused on establishing Base Camp and getting our initial warm up and training done — an interim goal. Then we focused on getting to Camp 1, and then Camp 2 and then Camp 3, and so on. We focused on eating well, exercising, and staying healthy.

When we set off for the summit my goal was not to make it to the top, but to make it to the top and back down again. The survival part trumped all, and I think because I had this very strong focus it gave me the power and the resolve to endure the physical and mental hardships.

Managing Change

Change is the only constant in life; it's long been a truism that those that cannot adjust to change will be left behind, whether in the world of business or in your personal life.

And perhaps one of the most important lessons I have learned involves how you manage the Circle of Concern and your Circle of Influence — for this will have a huge impact on how you deal with change. Try to focus your attention and energy on that which you have influence over and you will find that you have much greater success. You will probably also find that you have less stress in your life and can be happier.

Change on this expedition was constant from the very start — from our climbing restrictions and military presence to changing weather and climbing challenges — but as a team we agreed to focus on those things we could change or have influence over. As a result we made a great decision to throw a party on the mountain — simply because we realized with the military on the scene, there was nothing better to do to alleviate our stress!

learning in THIN AIR

Being Personally Accountable

Last but not least, being accountable for your attitude, your outlook on life, and being purposeful in your passion is critical to your success.

On Everest there were many people who did not make it to the summit — some would say they failed. Yet there can be many reasons for failure on Everest; lack of physical fitness, bad weather, lack of technical skills, and more. Sometimes failure happens on Everest simply because people are ill prepared for the challenge that lay ahead. Sadly, as we have seen in so many situations, this has led to tragedy.

Yet, other people who are well equipped to master Everest fail to make it to the summit — due to the fact that they burn themselves out by focusing on the Circle of Concern. Often these people will also lay the blame for their failure on an external force, rather than thinking about the personal reasons that might have held back their success.

I know people who were climbing Everest at the same time as I did and they did not make it to the top. They will tell you they failed because of the military, because of the government, or other factors beyond their control. The thing is, I was there too and I experienced these exact same factors and I was successful.

What makes for the difference? In any situation we make a conscious choice to play the victim (blaming something other than ourselves), or we can choose to be accountable.

When on Everest, or in any personal or business situation, we often find that we have a choice to make. That's what accountability is all about — it's the personal drive to succeed; the personal belief that one can do it; and by learning that it is better to focus on what we can influence rather than on what we can't.

Summit of Mount Elbrus 2010

Mountains
as a Metaphor

I WAS born 2 months premature weighing only 3lbs 6oz. The first several months of my life were a challenge and I guess somehow this set me on a course. Seeking challenge and adventure has always been a part of me. Who could have ever dreamed that I would go from such an early crisis to a full, rich and rewarding life that would see me climb the Seven Summits, build a rewarding and ever growing business, and have a wonderful and supportive family.

Each of my adventures has provided me with a continuous stream of lessons on life and more specifically on leadership and teamwork. And as you have read these experiences are often far from ordinary!

After a brief pause from Everest, my focus on climbing continued with summit number six - Mount Elbrus in Caucasus, Russia. At 5642 m Mount Elbrus is the highest point in all of Europe.

By the time of Mount Elbrus, I had a fairly active blog which chronicled my ongoing adventures for my friends, followers and business acquaintances; I would share my adventures and learning with anyone who was interested. I did not think that this minor expedition to Russia would be all too exciting, but I was quite mistaken. I would have thought my experiences with the military on Everest would have been once in a lifetime, but Russia did not disappoint.

As we flew from Mineralnye Vody back to Moscow after the climb our plane was hijacked! A few brief notes from a very lengthy blog gives you a sense of this 'adventure' as it unfolded.

The landing was also smooth and we were soon taxiing towards the gate. As I looked out the window I saw that our plane was following a car with flashing lights on top. ..... Our plane was guided to and stopped at an out of the way space away from the other parked planes.

It soon started to look like something dramatic was underway.

Then I looked out the window and saw that our plane was being surrounded by police in flack jackets. There was also a media crew filming our plane and a reporter was talking to the camera. None of us had any idea what was going on and the flight staff continued to play dumb.

We ended being held on the plane for over three hours before being released to a terminal building — all while being thanked by the crew for being so patient while waiting.

As I descended the stairs to the tarmac I saw for the first time the seriousness of the situation. There were dozens of police cars and what appeared to be Special Forces military vehicles around as well as half a dozen ambulances. I was left wondering what all the fuss was about. Since we could not speak Russian and nobody else around us seemed to know what was going on we just kept walking towards the waiting shuttle bus. At least it was over and we could get to our hotel in Moscow and go out for dinner.

Slowly through bits and pieces here and there we learned what had happened. Well at least parts of it. Apparently there was an attempted

learning in THIN AIR

hijacking of our plane. It happened in the front of the plane and since we were at the back we did not see or hear anything. All I know is that a person the police are calling a "terrorist" attempted to hijack the plane at some point as we were flying towards Moscow. I am not sure what happened next, but one story tells that the terrorist was subdued by passengers and a plain clothes security officer. The other story suggests that the terrorist was overpowered by Special Forces soldiers dressed as medical staff after the plane landed. Regardless of what actually happened the terrorist was captured, handcuffed, and led off the plane to an awaiting squad car.

The story didn't end there. We ended up being held by Russian security forces for over 14 hours. Each passenger underwent an 'interrogation' to determine if we might have been in on the 'terrorist plot.' I made it home safely, and quickly focused on my next goal — Mount Vinson.

Mount Vinson

MOUNT VINSON, at 4892 m, is the highest peak in Antarctica and would be the final climb of my Seven Summits. What an amazing place Antarctica is, and what a fantastic place to end this quest. My two climbing partners and I summited Vinson on November 28, 2011 on a cold, but clear day. It was so cold that our cameras all froze, but we were fortunate to get one photo of each of us on top to prove that we were there.

After the summit of Vinson most people cannot wait to leave, but not us. Our plane was not scheduled to fly us out for over a week so we skied off into the mountains. We went places and climbed peaks that had never seen a human foot print; truly spectacular.

These frozen and unforgiving slopes have taught me so much, but I must admit that while on the cold and desolate peaks of the mountains I had not done much thinking. This was often not a time for introspection and philosophizing. It was usually just cold. At home in the warmth of my family room, sharing stories with family and friends, is where this learning truly emerges.

Mountains are a metaphor for a life well lived

MOUNTAINS HAVE inspired adventurers, writers, artists, philosophers and intellectuals since the beginning of time. After all, who can stand on even the humblest of summits and not be moved in some way by the view spreading out before their feet? Who, having invested energy, sweat, skinned knuckles and blistered feet to attain the summit prize, can fail to connect the metaphors of the mountain to the challenges and triumphs of daily life? And who can fail to take away some of the mountain's power when the summit is left behind?

My passion and success in climbing transformed an aimless diversion into a powerful lever that I apply to all the challenges in my life. Through my business, keynotes, and teaching, it has allowed me to go from being a driftless teenager to someone who is helping to inspire others to achieve their goals.

To this day, climbing helps me frame almost any challenge in familiar and manageable terms. Whatever the challenge may be it is really no different than a climbing expedition. I know I need to have a clear picture of my vision, I need to have a high performance team, I need to have a plan, and my execution must be flexible to accommodate the unforeseen. Each new business project is a "mountain summit" to which I will apply all of my energy and skill.

My excitement for climbing spills over and raises my energy level for all pursuits.

Or you can see it through the eyes of Chris Darwin as he wrote in The Social Climbers...*"Life is brought down to the basics: if you are warm, regular, healthy, not thirsty or hungry, then you are not on a mountain. . . . Climbing at altitude is like hitting your head against a brick wall - it's great when you stop"*

CLIMB ON!

Scott on the summit of Mount Vinson in Antarctica

Acknowledgements

THIS BOOK is dedicated to the mountains that have inspired me to begin so many difficult and rewarding journeys, and to the people who have supported and encouraged me along the way.

This book was my second Everest and I think it many ways it was an even more difficult climb. I could not have done it without the support of a great team.

Nobody can do what I do without a very supportive and understanding family. My wife, Susan, has always been there for me and supports me in my continuing quest to climb. She looks after our two great kids, Amy and Colin, and runs the business while I am gone. She recognizes that climbing mountains, though it might appear foolishly dangerous to some, is part of who I am as a person, and that to not do it would be disastrous to me. She joins me in my hopes that, by pursuing my passions and facing these challenges, I am providing a good example to our children of what can be accomplished through dreaming, planning and hard work. I also hope that they gain an understanding that life is here for the taking, and that they should make the most of it.

I have many climbing partners to thank. These people have, through the years, shared my enthusiasm, sense of adventure and, in many cases, physical discomfort and pain. There are strong personal bonds forged between those unshowered and resolute companions who share sleep deprived nights in confined spaces for weeks on end, enduring the effects of searing sun, intense cold, blistering winds, altitude induced nausea and food that would (and does) fail to tempt a starving man. Thanks go to my early climbing partners, Walter, Chris, Julian, Sean, Kristin, Scott, and Colin.

Among my climbing partners I must single out my long time colleague and friend Angus, always dependable, always ready for the next big adventure,

learning in THIN AIR

whether it be Canada's highest peak or the world's highest peak. I would be remiss if I didn't also thank Angus' wife Sarah who, much to our mutual delight, encouraged him to go for the ultimate big adventure – Everest.

My team at Summit Team Building have made it possible for me to travel the world climbing while they keep the business thriving. Dave, Claudia, Susan, Alecia, Mary, and Melanie are an amazing and dedicated team and I could not have done this without them.

Jim Carroll, Christa Carroll, Dave Gibson, Olivia Hart, Catherine Bentzen-Bilkvist and Heidi Rampersad were invaluable in their guidance, insights, suggestions and editing of this book. The end product may never have come if it were not for them.

These last few words of appreciation are for my parents. As a child I was always encouraged to challenge myself through adventure. My mother was always supportive of what must have seemed, to her, my crazy pastimes. I'm sure she did not always understand why I did them, but she never held me back and consistently provided an environment in which I could thrive. My father was an avid outdoorsman who taught me to enjoy and respect the wilderness. Although he was not a climber, his love of the outdoors rubbed off on me in a big way. My Dad died too young, and it saddens me that I am not able to share with him my climb of Everest, my family, my various business successes and this book. Dad was a great writer, and he always hoped that I, too, would be a writer. Although I am nowhere near his ability, I'm sure he would have been proud of this book

About the Author

SCOTT KRESS is a highly accomplished leadership and team development trainer and an international keynote speaker.

He is the President of Summit Team Building and has created highly successful development programs for many of the Fortune 500 companies. Scott has only one goal; to assist teams, leaders, and individuals in reaching their peak performance. This is accomplished through combining the latest team and leadership theory with cutting edge experiential training to create one of the most effective training programs available today. Scott's team and leadership development programs are custom designed to meet each client's needs.

Years of experience, two undergraduate degrees and a Masters in Leadership and Training provide Scott with unique qualifications to design and deliver some of the most innovative corporate experiential based training available today.

Scott also teaches Leadership and Organizational Change for the Rotman School of Management (University of Toronto), the Odette School of Business (University of Windsor), and the University of Edinburgh Business School. Scott teaches in the Executive MBA, International Executive MBA, and MBA programs and has received several teaching awards including professor of the year two times.

Some of Scott's programs focus on; Teambuilding, New Team Formation, High Performance Team Development, Leadership Development, Values and Mission Creation, Communication Enhancement, Change Management, and Process Improvement.

learning in THIN AIR

Scott has also gained great insight into the inner workings of leadership and teams through over 25 years of leading climbing expeditions. He has guided and summited peaks throughout N. America, S. America, Africa and the Himalayas. Scott is the 51st Canadian to summit Mount Everest and in December 2011 became the 18th Canadian to climb the Seven summits (the highest mountain on each of the seven continents).

Since his ascent of Mount Everest and Mount Vinson, Scott has continued his passion for the climb and his enthusiasm for the trek, by engaging others in the pursuit. This has included a key role as a Civilian Team Captain and guide for the True Patriot Love series of expeditions. True Patriot Love is an organization that strives to raise awareness on the challenges faced by ill and injured Canadian soldiers as they transition from a life in the military to that of a civilian. The uniqueness of the True Patriot Love mission is its belief that wilderness expeditions can serve as a therapeutic retreat; and Scott signed on to this goal with enthusiasm. In 2013 Scott participated as Captain as True Patriot Love took a group of ill and injured soldiers and Canadian business leaders to Nepal on an expedition to Everest Base Camp, where they then achieved a successful summit to neighbouring Island Peak (elevation 20,305 ft, 6,180m). Then, in 2014, Scott again provided his passion and purpose by guiding a similar group to Canada's North Magnetic Pole. He continues to explore opportunities with the True Patriot Love organization to use the challenge and passion of the climb as a means to assist those who have served their country, in continuing to perform their best.

Through his dynamic background of education, training, experience, and adventure, Scott can help your teams and leaders reach the peak of their performance.

Prepare to be Engaged

SPECIFICALLY DESIGNED to energize, inspire and engage, Summit Team Building has been delivering successful team building and development programs across North America for the better part of 20 years.

We help you set the bar higher and bring outstanding value to your organization

Summit is a global team building firm that takes a human-centred approach in designing programs focused on unleashing a team's full potential.

Over fifteen years of experience has taught us that companies and organizations require different solutions at different times. To effectively address these needs, we've developed 3 distinctive service streams: Team Building, Team Development and Keynote Speaking.

Team Building

OUR TEAM building programs seek to find the perfect intersection of fun, adventure and shared experience, with an eye toward lasting results. Ideal for large or small groups, our programs can be a perfect energizer during a conference, a great kick off to a training day or a maintenance session to help keep your team on track.

Team Development

OUR DEVELOPMENT programs start off experientially to demonstrate the exhilaration found in great teamwork, followed by an understanding of how and why it is essential to focus on team performance. Then, using simple tools Summit has developed, we teach teams how to gain commitment, build trust, communicate effectively and, of course, get results.

Keynote Presentations

ONE CANNOT help but listen as Scott Kress engages his audience with tales of an audacious Everest climb where challenges went far beyond the norm. Scott then seamlessly ties these challenges into your world to provide insight, tools and strategies that will help you achieve your professional and personal goals.

In order to fully appreciate how Summit Team Building can help your organization build a high performance culture, focused on team and organizational goals, please join us at one of our 1/2 day showcases.

www.summitteambuilding.com/register-now-for-a-free-half-day-preview

scott.kress@summitteambuilding.com
www.summitteambuilding.com

For 10 years Summit has developed programs for us that are professional, engaging and successful. No matter the situation, Scott and his team have always delivered experiences that bring teams together for a long-term positive impact.

Carolyn Buccongelo, VP, HR, Microsoft Canada

Keynotes
by
Scott Kress

AN MBA Professor's lessons in leadership and team work from Mount Everest.

Summiting Mount Everest is a notable accomplishment at any time, but in May of 2008, an Olympics in China brought military blockades, arrests, deportations and chaos to Everest. Scott Kress witnessed first hand how teamwork, the ability to embrace change, and leadership were critical in overcoming unexpected obstacles.

Scott's gripping keynote presentation "Learning in Thin Air" will show you how he summited Mount Everest in these challenging conditions, and how the skills that his team excelled at are essential in finding success in business. It is a unique, powerful story rich in lessons for business and leadership.

While recognized worldwide for his unique business insight, Scott is truly at home in the mountains. As a climber and guide for over 25 years, Scott has summited peaks throughout the world. With his most recent summit of Mt. Vinson in the Antarctica, he is one of few among us who have finished climbing the "Seven Summits," the highest peak on each of the seven continents.

Through his inspiring story of triumph, challenge, determination, and sometimes failure, Scott shows audiences that we are all climbers looking to summit our own mountains. By rising to the challenge of change and continuous improvement, he demonstrates how the lessons learned in the mountains are directly applicable to any organization's challenges.

Contact Scott today to book a keynote for your next event!

scott.kress@summitteambuilding.com
www.summitteambuilding.com
905.257.8326